P9-ELV-443

WHAT
PHILOSOPHY
CAN DO

WHAT PHILOSOPHY CAN DO

Gary Gutting

W. W. NORTON & COMPANY

New York   London

For information about permission to reproduce selections from this book,
write to Permissions, W. W. Norton & Company, Inc., 500 Fifth Avenue,
New York, NY 10110

For information about special discounts for bulk purchases, please contact
W. W. Norton Special Sales at specialsales@wwnorton.com or 800-233-4830

Manufacturing by RR Donnelley Westford
Book design by Helene Berinsky
Production manager: Louise Mattarelliano

Library of Congress Cataloging-in-Publication Data

Gutting, Gary.
What philosophy can do / Gary Gutting. — First edition.
pages cm
Includes bibliographical references and index.
ISBN 978-0-393-24227-0 (hardcover)
1. Philosophy. I. Title.
B53.G88 2015
100—dc23

2015013783

W. W. Norton & Company, Inc., 500 Fifth Avenue, New York, N.Y. 10110
www.wwnorton.com

W. W. Norton & Company Ltd., Castle House, 75/76 Wells Street,
London W1T 3QT

1 2 3 4 5 6 7 8 9 0

To Anastasia
For all these wonderful years together

Contents

INTRODUCTION

The essays in this volume derive from shorter pieces I've written over the last several years for The Stone, the *New York Times* philosophy blog. Each piece had tens of thousands of readers. Typically there were hundreds of responses, many leading me to clarify, develop, and revise my thinking. Often my columns were highly topical—one group, for example, gave my take on various aspects of the 2012 presidential election. The essays here are much longer, treating similar issues but with more generality, depth, and detail.

Here, as in The Stone, I'm writing for non-philosophers, but my writing is philosophical in its emphasis on conceptual clarity and careful argument. I introduce technical concepts and distinctions not for their own sake but to illuminate the issues at hand. There is no need to have a philosopher's specialized training to profit from the application of philosophical ideas to a specific topic.

Philosophy today is an academic discipline—like physics, biology, or economics—and we professors of philosophy write mostly for one another. The exceptions are usually textbooks, meant to introduce students to the discipline, or popularizations designed to give laypeople a rough sense of what's going on in otherwise inaccessible technical discussions. My project, however, is not to bring the public into the halls of philosophy but to bring philosophy into the public arena.

I think of what I'm doing as *public philosophy*, which is both an application of and a complement to the more technical and specialized work of academic philosophers. Academic philosophy remains an autonomous discipline with its own problems, terminology, and standards of rigor. Public philosophy draws on academic work to tackle issues of general interest. At the same time, public philosophizing keeps its academic sibling in contact with the concrete human world, which is both the source of all philosophical questions and an important standard for judging answers to them.

Public philosophy does not offer ivory-tower solutions to real-life problems. The give-and-take of public discussion tests philosophical thinking as much as it contributes to public understanding. Scientific theories, no matter how well confirmed in the laboratory, are further supported—and sometimes modified—by practical applications. Similarly, public engagement both tests and improves philosophical ideas.

In these essays, I often put forward my views on disputed topics. But I am at least equally concerned with laying out issues and introducing considerations that people of differing opinions can use to think through, and perhaps refine and better defend, their own positions. An argument, in my book, is not a bludgeon to beat opponents into submission but a tool for intellectual development.

Those with particular interests will find that each chapter can be read independently. Readers who opt for a beginning-to-end approach will find that the book takes them through successively more extended and complex exercises in philosophical thinking. My goal is both to engage readers with major issues of public concern and to introduce them to the tools of philosophical thinking.

Each chapter presents philosophical principles, concepts, and distinctions that guide the discussion. Chapter 1 ("How to Argue about Politics") uses political disputes as an example to develop techniques for good thinking, techniques that will also apply in many other contexts.

The next six chapters focus on three of the most powerful forces in our society: science, religion, and capitalism. I employ relevant philosophical tools to make each force an object of *critical reflection*—where "critical" means not negative criticism or refutation but rather a careful assessment of value and limitations.

Chapter 2 ("Science: A Consumer's Guide") focuses on logical principles especially important for evaluating scientific claims. Chapter 3 ("Philosophy and the Limits of Science") covers a variety of philosophical issues that have attracted the attention of scientists and shows the problems that arise from not using philosophical resources in discussing these issues.

Chapter 4 ("The New Atheists") moves to a higher level of philosophical reflection, treating in considerable detail a single central question of the philosophy of religion: whether belief in God is rational. Here we see how to carry out a detailed analysis and critique of a philosophical position (in this case, that of the "new atheists").

Chapter 5 ("Religious Agnosticism") moves to the constructive task of developing and defending a positive view of how religious belief can be rational. Here I particularly emphasize that although I am putting forward my own views, the primary purpose is to provide readers with the philosophical tools needed to discuss religious belief and to illustrate what is involved in a sustained philosophical discussion.

Chapter 6 ("Happiness, Work, and Capitalism") and Chapter 7 ("Capitalism and Education") treat what initially seem very different topics: the nature of happiness, the value of work, the morality of capitalism, and the purpose of education. Our discussion shows how these topics are interrelated and combines them into an overall picture of what is involved in a good life. The result is a detailed illustration of philosophy's power of intellectual synthesis.

The next two chapters reverse direction, each showing what philosophy can contribute to a very specific public debate. Chapter 8 ("Thinking about Art") takes on the value of contemporary art and Chapter 9 ("Can We Stop Arguing about Abortion?") the morality of abortion. These chapters will give readers a sense of what the back-and-forth arguments of academic philosophers are like and how public debates can directly profit from philosophers' expertise.

Finally, Chapter 10 ("What Philosophy Can Do") develops a general account of philosophical thinking by reflecting on some key moments in the history of philosophy. It then uses a distinction (introduced by the twentieth-century American philosopher Wilfrid Sellars) between the *manifest image* (the world of everyday objects) and the *scientific image* (the world of molecules and atoms) to clarify philosophy's role in contemporary thought.

At the beginning of each chapter (or for Chapters 3 and 4, at the beginning of subsections), I give a schematic overview of the main philosophical tools—concepts, distinctions, and principles—the chapter will employ. These italicized introductions should allow readers to note the philosophical tools that guide each chapter and to track the increasingly complex role philosophy plays.

WHAT PHILOSOPHY CAN DO

1

How to Argue about Politics

Taking examples from recent political debates, this chapter explains and illustrates important logical principles and distinctions needed for effective argumentation. We first distinguish between real and bogus arguments and then discuss and illustrate the Principle of Charity, which shows how fairness to opponents can make arguments more compelling. Next, we examine the distinction between deductive and inductive arguments, and, regarding inductive arguments, explore the essential but often neglected Principle of Relevant Evidence.

The following section introduces the notion of convictions (and the related notion of pictures). Both concepts will have major roles in later chapters. Reflection on the part convictions play in arguments will lead to an important distinction between what is logical and what is rational.

Two further sections explore arguments between people who are equally competent on a given topic (epistemic peers), leading to a distinction between freedom of thought and correctness of thought, and an analysis of the logic of disagreement. Finally, we consider the value of arguments that fail to convince anyone else, formulating a Principle of Self-Understanding.

WHEN AN ARGUMENT IS NOT AN ARGUMENT

Often an "argument" is simply a heated exchange of views, an emotional encounter that's "won" by, say, reducing your opponent to silence or tears. Philosophers, however, are interested in argument as a rational process, an effort to convince someone of a view by providing good reasons. Unfortunately, in many cases—with politics as a primary example—the people we convince almost always already agree with us.

Why is this? One reason is that much of what we call political debate is in fact quarrel or mere disagreement, not argument. For the most part representatives of rival positions exchange one-liners: "The rich can afford to pay more" is met with "Tax increases kill jobs". Slightly more sophisticated exchanges may cite historical precedents: "There were higher tax rates during the 1950s postwar boom" versus "Reagan's tax cuts increased revenues". Such volleys don't amount to arguments in the logical sense of premises supporting a conclusion. (A simple example of a logical argument: "Over the last fifty years, only one of ten federal tax cuts has increased revenues; therefore it's likely that a tax cut will not increase revenues.") Even full-scale speeches by politicians are usually collections of slogans and factoids, hung on a string of platitudes. Candidates' pre-election "debates" are mostly exercises in looking authoritative, imposing their talking points on the questions, avoiding gaffes, and embarrassing their opponents with "zingers". We need to distinguish *real arguments*, which actually propose premises that support their conclusions, from *bogus arguments*, which at best cite facts that by themselves don't give us reason to believe the conclusion.*

---

* As we'll see later, an argument is logical (*valid* is the technical term) as long as the premises provide a reason for accepting the conclusion, even if the premises aren't true.

When political discussion does approach the level of genuine argument, we start with premises that seem obvious to us and draw from them what we see as the obvious conclusion. Two examples:

1. Obama is a tax-and-spend liberal, so of course his policies won't help our debt problem.
2. Republicans are only interested in helping the rich get richer, so we can't expect them to solve the problem of inequality.

But such arguments typically suffer from circularity. They are not *logically circular*: the premises do not themselves assert what the conclusions say. In example (1), increasing taxes and spending might stimulate economic growth that would lower the debt. In example (2), increased investment by the 1 percent might stimulate growth that did even more for the poor than it did for the rich. Still, the premises are circular in another sense. In both cases, even though the premise doesn't assume the conclusion, hardly anyone who doesn't already believe the conclusion is likely to believe the premise. In other words, the arguments are circular *in practice*: they won't convince anyone who doesn't already believe the conclusion. To be a bit more technical, we can say that such arguments move in an *epistemic circle*, where "epistemic" means having to do with knowledge (*epistémé* in Greek) that people have or claim to have.

THE PRINCIPLE OF CHARITY

If we break out of the epistemic circle and begin to look at things from our opponents' point of view, we have a chance to craft a better argument. Here, the philosophical *Principle of*

Charity becomes relevant. This principle, championed by Donald Davidson, has taken varying forms in complex philosophical discussions concerning meaning and truth. For our purposes, I'm going to appropriate the term as the injunction to develop our arguments in light of the best version of our opponents' position. Here "best" means the most plausible or defensible— at a minimum, a version that doesn't assume that our opponents are intellectually or morally bankrupt.

The first step in argumentative charity: render in neutral language the main elements of your opponents' position. Suppose, for example, that you are a liberal Democrat and want to argue against the conservatism professed by the mainstream of the Republican Party. Here's a typical Democratic statement of the Republican view (from Duncan Bowen Black, blogging as Atrios): The Republican Party is "all about enacting an elite consensus policy which involves kicking the poors and olds, funneling ever more money to Defense and Finance, and cuttings taxes on rich people."[1] This preaches to the choir, but conservatives will be unperturbed. They will, for example, argue that saying they merely want to enrich the wealthy at the expense of the poor ignores well-established laws of economics, which show that the wealth of the top economic classes is an engine of growth that allows everyone to prosper. Liberals may consider this claim a cover for capitalist greed, but it will remain an effective cover unless critics recognize its role and argue against economic claims that seem to support it.

A fairer formulation of the Republican position might be:

Conservatives favor minimal government action, particularly less regulation of business, less support for social welfare programs, and less control of ordinary citizens' lives. Economically, their goal is to balance the budget, pay off public debt, lower taxes and support the efforts of businesses to increase their profits and thereby generate new jobs. They also see it as crucial to support traditional religion and its ethical values, particularly on matters of sexuality, above all opposition to abortion and to same-sex marriage.

The next step on the path of charity: articulate, in the most positive terms, the reasons your opponent holds these views. For our example:

The conservative view is based on a general picture of the strengths of our nation and the dangers to its flourishing. The strengths are our free enterprise system and our religious/ethical heritage of hard work, individual responsibility and adherence to traditional moral standards. The working of the free enterprise system generates sufficient wealth to allow almost everyone to have at least an adequate standard of living and also produces innovations that continually improve that standard. Of course, there will be people who, because of bad luck or their own moral failings, wind up deprived of basic human goods. The primary remedy for this should be the charitable instincts of fellow-citizens living a life of faith, which is also the source of human fulfillment, beyond mere material prosperity.

On this conservative view, there are two great dangers to our way of life. First, there are the forces of secularism and relativism, which threaten our basic ethical values. Second, there is the perhaps well-intentioned but deeply wrong belief that governmental planning and regulation can significantly improve on the free enterprise system as a way of providing for our material needs. On the contrary, major interventions by government almost always make things worse. Maintaining the integrity of our ethical values and of our free enterprise system are the keys to solving our problems.

The Principle of Charity is not just a way of being nice. It lays the ground for a far more effective critique of conservatism. A proper appreciation of conservative strengths allows liberals to focus their arguments on points of genuine weakness, where the conservatives will not have an obvious response.

In this case, the Principle of Charity allows the liberal critique to home in on an essential bulwark of the conservative position: its assumption that a minimally regulated market— one in which all agents (employers, workers, buyers, sellers) act in their own selfish interests—will in fact maximize economic well-being.

This assumption can, of course, be challenged on purely economic grounds, and the charitable analysis suggests the issues such a challenge must address. But the charitable analysis also suggests another important line of critique: the apparent tension between conservatives' commitment to the free enterprise system and their religious ethical values. Christian morality in particular mandates a love for others and self-sacrifice on their behalf that hardly seem consistent with an economic system driven by self-interest. This problem is evident in the New Testament's unease with the wealthy and sympathy for the poor.*

---

* "The cares of the world and the delight in riches choke the word, and it proves unfruitful" (Matthew 13:22); "It is easier for a camel to go through the eye of a needle than for a rich man to enter the kingdom of God" (Mark 10:25); "Come now, you rich, weep and howl for the miseries that are coming upon you. . . . Your gold and silver have rusted, and their rust will be evidence against you and will eat your flesh like fire" (James 5:1, 3). (Revised Standard Version)

By implicitly recognizing the idea that the "invisible hand" of the market produces public goods out of private selfishness, our charitable analysis may seem to have blunted this ethical objection ahead of time. If we all act for our own selfish ends, so the argument goes, there will be far more material goods for us to share than there would be otherwise. But this is a *utilitarian* argument; that is, one that assumes actions are moral because they increase our worldly happiness. Christian morality, however, denies that moral good and evil depend on such considerations. Christian love and self-sacrifice, in particular, are *moral goods* in their own right, regardless of their worldly consequences. Conservative Christians would not countenance abortion or same-sex marriage, even if it turned out that doing so would increase worldly happiness. How can they consistently endorse an economic system that runs on selfishness as a morally acceptable means to prosperity?

This last line of criticism illustrates another way that the Principle of Charity can make a critique more effective. Many liberals, secular-minded and repelled by the fundamentalist tendencies of conservative religion, might simply denounce what they see as bigotry or naiveté in conservative believers. But the effort to appreciate conservative strengths exposes features of Christian ethics that at least seem to contrast with the utilitarian calculations of economics. The Principle of Charity opens the way to an argument that moves from your opponents' own premises to a denial of one of their key claims—a case of logically "killing with kindness".

Of course, this line of argument does not decisively refute the conservative position. But precisely because it is rooted in a sympathetic analysis of conservative ideas, it calls for a serious response. Such an argument is the beginning, not the end, of a fruitful discussion of fundamental political differences.

THE PRINCIPLE OF RELEVANT EVIDENCE

The Principle of Charity will keep us focused on the *issues* most relevant to making our case. But effective arguments also require appeal to relevant *evidence* (facts and principles supporting or opposing a position). Otherwise our political discussions will remain exercises in emotive expression instead of objective analysis. Appealing to evidence is not, however, as simple as it seems. To see the problem, consider a debate over President Obama's proposed 2012 federal budget.

In April, 2011, John Taylor, a distinguished economist at Stanford, put forward what he called a "fact-based" critique of Obama's proposal.[2] The centerpiece of his argument was a set of data showing federal government expenditures from 2000 to the present, along with Obama's projections of what he proposed to spend from 2011 through 2021. In 2000, government spending was 18.2 percent of our gross domestic product and had steadily increased, reaching 19.6 percent in 2007 and averaging 24.4 percent for the next three years. Obama's budget slightly reduced this rate to about 23 percent over its first few years, but then gradually increased it, ending with a rate of over 24 percent in 2021.

Given these facts and general agreement that we needed to reduce our deficit, Taylor asked why anyone should take seriously a budget that took Obama's "spending binge" from 2008 to 2010 into the indefinite future. If the federal government got along on spending 19.6 percent of GDP in 2007, why couldn't it at least reduce our spending to this level over the next ten years?

This seems like a good argument: given the evidence cited, the conclusion seems reasonable. But the equally distinguished economist Paul Krugman responded by pointing out that almost all the additional spending in Obama's budget addressed increases in the number of people eligible for Social Security and Medicare, expected increases in the cost of health care, and increased interest on the debt we incurred to overcome the Great Recession of 2007 to 2009.[3] The increased spending was tied not to new programs but to inevitable increases in the cost of existing programs.

Taylor in turn had a plausible-sounding response to Krugman. Yes, he said, "much of the increase comes in the form of mandatory spending", but Obama had the option to stop this spending.[4] He chose not to seriously reform the current social welfare systems (Social Security, Medicare, etc.) and decided instead to maintain them in forms that required large outlays. Krugman, however, responded that cost-cutting reforms would have unacceptable consequences, requiring, for example, that many Medicare recipients pay far more than they could afford for adequate medical care.

The evidence that both Taylor and Krugman used to make their arguments was not in dispute. Moreover, in each case, the evidence did support the conclusion for which each was arguing. There were no flaws in their logical moves from premises to conclusions. How could something be wrong with their arguments?

The answer lies in the crucial philosophical distinction between *deductive* and *inductive* reasoning—a distinction routinely ignored in political discussions. Consider a standard example of a good *deductive argument*:

All humans are mortal;
Socrates is human;
Therefore, Socrates is mortal.

Here the truth of the premises logically (on pain of contradiction) *requires* the truth of the conclusion. If the premises are true, the conclusion must be true. If Socrates is not mortal, then it simply cannot be true that he is human *and* all humans are mortal. When assuming the premises of a deductive argument requires accepting the conclusion (whether or not the premises or the conclusion are in fact true), the argument is *valid*. When, in addition, the premises are in fact true, the argument is *sound*.

In a *valid inductive argument*, accepting the premises does not require, on pain of contradiction, accepting the conclusion; the premises only make the conclusion *probable*, and so reasonable to accept given the evidence. For example:

Most humans will not live for one hundred years;
Socrates is human;
Therefore, Socrates probably will not live for one hundred years.

As in the case of a deductive argument, when an inductive argument is valid and its premises are all true, we say that the argument is *sound*. But whereas a sound deductive argument leaves no question about the truth of the conclusion (given the truth of the premises), a sound inductive argument merely shows that the conclusion is probable.

This is because there is a key difference between deductive and inductive arguments. In a deductive argument, adding further premises that might seem relevant to the conclusion will make no difference to the conclusion. Consider again the argument from the premises "All humans are mortal" and "Socrates is a human" to the conclusion "Socrates is mortal". Once we have the two premises we can be sure of the conclusion. Adding, for example, that Socrates is very young and that there will be major medical advances before Socrates reaches old age makes no difference to the conclusion of the argument.

But this point does not hold for an inductive argument—a key difference. From the premises "Most humans will not live for one hundred years" and "Socrates is a human", we can validly conclude "Socrates probably will not live for one hundred years". But in this case, adding further premises can *alter the conclusion*. If Socrates is young enough and subsequent medical advances will be great enough, it becomes probable that he will live to be one hundred. If we add still another premise—say, that Socrates is about to wander off a steep cliff—the conclusion of the argument will switch: Socrates probably will not reach one hundred.

This philosophical analysis of the difference between deductive and inductive arguments explains what was happening in the debate between Taylor and Krugman. Because they were arguing inductively for the probability of their conclusions, their reasoning was open to question simply by adding further relevant evidence, such as pointing out our aging population and increases in medical costs, or noting that serious reform of our welfare system was possible. Even a strong inductive argument from indisputable evidence is open to refutation unless we are assured that it has taken account of *all relevant evidence*.

The moral: we can rely on an inductive argument *only* if we have good reason to think that the premises include all the evidence relevant to the question of whether the conclusion is true. Let's call this requirement the *Principle of Relevant Evidence*.

To illustrate further the role of this principle, consider two arguments: one from Niall Ferguson,[5] a professor of history at Harvard, and one from David Frum,[6] a former speech writer for George W. Bush and a prominent Republican columnist. Both arguments supported a vote for Mitt Romney in the 2012 presidential election.

Ferguson's argument focused on Obama's major "political

mistakes": letting Congress pass inadequate measures on fiscal stimulus and financial market reform; supporting a healthcare plan (the Affordable Care Act) that didn't change the existing system and would increase the deficit; and failing to achieve a "grand bargain" with Republicans on deficit reduction. Of course, even if the mistakes Ferguson outlined amounted to an egregious failure, his argument still needed to give reasons to think that Romney would do a better job. Ferguson admitted, "Romney is not the best candidate for the presidency I can imagine", but went on to cite some facts in Romney's favor: for one, he made a very good choice of a running mate (Ferguson had met Romney's vice-presidential selection, Paul Ryan, at a dinner party and, he said, "Ryan blew me away"). Ferguson also pointed out that Romney has business and executive experience.

We can summarize Ferguson's argument as:

1. Obama made serious mistakes in managing the economy.
2. Romney was not the best candidate, but:
   a. His choice for vice president was very good.
   b. He had experience as a businessman and as an executive.
3. Therefore, Romney should be elected.

We might disagree with Ferguson's premises, but even if we assume they are true, the argument was strikingly ineffective. There were many other facts about Obama's presidency— foreign-policy achievements, educational reforms, the auto industry bailout, environmental policies—that could be plausibly put forward as relevant to who should be elected in 2012. As a result, there were likely millions of Americans who accepted the premises of Ferguson's argument (1, 2a, 2b) but still rightly saw no reason to vote for Romney. Ferguson might contend that consideration of any further facts would not alter the conclusion of his argument, but this is something he would need to defend.

Frum's argument was much more powerful. He acknowledged that Obama had done good things in his first term: ending a recession, passing the Affordable Care Act, working to reform education, and pursuing a sensible foreign policy. He also agreed that congressional Republicans had behaved irresponsibly in recent years and needed to be restrained. (Note his use of the Principle of Charity.) But, he said, elections are about the future, not the past. So what we have to ask is: Will Obama or Romney do a better job moving on from what Obama has achieved?

In Frum's analysis, the main tasks for the next president would be: (1) continuing to move the country out of recession in a responsible way; (2) successfully implementing the Affordable Care Act; (3) finding a better approach to educational reform; (4) continuing Obama's successful foreign policy; and (5) restoring some sanity in the conservative faction of the Republican Party. Given these future tasks, his argument for electing Romney was:

1. Romney's more fiscally conservative approach would be better for maintaining economic growth;
2. He would not, as some thought, try to repeal the Affordable Care Act, but would implement it with a greater sense of fiscal responsibility than Obama would;
3. His proposals for education reform were superior to Obama's approach;
4. He would basically continue Obama's foreign policy, just as Obama had continued George W. Bush's;
5. Republican conservatives would be less destructive without Obama to infuriate them. Also, given that the pres-

ident's party typically loses congressional seats in the midterm elections, a Romney win would result in less power for congressional Republicans.

6. Therefore, Romney was the better candidate.

In contrast to Ferguson, Frum presented an argument based on what at least approaches a *comprehensive account* of the issues relevant to his conclusion. He thereby provided a plausible overall framework in which the evidence (premises 1–5), if Frum was right about it, made a strong logical case for his conclusion.

Even assuming that Ferguson's premises were all correct, his argument fell flat because it ignored obviously relevant evidence (Obama's apparent achievements in foreign policy, education, economic recovery, and environmental policy). By contrast, Frum's argument, regardless of whether its premises were false, came closer to fulfilling the Principle of Relevant Evidence. It would be no trivial task for a critic to make a case that, assuming the truth of Frum's premises,* there are still further premises that would undermine the force of his argument.

Ignoring the Principle of Relevant Evidence creates false confidence in the strength of our positions in political debates. I put forward a barrage of indisputable facts that show, with a very high probability, that my view is correct. But you launch an equally impressive barrage for a contrary view. If, as often happens, we both focus only on our own arguments, we will both think we've made decisive cases—when, in fact, nothing has been settled, since we haven't taken account of all the relevant evidence.

---

* Of course, even many Romney supporters would not have accepted all of Frum's premises. But here the point is that, given those premises, Frum has a respectable argument. Even if you entirely accept Ferguson's premises, his argument doesn't come close to making his case.

You're no doubt asking, how do we know that we have taken account of all the relevant evidence? In the end, the best case for such a claim is simply that, after extensive efforts, no one has been able to find any more considerations that make a difference to the outcome of the argument. Any inductive argument for a conclusion is *an implicit challenge* for opponents to produce evidence that will reverse it. Here the Principle of Charity again enters the conversation. To have good reason to think that my argument adequately supports my view, I have to be thoroughly acquainted with my opponents' best arguments. Only then can I tell whether I have ignored any evidence relevant to my conclusion.

CONVICTIONS AND THE LIMITS OF ARGUMENT

So far we've been discussing principles that will help us argue more effectively. But, as the cynical line goes, what isn't worth doing isn't worth doing well. We need to consider whether there's any point in arguing at all.

We may believe that emotions and desires, not reason, drive politics. If that's so, why care about facts and arguments? Because among the whirl of our feelings, we possess a desire for our beliefs to be rational, to have support that would convince other sensible people. We're uneasy when they don't accept what we see as a strong case for our view, so we seek an explanation.

It is tempting to conclude that our political opponents are just irrational—or even crazy. At the height of the 2011 struggle over the once-routine increase of the federal debt limit, John McCain said that opposition to the debt-limit increase was "worse than foolish" and "bizarro".[7] Paul Krugman suggested that President Obama's desire to compromise on the debt limit might be "obsessive and compulsive".[8] Even a sober reporter such as Elizabeth Drew could observe, "Were they all insane? That's not a far-fetched question."[9] In less vivid terms, we might assert that a rival group's thinking is dominated by a mind-muddling ideology that cannot be supported by rational argument. I'm rational (of course!), but if my opponents aren't, there's no reason to try to argue with them.

Admittedly, we are all frequently irrational; we ignore obvious facts or make silly mistakes in reasoning. Often, however, we think our opponents are irrational simply because their arguments start from premises they can't prove and that we reject. For example, many Republicans assume the overriding importance of balanced budgets, and many Democrats assume the overriding importance of equal opportunity for minorities.

But the mere failure to support some of your basic claims with good logical arguments does not make you irrational. Any argument requires premises that it assumes and does not prove. (Aristotle made this point in the first book ever written about logic.) We may construct a further argument for an unproven premise, but that further argument will itself have unproven premises. That's why even mathematics, the most thoroughly rational enterprise we have, begins with unproven axioms. Just because my opponents start from premises they can't prove, it doesn't follow that they are irrational. Everyone, including me, must start from what they can't prove. Let's call these premises—the ones to which we are deeply committed but can't prove—*convictions*.

To illustrate the role of convictions, return to the debate between Paul Krugman and John Taylor over Obama's budget. We first considered it as an example of the Principle of Relevant Evidence. But when two economists as distinguished as Krugman and Taylor are concerned, it's reasonable to assume that the protagonists are aware—or will become aware in their interchanges with one another—of all the relevant evidence. If two renowned experts are both aware of all the relevant evidence, how can their conclusions be in conflict?

One explanation, of course, is that one of them is, consciously or unconsciously, misrepresenting the evidence. Krugman, for example, has said that some of Taylor's arguments are simply "dishonest".[10] But it is also possible that Taylor and Krugman are working from conflicting convictions.

Taylor's last salvo in the debate concluded:

> Krugman admits that the rate of increase in government spending is affected by Obama's policies, but he now gives reasons [quoting Krugman] "why federal spending shouldn't stay at or near the share of GDP it was at in 2007" arguing that Obama should not choose such policies. I disagree. Even with current demographic projections it is possible to institute good reforms which keep Medicare and Medicaid from rising so rapidly as a share of GDP and also deliver better health care services. And of course it is possible also to reduce other types of spending as a share of GDP, including national defense.[11]

At this point, Taylor appealed not to known facts but to projections of the future results of various economic policies. Moreover, although these projections make use of impressive mathematical models, in the end they rest on *convictions* about what sorts of policies are better. The "good reforms" that Taylor says will control medical expenses and provide better health care would work by decreasing government regulation and increasing free-market competition. Such an assertion expresses his conservative conviction about the privileged role of markets and the dangers of government regulation.

Krugman himself suggests that no comprehensive view of

the overall economy can be justified. Speaking of the predictive power of macroeconomics, he maintains that economists "will have to acknowledge the importance of irrational and often unpredictable behavior, face up to the often idiosyncratic imperfections of markets and accept that an elegant economic 'theory of everything' is a long way off. In practical terms, this will translate into more cautious policy advice".[12]

In our terms this means that any view of how the economy as a whole will behave—including Krugman's own liberal view—will depend on convictions, which we can't expect will be confirmed by predictions of the economic future. It does not, however, follow that Taylor's and Krugman's convictions are irrational. They have a certain intuitive plausibility, are not refuted by the evidence, and have been formulated in rigorous mathematical models. But in the end they express personal judgments, not established conclusions.

Convictions typically combine to constitute what I call *pictures*, coherent and comprehensive views of "the lay of the land" that guide our thinking on a given topic. Economic conservatives, for example, see business as primarily a source of social and economic goods, which are achieved by the market mechanism of seeking to maximize profit. They therefore think government's primary duty to businesses is to ensure that they are free to pursue their goal of maximizing profit. Liberals, on the other hand, think that the effort to maximize profit threatens at least as much as it contributes to society's well-being. They therefore think that government's primary duty regarding businesses is to protect citizens from their malpractice.

Both of these pictures have strengths and weaknesses, and there are cases where one or the other is particularly good at explaining economic events. Moreover, there are strategies available for modifying and adapting each picture to help it deal with recalcitrant facts. At a highly rarified level of economic debate, conservatives and liberals develop something like philosophical cases for their pictures.* But no one is able to make a logically compelling case, even if they are able to show that their view is one a rational person can accept.

This suggests another key philosophical distinction: between *logicality* (proof by logical argument—deductive or inductive) and *rationality*; it may be *rational* to accept a claim even if you can't prove it by *logical* argument. The distinction applies to truths we all accept as utterly obvious—that $2 + 2 = 4$, that the sky is blue—but cannot prove from anything more obvious. Such truths are rational even though they can't be proven logically. The distinction also applies to convictions that not everyone accepts. Such convictions arise from a complex mixture of family influences, schooling, personal experiences, discussions with friends, reading newspapers and blogs, and so on.

Formal arguments may play a role in the development of convictions, but they are not decisive—we simply come to feel convinced. Apart from clearly pathological cases, there's nothing inappropriate or irrational about this process. It's the way almost everyone forms convictions about serious matters, including not just politics but also morality and religion. Such convictions can be rational even if they aren't supported by logical arguments.

ARGUMENT AND DISAGREEMENT

As we have seen, argument as such is not pointless. Start from rationally held premises and you can argue to conclusions that

---

* Our discussion of Milton Friedman in Chapter 6 provides an example of a philosophical defense of an economic view.

anyone who accepts the premises will have to accept. But in politics and many other realms of life, the premises of opposing arguments are often conflicting convictions. Can there be fruitful argument among people who disagree on fundamental premises? Surprisingly, the answer is yes.

Although accepting a given picture (and the associated convictions) is not irrational, inflexible adherence to it may be. Rival pictures, particularly those developed through interactions with opponents, are often viable because they include *exception clauses* that grant validity to some aspect of the other picture. Adherence to the Principle of Charity can be an important factor here.*

Consider a proposal that would regulate a business to advance the public good. Stated in the abstract, it's entirely appropriate (and rational) for liberals to be inclined to support such a measure and for conservatives to be inclined to oppose it. But both sides will need to attend to the facts of the situation to see if they warrant invoking an exception clause. The risks of radiation leakage from a nuclear plant, for example, may be too great to preserve free-market principles, or the severity of unemployment may make it worthwhile to exempt small businesses from some regulations. When liberals or conservatives become incapable of thinking this way, their positions can become irrational.

Aristotle offers some helpful terminology. *Sophia* (roughly translated as "theoretical knowledge"), he says, grasps universal truths, whereas *phronesis* (roughly, "good practical judgment") is required to apply these truths properly to particular instances. Although Aristotle himself might disapprove, members of a

---

* Chapter 9 discusses two other important modes of fruitful argument among those who strongly disagree: *overlapping consensus* and *immanent critique*.

deeply pluralistic society need to admit the availability of diverse, even conflicting sources of *sophia*—the rival pictures we've been talking about. Discussions about the theoretical truth of pictures are important, but they offer little value in the trenches of practical policy-making. Policy-making does, however, often require Aristotelian *phronesis*, particularly the ability to recognize salient facts that require invoking the exception clause of a guiding picture. When participants in a political dispute lack *phronesis*, we are entitled to judge them irrational. In fact, a lack of such *phronesis* is a good definition of fanaticism.

Finally, sustained engagement with rival pictures can narrow the distance between opposing positions and make political conversions possible. Even though no particular argument has convinced me that I'm wrong, I may, after much thought and discussion, find old convictions fading away and new ones developing. Eventually, I may see the world pretty much the way my erstwhile opponents do. Even without a decisive role for arguments, this process of conversion may be quite rational. Admittedly, such conversions are more likely among ordinary voters than among politicians themselves. For them, apparent changes in fundamental views are more likely to be a matter of feeling the heat than of seeing the light.

EPISTEMIC PEERS AND THE HARD PROBLEM OF DISAGREEMENT

We've seen how political debate can be fruitful even when it involves people with opposing convictions. We may reach consensus about practical action through the exception clauses of opposing convictions, or even convert opponents to new convictions.

But what about the case—very frequent—in which even after

the most thorough, fair-minded, and good-willed discussion, we remain in disagreement on issues of public policy?

It should be obvious that major policy disputes are complicated issues on which knowledgeable and reasonable people may disagree, yet we rarely acknowledge this truth in our public debates. The typical op-ed column or letter to the editor implies that anyone competent to judge the issue should agree with its view. Dissent, we are told, must emerge from lack of knowledge or poor reasoning skills (if not from moral depravity).

Of course it's highly unlikely that all of our opponents know less or reason more poorly than we do. On honest reflection, we should admit that, no matter what our political views, there are people on the other side who know at least as much about the issues as we do and are at least as good at drawing conclusions from this knowledge. Most of us, for example, would not fare well in a debate on economic policy with Paul Krugman or John Taylor.

On most political matters, then, we have what philosophers call *epistemic peers*—people at least our equals in the intellectual qualities needed to make good judgments about a given matter—who disagree with us. What should we make of this? There's a temptation to claim it doesn't matter. I have a right to my opinion, no matter who might disagree with me. That's freedom of thought.

But *freedom of thought* does not imply *correctness of thought*: my political right to assert my views does not mean that I have good reasons for holding them. Don't I, after all, think my opponents have a right to their opinions but can't adequately support them with facts and reasons? They have a right to their views, but I don't see their views as rationally justified.

We must ask: When my epistemic peers disagree with me, do I have a good reason to question my views? Shouldn't I see their disagreement as another piece of evidence in the debate, one that may tip the balance against my position? If so, then the fact of disagreement seems to undermine everyone's political convictions. Why should I continue to hold views that are no more justified than my peer's denials? This line of thought invites a debilitating skepticism; in the face of irresolvable disagreement among epistemic peers, we would all withhold judgment on a controversial issue.

David Christensen, a philosopher at Brown University, offers a simple example that has focused much recent philosophical work on disagreement.[13] A friend and I have agreed to split the check at lunch equally. When the bill arrives we each look it over, add a 20 percent tip (on food and drink), and put the amount we owe on the table. But my friend has put down five dollars less than I have. In most cases, we will see each other as epistemic peers in carrying out such a simple calculation, both equally reliable at the task. Neither of us will insist that his or her calculation is correct. We will instead agree that we each have an equal chance of being wrong and so redo the calculation until we agree. But until we do agree, neither of us will claim to be right.

Political disagreements between peers are more complicated, but have the same logical structure: two people, equally reliable, disagree about a claim. If in the restaurant case the two parties should doubt their conclusions until they can agree, why should the political case differ?

Of course, in the political case the peers will likely never agree. They might appeal to the opinions of experts, but there will be equally qualified experts on both sides. So shouldn't both parties permanently doubt their claims and admit they don't know whether, say, we should repeal the Affordable Care Act? But very quickly this leads to an absurd choice between abandoning our political views altogether or continuing to hold them for no good reason.

To avoid this conclusion we must find some relevant difference between the restaurant case and political disagreements. One difference is that the two diners have merely checked the bill quickly, whereas those embracing political views at least sometimes have carefully worked out their reasons. If I had rigorously determined my share of the bill (using a calculator, checking each step several times), wouldn't I be confident in my result, no matter what my friend had concluded? But suppose I knew that my friend had done the math with equal care? Shouldn't that require me to recalculate?

The restaurant disagreement is also highly localized. Our different tallies do not mean we disagree on other topics. Political disagreements, however, can range wide and deep. If we disagree about health care, we likely also disagree on welfare, budget deficits, and regulating business. And this range of disagreements may stem from differences in our fundamental convictions. Perhaps such thoroughgoing differences suggest to us that the people on the other side are not our epistemic peers. If I think they are so wrong about so many things, why should I agree that they know as much and judge as well as I? On the other hand, if I have good evidence for thinking my opponents as knowledgeable and intelligent as I about topics on which we mostly agree, why should I think that I'm superior when we disagree?

We may think the restaurant example is too simple to catch the complexities and subtleties of actual political disagreements. Unlike the dispute over the check, such disagreements often derive from differences over moral values and involve powerful, conflicting emotions, interests, group pressures, and ideologies. Moreover, many political disagreements are highly nuanced and cannot be reduced to a simple yes or no.[14]

The restaurant example, however, illustrates that we often follow a principle: *When epistemic peers disagree, they should withhold judgment until the disagreement is resolved.* The question is, should this principle apply to more complex cases like political disagreements? Making the correct point that these cases are different does not mean we should not apply the same principle. We need to explain why the complexity (values, emotions, ideology, etc.) should allow us to keep holding political views in the face of our peers' disagreement.

At first glance, in fact, the inherent complexity would seem to support keeping to the principle. Political disagreements differ from the simple restaurant case because they involve irrational factors that can't be resolved by any amount of reasonable discussion. But if irrational views cause our political disagreements, doesn't it follow that we should discard the views?

Perhaps; however, our fundamental convictions, especially about values, are—at least sometimes—not so much irrational as deeper than the rationality at work in the restaurant-check case, where there is a simple, objective method of deciding who's right. In particular, convictions about fundamental values may express my moral integrity as a person, something it makes no sense for me to compromise simply because an epistemic peer does not see things as I do. Should Socrates, Jesus, and Gandhi— or any of history's other great moral heroes—have given up their fundamental convictions because other equally knowledgeable and rational people disagreed with them? Here basic moral differences trump knowing facts and reasoning well.

The view emerging here is similar to what the late British philosopher Bernard Williams put forward in his critique of utilitarian morality. In the utilitarian view, we should always act in the way most likely to most increase the happiness of society as a whole.* Williams put forward an example that he thought undermined the utilitarian view.[15]

Here's a quick summary of the example: George, a new biochemistry Ph.D. in a very tight job market, is desperate to find work to support his family. One of his mentors offers him an inside-track to a job developing biochemical weapons. The mentor knows that George is a pacifist and, in particular, strongly opposed to biochemical weapons. The mentor is sympathetic to George's position but points out that if George doesn't take the job, it will go to another equally qualified candidate who happens to strongly support the biochemical weapons program. The mentor suggests, therefore, that not only George and his family, but also the whole world will be better off if George takes the job.

Williams maintains that George should not take the job (or, at least, that the mentor's utilitarian case for taking it doesn't automatically trump the job's conflict with George's pacifist identity).

Similarly, considerations of personal integrity can outweigh the disagreement of epistemic peers. In both cases, the preference for personal integrity is based on the moral absurdity of saying that I should give up any or all of my most fundamental convictions because some epistemic peers disagree with them. This, in Wittgenstein's phrase, is where "my spade turns", where I hit the bedrock of convictions for which the disagreement of my peers does not matter.

But what about cases where personal integrity isn't at stake?

---

* There are lots of complications about how to define happiness and how to determine the "amount" of happiness produced by a given action, but these issues aren't essential to the point we're discussing.

Should I then give up (not deny, but withhold judgment on) my convictions when my epistemic peers disagree? Here we need to consider the extent of the disagreement. There's no reason to retreat when an equal or greater number of peers still agree with me or, indeed, until there's a clear majority who disagree. But even in the face of the overwhelming disagreement of peers, it may be reasonable to hold fast to my convictions even while acknowledging (at least to myself) that they may be wrong. As long as there's a non-negligible chance that a position is correct, it makes sense to have it represented in public debate, and who better to articulate it than someone strongly inclined to accept it?

WHAT GOOD IS ARGUING?

We see, then, that I can be justified in holding onto my convictions in the face of unresolvable disagreement with epistemic peers. But even here engaging the argument is valuable, since it can help uncover what my convictions are and how deeply I hold them. Here we need to invoke one last principle: *The Principle of Self-Understanding.* Yes, public debates are valuable because they give us an opportunity to support our views. But they are equally valuable for the chance they offer us to reflect on those convictions. Through debate we are forced to consider how central our convictions are to our sense of personal integrity. Sometimes what I accept without question on a controversial issue is not really a conviction but merely a belief I've picked up without having thought about whether I'm really convinced of it. On controversial issues, only what has withstood sustained reflection and testing can have the status of a rational conviction. I also, to the extent possible, should try to understand the nature and the depth of my opponents' convictions.

Given such understanding, I can assess what is truly at stake in political debates: where I should be open to changing my mind because an issue doesn't involve my convictions; where a conviction is not a matter of personal integrity and so can be relinquished in the face of peer disagreement or compromised to achieve a goal that matters more to me; and where I must say, "Here I stand, I can do no otherwise". Without this kind of hard-won self-understanding, political debate can readily become a mere game, a form of intellectual competition in which I have no ultimate goal except to win.

We know that political debate alone is unlikely to settle any important issue. That's why, in a democracy, we vote. Debate is the prelude to voting. But how does my vote relate to the debate that preceded it? Not, as we might think, by expressing my view of who won the debate. My vote simply signals who I want to hold a position of authority (or, in the case of a referendum, what law should be adopted). What should determine my vote varies, ranging from my individual self-interest to the interests of various groups I belong to, even to the common good of the nation or the world.

In every case, however, knowledge has weight in my voting for what I really want. If I want to vote my self-interest, then I need to know whether paying lower taxes is really in my self-interest and, if so, whether a given candidate is likely to lower my taxes. More generally, if I want to vote to achieve a certain goal, then, for any policy, I need to know that it will fulfill this goal and whether a given candidate will in fact carry out that policy.

No-holds-barred public debate is the most reliable process for attaining such knowledge, since other processes—accepting another's authority, following emotions, agreeing with the most attractive advertising, acting on gut-instincts—are not directed toward knowledge and reach it only by accident. The higher the level of public debate—that is, the closer public debate comes to fulfilling the various principles we have discussed—the better chance there is that I will vote for what I really want, no matter what theory underpins the decision.

WE HAVE SEEN how philosophical methods and concepts provide guidance for fruitful political debates as well as an understanding of the types of results we can expect those debates to yield. Further, the principles and concepts developed in this chapter apply to the issues in the following chapters. Throughout, we will need to put arguments on both sides in their strongest forms, take account of all relevant evidence, keep in mind the role of convictions and the resulting limits of argument, and assess responsibly the significance of the disagreement remaining when argument has done what it can.

The next two chapters will show how philosophical considerations can help us in assessing claims made in the name of science.

2

SCIENCE: A CONSUMER'S GUIDE

A few years ago space scientists announced that large solar flares were likely to produce strong electronic effects on Earth. Airlines adjusted flight patterns, power companies monitored electric grids for surges, and people in northern states made plans to look for the aurora borealis. This is a simple but striking example of the *cognitive authority* of science in our society. Outside of science, there are no claims to knowledge, beyond common sense, that we readily and generally accept. If you want people to pay attention when you're selling them soap, urging them to support your cause, or telling them how to raise their children, you need to present what at least looks like scientific evidence.

Chapter 1 introduced a variety of concepts, principles, and distinctions that are relevant to discussions of public issues. We now turn to philosophical tools that help assess appeals to the authority of science.

We begin with the Principle of Predictive Success, which allows us to distinguish reliable sciences like physics and chemistry not only from pseudosciences like astrology but also from

legitimately scientific disciplines (mostly in the human sciences)
that should have a far more limited role in guiding public policy.
There are a series of crucial philosophical distinctions that allow
us to evaluate claims in popular media regarding the results of
human sciences.

The distinction between correlation *and* causation *helps*
assess claims from biomedical sciences. A further distinction
between the laboratory *and the* world *raises questions about*
the phenomena of "priming" in experimental psychology.

We next look at the limitations of evidence-based public policy
(in education and elsewhere), using the distinction between what
works in one situation *and* what will work in another situation *and noting the* problem of self-refuting knowledge.
Finally, we turn to climate science, where current debates require
reflection on the logic of appeals to authority *and the role of*
probabilities *and* values *in making decisions.*

THE PRINCIPLE OF PREDICTIVE SUCCESS

Not everything that presents itself as "scientific" deserves our
confidence. There are clear examples of trustworthy sciences—
especially in the core natural sciences of physics, chemistry,
and biology—and clear examples of untrustworthy pseudosciences—astrology, phrenology, homeopathy. What distinguishes a true science from a pseudoscience? The historian and
philosopher Thomas Kuhn[1] made a good case for a feature of
successful science that he called a *paradigm*: a distinctive achievement so successful that everyone in an area of research uses it
as a model for subsequent work. Newton's discovery of his three
laws of motion and his law of gravitation has long been the paradigm for work in many areas of physics. Scientists following him
accepted both his results (the laws) and the methods he used

to discover them (theoretical reasoning based on the mathematics of the calculus, confirmed by precise observation and experimentation). James Maxwell's discovery in the nineteenth century of the equations named after him likewise became the paradigm for physicists working on electromagnetic phenomena, as did, in biology, Darwin's account of evolution via the process of natural selection.

On one reading, Kuhn's paradigms are social rather than epistemological. That is, they indicate *consensus* among a group rather than *knowledge* (*epistémé*) independent of that consensus. While science undeniably requires social consensus on methods and results, a discipline's cognitive authority—specifically, its reliability as a guide to the future—requires more than consensus. Our believing that something is going to happen does not in general have any effect on what *does* happen. Ultimately, the only good reason for thinking that science (or anything else) can predict the future is evidence that it has done so previously. In Kuhnian terms, predicting the future is integral to a scientific paradigm's success.

A discipline may be surrounded by the *paraphernalia of science*, including technical terminology, mathematical equations, empirical data, carefully designed experiments, and even consensus among practitioners. Such disciplines may even conform to the principles we discussed in Chapter 1: practitioners may follow the Principle of Charity in discussing disputed issues, they may take account of all relevant evidence, and they may even arrive at a strong consensus that minimizes any lingering disagreement. But unless a discipline has a strong record of predicting the future, we have no basis for relying on it as a guide to what will happen.

Since we often use "science" to refer to any organized effort to study the world in a scientific way (that is, displaying the par-

aphernalia of science), not all sciences are reliable for predicting the future. We need, therefore, to distinguish *sciences* from
predictively successful sciences. A science with few or no predictive
successes may be valuable in other ways; it may, for example,
accurately describe and perspicuously organize a body of data.
But it is not a reliable guide for practical decision-making. Further, there are degrees of predictive success, and different parts
of a given science may have different degrees of reliability.

Predictive power is an issue even in the natural sciences, which
have so many spectacular predictive successes, from eclipses to
nuclear power. Theorists of fundamental physics (cosmology
and elementary particle theory) argue about whether string
theory, long regarded as a powerful mathematical tool, has or
even could generate any predictions. Questions have also been
raised about evolutionary biology, where because of the huge
time scale encompassed, making and testing predictions (say
of the emergence of new species) is practically impossible. But
a little reflection shows that evolutionary theories can be highly
successful at predicting what we will find in the fossil record.
Darwin, for example, correctly predicted that earlier forms of
trilobites would be found in rocks from the pre-Silurian geolog-
ical period. (Such predictions of what we will find out about the
past are called *retrodictions.*)

It might seem that *explanation* rather than *prediction* grounds
the cognitive authority of science. Explanation, after all, tells us
why something happens (its cause), not only *that* it will happen.
But there are often various possible explanations of an event.
For example, when Uranus's orbit deviated from what astronomers' calculations predicted, they postulated another planet,
Neptune (with an appropriate mass and location), to explain
these deviations. But the deviations could likewise have been
explained by, say, postulating moons of Uranus, revising our

estimate of Uranus's distance from the Sun, or even slightly modifying the law of gravitation. Neptune's existence may have been the most likely explanation, but until the astronomers' telescopes verified the prediction of its location and mass, Neptune would remain a hypothesis. A successful explanation—one that reveals the cause of what happens—must be underwritten by its predictive success.[*]

Questions about predictive power are most acute in the human sciences—biomedicine; psychology; and the social sciences of economics, sociology, and anthropology. Since these are also the sciences that seem most relevant to practical decisions about personal behavior and public policy, it's particularly important to understand how to evaluate claims that they make.

I will not attempt a comprehensive discussion of prediction in the human sciences. My focus is on results in these sciences that popular media reports present as relevant to personal and public decisions. The goal is to provide non-expert readers some philosophical tools for assessing these claims of relevance.

CORRELATIONAL STUDIES AND THEIR LIMITS

Biomedical science has, of course, produced some of the most spectacular and useful predictive science ever. With antibiotics, vaccines, and other drug therapies, along with advanced imaging and surgical techniques, we have unprecedented power to control medical outcomes. But the very success of

---

[*] We'll see more about the relation of causation and prediction below, when we discuss the distinction between *correlation* and *causality*.

biomedicine, combined with our life-and-death interest in its resources, has led us to misjudge and misrepresent some of its achievements.

Almost every day we read about a new medical study that says we would be healthier if, for example, we ate more fish, drank red wine rather than white, took echinacea, or began practicing yoga. Do such studies represent a body of knowledge to which we should pay attention?

On the whole, no. To understand why, we need some background in the philosophy of scientific methodology. I say *philosophy* because the study of scientific method is not a purely empirical discipline. Its goal is not to describe how in fact science is done but to determine how it ought to be done. The empirical methods of science cannot by themselves tell us what ought to be done; they provide us with facts but have nothing to say about the value of those facts. Even when scientists offer answers to methodological questions, they are not appealing to experimental facts but to their philosophical reflections about how we ought to do science.*

A first crucial methodological point is that the biomedical "results" that popular media most often report are *observational studies*. Such studies can tell us that certain practices are *correlated* (or *associated*) with better health, not that the practices *cause* us to be healthier. (A simple example of the distinction between correlated events and causes: as children grow taller, their vocabularies increase; so growing taller is correlated with

---

* This is not to say that the study of scientific method cannot appeal to historical facts about how science is practiced. But such factual information becomes relevant only if we already know that the practices in question meet the standards for good science. These standards express value judgments that cannot be determined simply by looking at facts. The same point applies to results of psychological or sociological studies of scientific behavior.

larger vocabulary. But we can't say that growing taller *causes* an increased vocabulary.)

Correlations are relatively easy to establish: simply compare people who have a certain feature (larger vocabulary) with those who don't and see if more of them have another feature (greater height). To show causation is much more difficult. We have to be sure that the two groups we are comparing have no other relevant differences than the one that we suspect may be the cause—if there are other relevant differences, one of these actually may be the cause. The most common way of excluding other relevant differences is through a *randomized controlled trial* (RCT).

Here's a simple example of an RCT. Suppose I want to know if students will do better on a test when they know their grades on the previous test. I select a group of students—say the two hundred in my large Introduction to Philosophy class—as the "subjects" of an RCT. I then divide the students into two groups: those that will be told their previous grade (the *experimental group*) and those that will not (the *control group*). This division is what makes the trial *controlled*. To make the trial *randomized*, I choose who goes into which group by a random (chance) process (e.g., by flipping a coin for each student—heads puts you into the experimental group, tails into the control group). I then give the test and see if there's any difference in the average grades of the two groups. If there is, I conclude that the difference was caused by the control group knowing their previous grades; if not, I conclude that knowing the grades made no difference.*

---

* In practice, RCTs are far more complex and difficult to carry out than this example might suggest. Among many other problems, it is not easy to be sure that the separation of the experimental and control groups has in fact been random.

The logic behind the RCT is this: Since students were assigned to the two groups by chance, there should be no differences on average between the two groups prior to the trial. In particular, any other possible causes of doing better or worse on the test—class attendance, previous grades, year in college, gender, etc.—should be equally distributed between the two groups. Therefore, the only possible cause of a difference in grades would have to be the fact that one group knew their previous grades and the other didn't.

RCTs are not always possible. Sometimes there is no way to assign subjects randomly and/or no reasonable way to control the possible causes operating on the groups. For example, scientists wanting to know if marrying early (before age twenty) affects men's income couldn't practically (or ethically) assign an experimental group to marry before they were twenty and a control group not to do so. In such cases, we can fall back on *observational studies*, which typically tell us that two factors always (or often) accompany one another. So, for example, we could compare IRS data giving the salaries of married and unmarried men. But even if we found that, say, men who had married early had lower incomes, we couldn't conclude that it was being married that made the difference. It might be that men who are likely to make more money are also less likely to marry early, or that some other factor (perhaps not going to college) leads to both early marriage and lower income.

Observational studies do often suggest causal connections—after all, a cause and its effects are correlated—but generally remain tentative until confirmed by more rigorous RCTs. For example, since at least 2004 we have been reading about studies that show "vitamin D may prevent arthritis."[2] A 2010 Johns Hopkins Health Alert announced, "During the past decade, there's been an explosion of research suggesting that vitamin D plays a significant role in joint health and that low levels may be a risk factor for rheumatologic conditions such as rheumatoid arthritis and osteoarthritis."[3] Then, in February 2013, an RCT called the previous studies into serious question.[4] Similarly, despite many studies suggesting that taking niacin to increase "good cholesterol" would decrease heart attacks, an RCT showed niacin had no effect.[5]

In some cases, sophisticated observational studies can establish a causal connection; this was the way scientists proved that smoking tobacco causes cancer. But less rigorous observational studies are far more common and, without clear indications to the contrary, we should assume that we can't rely on the results reported in popular media.

Media reports frequently suggest that the biomedical results they report are valuable to our decisions about our health and that, taken as a whole, these reports form a vast body of practical medical knowledge. In fact, most biomedical results are of no immediate practical value. What they do is move scientists one small step closer to a final result that may be truly useful. In journalistic terms, most correlational studies are "news" only for scientists who are looking for hypotheses that may be worth further testing. For those of us interested in science we can rely on to improve our lives, such studies are irrelevant. They are part of the scientific process but not a reliable product of that process.

THE LABORATORY VS. THE WORLD

Even when our experiments give us a causal relation, they may not allow us to make useful predictions. Consider, for example, psychological experiments that reveal the often surprising effects of "priming" on human behavior.

Priming occurs when a seemingly trivial alteration in an experimental situation produces major changes in the behavior of the subjects. The classic priming experiment asked college students to form various sentences from a given set of words. One group was given words that included several associated with older people (e.g., "bingo", "gray", "Florida"). Another group was given words with no such associations. After the linguistic exercise, participants were instructed to walk down a hallway and leave the building. Although the participants were unaware of it, the experimenters timed their walks down the hall. Students from the group given words associated with old people walked more slowly than those in the other group. This group had been successfully "primed" to walk more slowly.

Similar experiments have revealed a cascade of priming effects operating on the whole range of human behavior. People primed with thoughts of larger numbers are willing to pay more for merchandise and give higher estimates of people's ages or the size of cities. Those primed by engaging in abstract thought are more willing to agree with the idea of killing one person to harvest organs to save the lives of many others, while those who have been thinking of money are less willing to help strangers who have dropped pencils.[6] There has been considerable controversy raised by experimenters unable to replicate some prominent priming effects.[7] This needs sorting out, but the sheer number of scientific reports of such effects over many years makes it unlikely that the phenomenon doesn't exist.

Priming experiments are fascinating to read about, provide great conversation starters, and are reminders of how vulnerable we are to irrational forces. But often much more is claimed for these experiments. In particular, they are often thought to provide powerful new tools for influencing human behavior. But a closer analysis does not support such claims.*

Priming experiments do not tell us how important priming is in *realistic* situations. (As psychologists put it, experimental validity does not imply "ecological validity".) We know that priming has striking effects under highly simplified and controlled *laboratory conditions*, where the subjects are exposed only to carefully selected stimuli. But we seldom know how effective priming stimuli (e.g., thinking about money, large numbers, abstract questions) would be in *real-life, uncontrolled environments*, where all sorts of stimuli might be in conflict with one another. Also, there is seldom reason to think that even strong effects of priming stimuli would last long enough to make a significant practical difference.

John Bargh, a Yale psychologist who has done some of the most important work on priming, acknowledged in a 2006 article the failure to extend priming to real-life situations.[8] Priming studies, he said, had come to their "childhood's end". Now, "we must seek to extend the findings of nonconscious perceptual, appraisal, motivational, and behavioral effects from our laboratories, where they have mainly been studied in isolation from each other, into the complex and noisy real world in which they all combine, somehow, to drive our actions." However, in a detailed 2012 survey of recent work on priming, Bargh and colleagues cite no applications to real-world situations.[9] All the studies they cite are laboratory or carefully controlled field experiments.

Popular reports often call the results of priming experiments "significant." This language, however, refers to *statistical significance*, which speaks only to the probability that the observed

---

* My discussion focuses on priming, not on the broader field of behavioral economics, which covers many other irrational influences on our decisions that would require separate evaluations.

effect is real and not attributable to chance. It says nothing at all about the *practical* significance of the effect. Statistical significance tells us how certain it is that the effect *exists*. Scientific journals typically require a certainty of 95 percent: if the same experiment were carried out twenty times, there would be, on average, only one experiment that did not find the effect. But this in itself does not tell us *how much* difference (or how important a difference) the effect would make in practice.

There is, then, no automatic transfer of a laboratory result to the real-world events we want to control. In the natural (non-human sciences) we can typically control and probe inert bodies any way we like in our efforts to yield precise quantitative measures of effects. But the complexity of humans, the interdependence of key variables, and ethical limitations on constraining human subjects make such control far less likely in the human sciences.

The limits of priming experiments are illustrated by Richard Thaler and Cass Sunstein's best-selling book, *Nudge*.[10] The authors begin with excellent discussions of priming and similar experimental results and then put forward numerous public policy proposals, most of them quite sensible, allegedly inspired by these scientific results. But in fact hardly any of their proposals depend on the results of priming and other scientific studies. Their ideas usually chime with common sense or strategies long practiced in the business world. They recommend that when giving people options (regarding, for example, retirement plans or organ donations), you should make the choice you prefer the default; give more or less information on a credit card bill depending on whether you want people to pay just the minimum amount each month; arrange food in a cafeteria or supermarket so the items you most want to sell are most accessible. As Benjamin Friedman, a Harvard political economist, pointed out in his review of the book, "we don't need behavioral economics . . . to think such proposals might be helpful."[11]

This point was further illustrated on the book's website in an interview with John Kenny, a senior executive at a major international advertising agency. The executive asserted the great importance of "behavioral economics" for his agency's work, but his examples reflected common sense rather than scientific surprises: having free WiFi available for customers, providing coupons to share with friends, and (his favorite) the idea that "the best way to persuade [young men] that a video game is cool is to tell them their mom hates it."[12]

Priming experiments remain important sources of information about the details of how our minds work. But claims that they have major practical consequences have little support. Causal principles established in controlled laboratory conditions do not in themselves help us control events outside the laboratory.

"Works Here" vs. "Works There"

Even when we have established that *C* causes *E* in one real-life context, we cannot automatically extend the result to other contexts. As Nancy Cartwright, a prominent philosopher of science, has emphasized, the very best randomized controlled test in itself establishes only that a cause has a certain effect in a particular kind of situation.[13] To borrow an example from physics, a feather and a lead ball dropped from the same height will reach the ground at the same time—but only if there is no air resistance. Typically, scientific laws allow us to predict a specific behavior only under certain conditions. If those conditions don't hold, the law doesn't tell us what will happen.

In dealing with the natural world, we are often in a position to establish conditions that are sufficiently close to those that make a law relevant. In the human (and especially the social) world the high degree of complexity and interconnectedness makes this fiendishly hard to do. A method of teaching fifth-grade math that is highly effective for the students and teachers in one school district may well not work for the students and teachers in another school district.

It follows, then, that even when we have reliable results from "pure science", we need the social equivalent of engineers: people who can tell us whether and how these results apply to the situations we are dealing with. For the natural sciences (physics, chemistry, biology) we have well-established engineering disciplines. But the engineering equivalent for the human world is, with few exceptions, still a very long way off.

Cartwright offers a powerful example.[14] During the 1980s, a project was developed for improving the nutrition of children in the Indian state of Tamil Nadu (TINP, or Tamil Integrated Nutrition Project). The program was a success and greatly decreased malnutrition. The World Bank sponsored a rigorous study by social scientists that showed the program had caused half to three-fourths of the decline. During the 1990s essentially the same program was deployed in Bangladesh (BINP), where it had almost no effect. In both cases, the program involved a specific, integrated system of educating mothers about nutrition as well as providing supplemental food and access to health care.

BINP failed for two main reasons. Whereas in Tamil Nadu mothers are responsible both for buying food and deciding what to feed their children, in Bangladesh, fathers typically buy the food; and decisions about what children should eat are often made not by mothers but by their mothers-in-law. As a result, educating mothers about nutrition—a key element of TINP—was irrelevant in Bangladesh. It was not surprising that the program failed.

Cartwright sums up the situation in the motto "It worked here, does not imply that it will work there." Put so simply, the point seems obvious and trivial. But it's easy to ignore, particularly if we think of social sciences as quite like the physical sciences, where causal principles can often be generalized and the conditions of their application modified to produce the effects we want. But as Cartwright points out, the causal principles we need to solve social problems are both *local* and *fragile*: local because they are closely tied to the precise organization of a specific socioeconomic system, fragile because even minor efforts to modify this system are likely to render the principles inapplicable. * Locality and fragility express the distinctive complexity and interrelatedness of social as opposed to natural systems, and they explain why we are so seldom able to generalize specific successes in applied social science.

We can still apply causal principles to local and fragile systems, provided we have a detailed understanding of how the causes operate (a thorough theoretical understanding of the system) and of what external factors might impede their operation (background knowledge of the context in which the system exists). This combination of theoretical understanding and background knowledge is frequently available in the physical sciences but seldom in the social sciences. This is why we can be confident that an automobile will work almost anywhere, but not that a successful method of teaching reading will work in another school or another country.[15]

EVIDENCE-BASED PUBLIC POLICY

Evidence-based public policy is an influential movement modeled on the project of evidence-based medicine. As we've seen,

---

* Cartwright notes that this terminology comes from the Chicago School of economists.

evidence-based medicine is a sensible pursuit, as long as we are talking about RCTs that, after long and careful efforts, establish generalizable causal principles. Evidence-based public policy is considerably less promising.

For example, Jeffrey Liebman, a Harvard political scientist, has proposed that we "identify ten social-policy problems where it is a national priority to find solutions" and then fund one hundred communities (ten for each problem) that put forward the most promising projects for solving the problems over five to ten years. "The goal", he says, "would be to discover two or three transformative approaches for each policy problem—solutions that could then be applied nationwide".[16] But Liebman's project assumes that the solutions to problems in his test communities would transfer to the rest of the nation—ignoring the locality and fragility of causal principles in the social sciences.

Another example illustrates several of the problems we've found with research in the human sciences. A highly praised study of teacher effectiveness purported to show a connection between better teachers and long-term success for students.[17] The study analyzed a massive amount of data about teachers and students in a large urban school system for grades four through eight over a period of twenty years (1989–2009). Its focus was on the "value added" by a teacher. The value added (VA) was defined as the average increase in the standardized tests scores of students in a given teacher's classes. (The measure of VA was adjusted to equalize factors that might affect the test results, such as class size and students' previous test scores.)

The study's first result was a demonstration that "VA accurately captures teachers' impacts on students' academic achievement [as measured by test scores]". Students' performance on the tests was caused by, not just correlated with, what the teacher had done. It was not, for example, that parents with high-achieving children got them placed in the classes of high-VA teachers.

The second and most striking result was the effect that higher-VA teachers had on their students' subsequent lives. The study found that "students assigned to higher VA teachers are more successful in many dimensions. They are more likely to attend college, earn higher salaries, live in better neighborhoods, and save more for retirement. They are also less likely to have children as teenagers." The economic results were particularly impressive: "Replacing a teacher whose true VA is in the bottom 5% with one of average quality would generate cumulative earnings gains [in current dollars] of more than $250,000 per classroom."

Initial media response to the study was enthusiastic. Nicholas Kristof, in his *New York Times* column, hailed a "landmark" study showing that "the obvious policy solution is more pay for good teachers, more dismissals for weak teachers."[18] In fact, he said, the study's data show that, if a great (high-VA) teacher planned to leave a school, it would make excellent sense for the parents of students in the teacher's classes to offer her a bonus of $100,000 (about $4,000 per student) to stay just one more year. Conversely, the parents should be willing to pay a poor (low-VA) teacher $100,000 to quit (assuming there's an average-VA replacement available). The report also was well received among policy makers, with President Obama citing it in his 2012 State of the Union address: "We know a good teacher can increase the lifetime income of a classroom by over $250,000."

But how sensible would it be to use this study as a guide to policy? Keeping in mind the distinction between correlation and causality, we first note that the study was not an RCT; there was no assignment of a random group of students to high-VA teachers and another to low-VA teachers and then systematic tracking of how these students did throughout their lives. The study was, on the other hand, a complex and sophisticated effort to tease out causes from a large body of correlational data by, for example, treating certain sets of data as effectively "natural experiments" that could be regarded as meeting something like laboratory standards. But it still remains less reliable than a genuinely controlled test.

More important is the question of the practical significance of the results. The headline-grabbing $250,000 salary increase reflects the combined salaries of about twenty-five people over several decades. For an individual in a given year, the dollar value of a high-VA teacher was about $1,000, or about 3 percent of an American worker's median salary. Similarly, having a high-VA teacher made a student only 1.25 percent more likely to attend college (and, for female students, 1.25 percent less likely to become a teenage mother).

Even if we ignore these limitations, Cartwright's distinction of "works here" versus "works there" raises a serious question, since the study at best demonstrated the importance of high-VA teachers only in the particular school district it examined. It would require considerable work to show that what happened in this district would happen in others.

Finally, there is a major problem with what most people have embraced as the policy implication of the study: to evaluate teachers by their effect on their students' test scores. The authors themselves make the point: "While our findings show that improving teacher value-added would have large returns for students, it's less clear how to achieve this goal in practice. One problem is that evaluating teachers using test scores could encourage counterproductive behaviors, such as teaching to the test or even cheating." This is an instance of a common and well-known difficulty in applying results of the human sciences. Once people know what the science-based policy is, they are likely to adjust their behavior in ways that confound the science. (Here we can speak of the *problem of self-refuting knowledge*.) Given this reservation, the authors, unlike their more enthusiastic readers, suggest that "the best way to rate teachers most likely combines test score value-added ratings with other information, like principal or peer evaluations based on classroom observation." But still, their study relied on just test scores to evaluate teachers.

Taking account of all these problems, there is nothing "landmark" or otherwise decisive about the study. It, like most psychological and social scientific work, cannot be a primary guide to setting policy. Contrary to the hopes of "evidence-based" policy proponents, such work will typically supplement the general knowledge, practical experience, good sense, and critical intelligence that we hope citizens and their leaders possess.

Climate Science

Climate science is a natural science, based on the laws of physics and chemistry, not a human science. But the sheer complexity and multitudinous interactions of the causes of climate (including human interventions) make its predictions considerably less reliable than those of many other natural sciences.

Nonetheless, climate science has established at least this much: (1) the average temperature of the Earth has been increasing and will continue to do so, and (2) some of this increase is due to human activities (e.g., burning fossil fuels such as coal and oil) that put carbon dioxide into the atmosphere. These two results are based on reliable observations and well-understood physical processes.

Beyond this, climate science has produced a number of

empirically based, sophisticated mathematical models that predict a range of effects from global warming over the next century or more. These models do not offer precise predictions of how much global warming is likely to take place and, in particular, of just what its effects will be. But they do establish a range of probabilities. Roughly, there's a high probability that some very bad things will happen (flooding of cities, life-threatening heat waves and storms, serious droughts). There is some (lesser) chance that things will not be so bad, but at least as much chance that they will be much worse.[19]

Following standard terminology, let's call this view "anthropogenic global warming" (AGW). It is a view well supported by the evidence, and there is a strong consensus among climate scientists that it is correct. My concern here is not with the details of this view or of its scientific justification, but with questions of how to form policy in the light of such information.

There are a small number of climate scientists who doubt or deny AGW, and non-expert opponents of AGW usually base their case on criticisms of the consensus view raised by this minority. But such an argument misunderstands the *logic of appeals to authority*. To see why, we need some philosophical reflection on this logic. (This will add to our discussion of disagreement in Chapter 1.)

When we appeal to expert authority, we need to decide who the experts are on a given topic. Until there is agreement about this, expert opinion can have no persuasive role. There must also be a consensus among the experts about what evidence is relevant and how to interpret it. Precisely because we are not experts, we cannot adjudicate disputes among those who are. Finally, given a consensus on a claim among recognized experts, we non-experts have no basis for rejecting the claim. When non-experts accept the authority of a discipline, they have no basis for rejecting the strong consensus of experts in that discipline.

Returning to the debate over global warming, all creditable parties to this debate recognize a group of experts designated as "climate scientists," whom they cite either in support of or in opposition to their claims. In contrast to astrology or homeopathy, there is no serious objection to the very enterprise of climate science. The only questions involve the conclusions about global warming this science supports.

There is a strong consensus among climate scientists on the existence of AGW.[20] Even those who doubt or deny this claim show a clear sense of opposing a view that is dominant in their discipline. Non-expert opponents of AGW base their case on various criticisms that this small minority of climate scientists has raised against the consensus view. But, as we've seen, as long as non-experts accept the authority of climate science, they have no basis for supporting the minority position. Critics within the community of climate scientists may have a cogent case against AGW, but, given the overall consensus of that community, the logic of appeals to authority implies that we non-experts have no basis for concluding that this is so. It does no good to say that we find the consensus conclusions poorly supported. Since we are not experts on the subject, our judgment has no standing.

A non-expert who wants to reject AGW can do so only by arguing that climate science lacks the scientific status needed for us to take seriously its conclusion about AGW. But in fact opponents don't do this. They appeal to the view of (some) climate scientists, and if there were a consensus of climate scientists against global warming, they presumably would accept it.

Once we have accepted the authority of a particular scientific discipline, we cannot consistently reject its conclusions. To adapt Schopenhauer's famous remark about causality, science is not a taxi cab that we can get in and out of whenever we like. It is, rather, an express train that, once we board it, we must take wherever it may go.

SCIENCE AND CLIMATE POLICY: PROBABILITIES VS. VALUES

Nonetheless, science cannot be the sole arbiter of climate policy. In discussions about AGW, the basic problem is how to balance scientific information about the *probabilities* of what will happen against what we see as the *values* of the various possible outcomes of an action.

To take a very simple example, suppose we had a plan for reducing the amount of CO_2 in the atmosphere that, our scientists tell us, would cost \$12 billion but would save us \$20 billion in environmental damage, for a net gain of \$8 billion. If it isn't successful, we just lose the \$12 billion. Measured in billions of dollars, the value if the plan succeeds is 8 and the value if it fails is –12. Suppose, further, that we have good reason to believe that the plan has a 70 percent chance of success (and, correspondingly, a 30 percent chance of failure). To decide what to do, we need to balance the possible savings against the risk of failure. *Decision theory* (a well-developed part of mathematics) shows us how to do this.

Decision theory tells us to weigh the values of the two outcomes in terms of their probabilities of happening, each counting in proportion to how likely it is. The result of this weighting is called the *expected value* of an outcome. In our example, the expected value if the plan succeeds is .70 x 8 = 5.6, and the expected value if the plan fails is .30 x (–12) = –3.6. This would seem to show that the plan is worth implementing. The expected gain from success is greater than the expected loss from failure. Put another way, the plan is worth implementing when the sum of the two expected values is positive—as it is in this case: 5.6 + (−3.6) = 2.

This simple example might suggest that we could arrive at an entirely scientific solution to the climate change debate. Obviously, we would have to take into account a wide variety of possible plans (including doing nothing at all) and these plans would have complex outcomes that would need to be carefully evaluated. But once we knew the relative costs and benefits of each plan, and the probability of success, we could calculate the best action.

Unfortunately, this promise is specious. Decision-theory calculations can clarify our thinking, but they carry with them a false sense of mathematical rigor. For example, in most real cases scientific knowledge will not give us a precise probability for an outcome but only a range of probabilities. Going back to our example, we'd be lucky to know that the probability of success was between 70 percent and 60 percent. But if we substitute .60 for .70 (and, correspondingly, .40 for .30) in our calculations, the expected value if the plan succeeds becomes .60 x 8 = 4.8, and the expected value if the plan fails becomes .40 x (−12) = −4.8. Since the sum of these two expected values is 0, there would be no advantage to carrying out the plan. A small change in a difficult-to-estimate probability leads to a very different practical result.

Turning to value, even dollar estimates of gains and losses will be at best educated guesses, but most problems will require judgments that go far beyond monetary value. Such judgments will usually be far more subjective and will allow us to assign only very approximate numbers. In the debate over climate change, for example, how are we to value our needs against those of future generations? Or the conflicting concerns of advanced and developing nations? There may be reasonable answers to such questions, but we will not read them off of a table of expected values. Despite all the power of mathematical decision theory, we need to realize that—to borrow an expression of the great British mathematician and philosopher Alfred North Whitehead—"the exactness is a fake".[21]

Sometimes the logical gap between scientific facts and policy decisions is of little significance. If there is a high probability that a category-five hurricane will strike New Orleans, there is good reason to order an evacuation of the city. It would be otiose to point out that the argument from "A category-five hurricane is likely to strike" to the conclusion "We ought to evacuate the city" is not valid without premises stating that staying in the city would be very dangerous, that evacuation is a sensible response, that the probability of the storm's striking is high enough to act on, etc.

But in cases like global warming—and many other science-related policy issues—the additional non-scientific premises are not obvious and require substantial discussion. The fact of AGW alone does not lead us to any obvious specific response. Appeals to science alone will not be decisive and will often require messy arguments over values. Even if scientists agree on a policy recommendation, their scientific expertise does not extend to the value judgments implicit in their advice.

We cannot, then, replace Plato's philosopher-kings with scientist-kings. First, we can't just take at face value a group's claim to scientific authority; we have to decide whom to accept as experts. Further, there will often be a non-trivial logical gap between established scientific results and specific policy decisions; and, even 2,400 years after Plato, there are no experts who can speak with one voice on questions of fundamental values. It's left to us non-experts to figure out what to do—using, we can hope, Chapter 1's techniques for arguing about politics.

As we've seen, a discipline can display the paraphernalia of science—observation, experiments, mathematical formulations —and still not offer reliable practical guidance. There is a marketplace of purportedly scientific claims. This chapter has provided philosophical tools to sort out the ones that are worth buying. Our next chapter will show how some apparently scientific conclusions in fact involve philosophical assumptions and as such require not only empirical support but also support from philosophical reflection.

3

PHILOSOPHY AND THE LIMITS OF SCIENCE

S peaking to Google's Zeitgeist Conference in 2011, Stephen Hawking proclaimed that "philosophy is dead" because philosophers "have not kept up with modern developments in science."[1] Once upon a time, most sciences were part of philosophy. Aristotle was in some sense an astronomer, a physicist, a biologist, a psychologist, and a political scientist. As various branches of philosophy found ways of treating their topics with empirical rigor, they separated themselves from philosophy, which increasingly became an armchair enterprise that worked not from controlled experiments but from common-sense experiences and conceptual analysis.

In a return of sorts to their origin, the sciences have in recent years tried to use empirical research to answer questions previously considered the exclusive domain of philosophy. Physicists like Hawking are not hesitant to claim that their work supplants philosophy. There are neuroscientists who think they are at least close to providing an entirely physical account of consciousness and proving that there is no such thing as free will. Some psychologists have claimed to answer fundamental ethical questions about morality and happiness, and others think they have revealed the clay feet of reason, the idol of philosophy. There are physicists who think they have the right tools to answer what many have seen as the deepest philosophical question of all: Why is there something rather than nothing?

In the first two chapters, philosophy guided our discussions of non-philosophical topics (in politics and science) using concepts and principles that clarified the general logic of arguments. In this chapter we turn to distinctively philosophical topics, focusing on those that have also attracted scientists with philosophical interests. What light does philosophy bring to these topics and how does its contribution compare to that of science?

CONSCIOUSNESS AND THE BRAIN

We begin with two fictional scenarios ("thought experiments") popular among philosophers interested in the nature of consciousness. These thought experiments challenge the idea, suggested by neuroscience, that there is no ultimate difference between the mind and the brain. They suggest instead that, where the mind is concerned, we need a fundamental distinction of the subjective *from the* objective *(roughly, an* inside/private *view of the mind versus an* outside/public *one). This distinction supports* dualism, *for which consciousness depends on the brain but isn't identical with it. Dualism is opposed to* materialism, *which claims that we need look to the brain alone to understand what consciousness is. In our review of the debate between materialism and dualism, we will make use of the distinctions between* logical *and* physical possibility *and between* phenomenal *and* psychological consciousness.

We trust science because it is ultimately based on direct observations of the world. But these observations arise from our experiences, which themselves are subjective realities that appear to elude the objectivity of scientific understanding. We know that our experiences depend on material systems like the brain that science can, in principle, exhaustively explain. But we find it hard to make sense of the idea that experiences themselves—seeing red, feeling, pain, falling in love—could be purely physical. No doubt experiences *correlate* with or even are *caused* by objective physical facts, but, as subjective realities, how could they *be* such facts? When I feel intense pain, scientists may be able to observe brain events that produce my pain, but they cannot observe the very pain that I feel. Could the stream-of-consciousness descriptions of James Joyce and Virginia Woolf really be translated into the language of neuroscience? What science can observe is *public* and *objective*; what I feel is *private* and *subjective*.

Some of the most interesting recent philosophical discussions have centered around two *thought experiments* designed to show that experiences cannot be physical. (A thought experiment is a description of a possible situation designed to make a point apparent.) These thought experiments have by no means settled the issue, but they have convinced quite a few philosophers and have posed a serious challenge to the claim that experience is entirely physical.

MARY AND THE ZOMBIES

The Color-Blind Neuroscientist
Mary, a leading neuroscientist who specializes in color perception, lives at a time in the future when the neuroscience of color is complete, and so she knows all the physical facts about

colors and their perception. (Here "physical" means entirely objective, with no subjective aspect). Mary, however, has been totally color-blind from birth, seeing only as in a black-and-white movie. (Here I deviate from the story's standard form, which has her sighted but—for obscure reasons—having lived in an entirely black-and-white environment all her life.)

Fortunately, as a result of research Mary herself has done, there is an operation that gives her normal vision. When the bandages are removed, Mary looks around the room and sees a bouquet of red roses sent by her husband. At that moment, Mary for the first time experiences the color red and now knows what red *looks like.* Her experience, it seems clear, has taught her a fact about color that she did not know before. But, remember, before this she knew all the *physical* facts about color. Therefore, there is a fact about color that is not physical: what that color looks like. It follows that physical science cannot express all the facts about color.[2]

Your Zombie-Twin

Here we are thinking not about the brain-eating undead of movies, but *philosophical zombies,* defined as identical to you or me except that they are utterly lacking in internal subjective experience. Imagine that you have a twin, not just genetically identical but identical in every physical detail—made of exactly the same sorts of elementary particles arranged in exactly the same way. Isn't it logically possible that this twin has no experiences?

Of course it may be true that, in our world, the laws of nature require that certain objective physical structures be correlated with corresponding subjective experiences. It may, for example, be a law of nature that when the brain is in a certain physical state, I will feel pain or see red. But laws of nature are not *logi-*

cally necessary but only *physically necessary*. A world with different laws of nature could exist; that is, there is no contradiction in the idea of such a world. For example, water could freeze at 22°F rather than 32°F. If there were no distinction between logical and physical necessity, we could discover laws of nature as we do laws of logic or mathematics, by pure thought independent of empirical observations. Therefore, even if the laws of nature require that a given state of the brain produce a given conscious state, there could (logically) exist a being physically identical to me but with no experiences: my zombie-twin.

But if a zombie-twin is logically possible, it follows that my experiences involve something beyond my physical makeup. For my zombie-twin shares my entire physical makeup, but does not share my experiences. This means that physical science cannot express all the facts about my experiences.[3]

It's worth noting that philosophers who find these thought experiments convincing still allow that there is a sense in which an experience is physical. Seeing red, for example, involves photons striking the retina, followed by a whole string of physical events that process the retinal information before we actually have a subjective sense of color. There's a purely physical sense in which this is "seeing", which is why we can say that a surveillance camera "sees" someone entering a room. Philosophers call this *psychological consciousness* (an objective reality observable from the outside). But the "seeing" camera has no subjective experience; that is, no *phenomenal consciousness* (a subjective reality, observable only by introspection). Subjectivity comes into the picture only when *we* look at what the camera recorded. The claim that experience is not physical applies only to experience in this sense. But, of course, experience in this subjective sense is what populates the rich inner life that matters so much to us.

Few philosophers think these thought experiments show that there are souls or other sorts of supernatural entities. Most maintain that there is no world beyond the natural one in which we live. Their claim is rather that this world contains a natural reality (consciousness) that escapes the scope of physical (purely objective) explanation.

David Chalmers, in particular, supports a "naturalistic dualism". Not only are there the physical realities (entirely objective, with no subjective aspect) that the natural sciences have so successfully studied but there are also, he thinks, nonmaterial realities with subjective aspects that are needed for understanding our minds. This is his *dualism*. But Chalmers also thinks that these nonmaterial realities are part of the natural world and that we could develop a unified scientific account of how the material and the nonmaterial work together to produce our subjective experiences. This is why his dualism is *naturalistic*: he doesn't think there are any supernatural realities beyond the natural world that we know through science.

How can a materialist (someone who thinks consciousness is entirely physical) respond to these two examples—or, more generally, to the claim that there is an unbridgeable gap between scientific objectivity and our subjective experience? Perhaps the most attractive response is that it's hard to understand how experiences could be physical only because we lack the relevant scientific concepts. After all, before we had the concepts of biochemistry, we couldn't understand how living things could be entirely physical. Why think it's impossible that experiences are physical?

For example, Daniel Dennett, one of the most prominent philosophical defenders of materialism, admits that, intuitively, zombies seem to be logically possible: "I can feel the tug as well as anybody else". But he points out that, over three hundred years after Galileo, the sun still *seems* to move around the earth. He foresees "a day when philosophers and scientists and lay-people will chuckle over the fossil traces of our earlier bafflement about consciousness: 'It still *seems* [they will say] as if these mechanistic theories of consciousness leave something out, but of course that's an illusion. They do in fact explain everything about consciousness that needs explanation".[4]

To undercut the case against materialism, Dennett offers his own versions of the two thought experiments ("intuition pumps" in his terminology). Regarding the zombie twin, for example, he introduces the notion of a *zimbo*: a kind of zombie that not only has unconscious parallels to our ordinary subjective states (seeing, thinking, etc.) but also unconscious parallels to our subjective awareness of these states. Dennett imagines a conversation with Zeke (a zimbo) in which he questions Zeke about his thoughts and feelings: "Zeke, do you like me?" . . . "Of course I do". . . . "Did you mind my asking?" . . . "Well, yes, it was almost insulting". . . . "How do you know?" . . . "I just recall feeling a bit annoyed or threatened".[5]

In Dennett's view, going into this much detail about what is involved in the idea of a zombie should lead us to see that to claim such a being is different from us makes no sense. There's no way to tell whether an alleged zombie is really unconscious: "Why would you care whether Zeke is a zimbo? Or, more personally, why would you care whether you are, or became, a zimbo? In fact, you'd never know".[6]

Similarly, Dennett argues that thinking through what it would mean for Mary to "know everything" about color will cast doubt on the assumption that she wouldn't really know what red looks like until she had seen it. Imagine, for example, that when Mary first sees colors, her husband tries to trick her, presenting not red roses but a bunch of bananas painted blue. But, Dennett says, Mary would immediately recognize the trick. Why? Precisely because she knows *everything* scientifically knowable about colors, she would have known ahead of time exactly what thoughts seeing a blue banana would cause her to have. When she had these thoughts (e.g., "he's trying to trick me"), she would know she was seeing blue, not yellow.[7]

Here I'm not concerned whether Dennett's discussion successfully undermines the case against materialism. My point is that his critique is philosophical, not scientific. That is, he does not put forward further empirical evidence to refute the anti-materialist argument. Rather, he tries to get us to see conceptual points: that the idea of a zombie makes no sense, that having complete scientific knowledge of colors does mean being able to tell what it's like to see a color. The point is that whether we accept or reject the anti-materialist case depends on philosophical, not scientific thinking; it depends on what "consciousness" and "seeing" mean, not on scientific facts about them.

Of course, scientific facts are relevant. To draw a firm conclusion about whether a complete scientific account of consciousness expresses every truth about it, we might well need something at least close to such an account. Otherwise, it would be hard to understand what it means to have a "complete scientific account". But even if we knew all that science could know, we would still need a philosophical understanding of consciousness to determine whether consciousness, properly understood, involves anything beyond matter.

Dennett himself seems to recognize this. If, he says, once science has answered all the questions it can about consciousness, "there is still a deeply mysterious residue, it will then be time to reconsider our starting point and cast about for some radical departure from current assumptions about biology, physics, and even logic".[8] To judge whether there is a "mysterious residue" will be the business of philosophy, not science. If the best scientific account implied that I was not in pain despite my subjective experience of agony, I could be sure there was something wrong with the account.

Dennett is right that we can't predict how things would look if and when science has done all it can to explain consciousness. Perhaps we would then understand how an entirely objective account of consciousness is consistent with everything we know from our subjective experience. But one thing is clear: we can't be sure about this ahead of time. At the present stage of science, we simply don't know whether materialism is true. We may have strong feelings about how things will turn out, but these feelings are based on faith, not on decisive evidence.

As a philosopher of mind, Valerie Gray Hardcastle, has put it: "I am a committed materialist and believe absolutely and certainly that empirical investigation is the proper approach in explaining consciousness. I also recognize that I have little convincing to say to those opposed to me." Rather, she says, she has a "total and absolute faith that science as it is construed today will someday explain [consciousness] as it has explained the other so-called mysteries of our age".[9] At our present level of scientific and philosophical understanding, both Chalmers-style dualism and Dennett-ish materialism remain matters of faith.

NEUROSCIENCE AND FREE WILL

We consider laboratory experiments thought to show that free will is an illusion. Our discussion will make use of the philosophical distinctions between causing *and* compelling, *between a* fact *and its* meaning, *and between an* action *and an* event. *These will lead to the idea of* compatibilism, *the philosophical view that, properly understood, our choices can be simultaneously free and caused. We will also discuss the limitations of the* operational definition*s scientists use to test hypotheses about freedom.*

"We feel that we choose," says neuroscientist Patrick Haggard, "but we don't".[10] His claim is based on experiments he and Benjamin Libet (who first developed this approach) conducted to find out what causes an action. Subjects were asked to look steadily at a rotating clock hand and to move their wrist whenever they chose. They then reported the position of the clock when they first became aware of their decision to move the wrist. The moment at which the action itself began was determined with scalp electrodes that measure the readiness potential (RP) in the area of the brain associated with the wrist's movement. As Haggard explains, "The RP is a well-established gradual increase in electrical activity in the motor cortical regions, which characteristically precedes willed actions".

Haggard then lays out the logic behind the experiments as tests for free will:

> If the moment of conscious intention preceded the onset of the readiness potential, then the concept of conscious free will would be tenable: the early conscious mental state could initiate the subsequent neural preparation of movement. But if the moment of conscious intention followed the onset of the readiness potential, then conscious free will cannot exist: a conscious mental state must be a consequence of brain activity, rather than the cause of it.[11]

As it turned out, in test subjects, the beginning of the action (measured by the RP) measurably preceded the conscious intention by from one-third to one-half of a second. By the logic of the experiment, there was no free will, despite the subjects' subjective experience of having freely decided to move their wrists; the decision occurred after the action began and therefore could not have caused the action.

There are some purely scientific challenges to accepting these experiments as proof that the subjects' movement was not free. How accurate could subjects be in their self-reporting of when they decided to move their wrists? Recalling the distinction of *correlation* and *cause*, are we certain that the RP is a cause of the motion and not just correlated with it? Mightn't the RP cause the motion only because there was no subsequent decision to stop the motion? (Libet himself suggested that this possibility might save free will, but subsequent experiments refuted that idea.)

Let's suppose, however, that all such objections are overcome by subsequent experiments and that there is substantial scientific proof that our apparently free decisions are in fact caused by prior physical events in the brain. Does this show the decisions were not free?

Here we need a philosophical understanding of what it means for an action to be free. It might seem that a choice can't be free if it is caused, but, on the other hand, how could a choice that was not caused be free? If a choice has no cause at all, it's a random event, something that occurred out of the blue. Why say that a choice is mine if it doesn't arise from something occurring in my mind (or brain)? And if a choice isn't mine, how can we say I made it?

Following out this line of thought, many philosophers, and particularly David Hume, have argued that a free choice must be caused and that, therefore, freedom and causality must be compatible (which is why we call this view of freedom *compat-*

ibilism). Of course, some ways of causing a choice will exclude freedom. If I choose to remain indoors because I'm in the grip of a panic attack at the thought of going outside, then my choice isn't free. Here we might say that I'm not just *caused* to choose as I do, I'm *compelled*.

But perhaps I stay inside because I want to continue reading an interesting book. Here my desire to continue reading causes me to stay inside, but it seems wrong to say that it compels me. So perhaps a choice is free when it's caused by my desire rather than compelled (that is, caused against my desire). A choice is not free when it's uncaused; it's free when it's caused in the right sort of way: that's compatibilism.

We can also formulate compatibilism in terms of an important philosophical distinction between *an action* and *an event*. Roughly, an action is something that I do, whereas an event is something that happens to me. The standard example is the difference between my raising my arm (an action) and the mere fact that my arm rose (an event). From a compatibilist standpoint, the very same motion can be an action that is free because I do it *and* an event caused by other events that precede it.

Philosophers favoring compatibilism have worked out elaborate accounts of what's involved in a choice's being caused "in the right sort of way", therefore making it free.[12] Other philosophers have argued that compatibilism is a blind alley, and that there must be some sense in which a free choice has no cause. These efforts have led to many important insights and distinctions, but there is still lively debate about the required conditions for a choice to be free.

The logic of Libet's and similar experiments simply *defines* a free choice as a choice not caused by physical changes in the brain. This is what philosophers of science call an *operational definition*: a definition of a concept in terms of the scientific procedures or operations used to detect and, often, measure it. Operational definitions are essential for scientific observation, since they tell us precisely what the results of our observations mean. But this "operational meaning" may not be an especially good fit with what we are actually interested in. Think, for example, of when a doctor asks you where you'd place your pain on a scale of zero (no pain at all) to ten (the worst you can imagine). The simple test is replacing a complex phenomenon (the subjective feeling of pain) with something much easier to observe (the utterance of a numeral). This can be a useful device for getting a rough sense of a patient's distress, but it obviously doesn't tell what it means to be in pain, nor does it provide a precise measure of how much it hurts.

For a complex and controversial concept such as freedom, any operational definition requires thorough scrutiny before we draw conclusions about it from an experiment. In particular, Libet-style experiments employ an operational definition of freedom that assumes that if a choice has a physical cause, it can't be free. This is a philosophical assumption about freedom that is not supported by any scientific evidence.

Figuring out what makes a choice free is essential for interpreting scientific experiments about freedom but does not itself involve making scientific observations. This is because "What makes a choice free?" is not a question about *facts* but about *meanings*. Introducing an operational definition for the sake of getting observable results ignores this crucial distinction. Haggard himself seems to have some sense of this point. Toward the end of his discussion of Libet's and his experiments, he suggests that interpreting the experiments may well depend on the "largely philosophical [issue of] what is chosen in voluntary action".[13]

The fact that I moved my arm can be established by scientific observation—even by the impersonal mechanism of a camera. But whether I was waving in greeting or threatening an attack is a matter of interpretation. The camera catches the *fact* of my arm's moving but offers no insight into the *meaning* of this motion. Similarly, scientific observations might show that a brain event caused a choice. But whether the choice was free requires knowing the meaning of freedom. If we know that a free choice must be unpredictable, or uncaused, or caused but not compelled, then an experiment may tell us whether a given choice is free. But an experiment cannot of itself tell us that a choice is free, any more than a photograph by itself can record a threat.

It doesn't follow that freedom is some mysterious immaterial quality beyond the ken of science. That may or may not be so. For us the essential point is that we do not have a sufficiently firm idea of what we mean by freedom to design a scientific test for it. We don't, in other words, have an adequate operational definition of freedom. More precisely, we don't know enough about how a free choice might still depend on the brain events that typically precede it. (By contrast, we do now know enough to judge that psychotic behavior triggered by a brain tumor is not free.)

Brain science can give us specific information about how brain events affect our choices. This allows our philosophical discussion of the conceptual relation between causality and freedom to focus on the real neurological situation, not only abstract possibilities. It may well be that philosophers will never arrive at a full understanding of what, in all possible circumstances, it means for a choice to be free. But, working with brain scientists, they may learn enough to decide whether the choices we make in ordinary circumstances are free. Science and philosophy together may reach a solution to the problem of free choice that neither alone could achieve.

THE PSYCHOLOGY OF HAPPINESS AND MORALITY

Recent years have witnessed a boom in empirical studies of the psychology of happiness, which is often taken to be the ultimate value of human existence, and of morality as the guide to how we should live. We discuss the limits of such studies using philosophical distinctions among various senses of happiness, a distinction between fact and value, and a distinction between intuition and reason. Plato's views on intuition and reason offer special insight.

Psychologists have accumulated a vast amount of empirical data suggesting correlations (or lack thereof) between happiness and various genetic, social, economic, and personal factors. Some of the results are old news: wealth, beauty, and pleasure, for example, have little effect on happiness. But there have been surprises. There are studies suggesting that serious illness typically does not make us much less happy, and that marriage in the long run is not a major source of either happiness or unhappiness.

The new research has both raised hopes and provoked skepticism. Psychologists such as Sonja Lyubomirsky have developed a new genre of self-help books purporting to replace the intuitions and anecdotes of traditional advisors with scientific programs for making people happy.[14] At the same time, there are serious questions about the methods the studies use: Can we trust individuals' self-reports of how happy they are? Can we objectify and even quantify so subjective and elusive a quality as happiness? As in the case of consciousness, we need to distinguish happiness as *objective* (measurable by science from the outside) and happiness as *subjective* (lived from the inside).

As with free choice, the most powerful challenge to happiness research concerns its meaning and value. Once again, the problem is finding an operational definition that will catch what we really mean by happiness. When researchers ask people if they are happy, the answers tell us nothing if we don't know what our respondents mean by "happy". One person might mean, "I'm not currently feeling any serious pain"; another "My life is pretty horrible but I'm reconciled to it"; another "I'm feeling a lot better than I did yesterday". Happiness research requires a clear understanding of the various meanings of the term. For example, most researchers distinguish between happiness as a *psychological state* (e.g., feeling overall more pleasure than pain) and happiness as a *positive evaluation of your life*, even if it has involved more pain than pleasure. Above all, there is the fundamental question: In which sense, if any, *should* happiness be a goal of a human life?

Empirical surveys can provide a list of the different ideas people have of happiness. But research has shown that when people achieve their ideas of happiness (marriage, children, wealth, fame), they often do not regard themselves as happy. Other studies suggest that we are sometimes most content doing things that we don't think make us happy (work, for example).[15] There's no reason to think that the ideas of happiness we discover by empirical surveys are sufficiently well considered to lead us to genuine happiness. For richer and more sensitive conceptions of happiness we need to turn to philosophers, who, from Plato and Aristotle, through Hume and Mill, to Hegel and Nietzsche, have provided some of the deepest insight into the possible meanings of happiness.

Even if empirical investigation could uncover the full range of possible conceptions of happiness, there would still remain the question of which conception(s) we ought to try to achieve. Here we have a question of *value* rather than *fact*: what is good to aim for, regardless of what anyone does in fact aim for. (This corresponds to a distinction between *happiness as desired* and *happiness as desirable*). Empirical inquiry alone is unable to answer such questions, which also require philosophical thinking.

This is not to say that we can simply appeal to expert philosophical opinion to tell us how we ought to live. We all need to answer this question for ourselves. But if philosophy does not have the answers, it does provide tools for seeking them. If we are inclined to think that pleasure is the key to happiness, John Stuart Mill shows us how to distinguish between sensory and intellectual pleasures. Robert Nozick (as we will see in more detail in Chapter 6) asks us to consider whether we would choose to attach ourselves to a device that would produce a constant state of intense pleasure, even if we never achieved anything in our lives other than experiencing this pleasure.

On yet another level, Immanuel Kant asks whether happiness should be the goal of a good human life, suggesting that we should do the right thing even if it seems opposed to our happiness. Nietzsche and Sartre ask whether morality itself is a worthy goal of human existence, Nietzsche suggesting that it glorifies weakness over strength, Sartre that morality is a way of denying our responsibility for our free choices. These essential questions are not empirical, and cannot be answered by the psychology of happiness. No matter who discusses them, they require conceptual clarifications and distinctions that cannot be discovered by scientific observation.

Similar problems arise when psychologists address the question of morality. Here one of the best contemporary examples is Jonathan Haidt, who explicitly presents his psychological account of morality as a direct challenge to traditional philosophical views.[16] Specifically, Haidt purports to refute Plato's central argument in the *Republic*, which tries to show why a *just* (morally good) life is superior to an *unjust* (immoral) life.

In the *Republic*, Socrates (as usual, Plato's spokesman) responds to a view put forward by his young friend Glaucon. On this view, someone who devoted his life to nothing but satisfying his selfish desires could be entirely happy. At the most, Glaucon suggests, happiness would require a person's keeping his selfishness secret and enjoying a reputation for virtue. Glaucon does not believe this claim, and he hopes to see Socrates refute it and show how morality, by itself, brings happiness.

Haidt pithily summarizes Socrates' argument: "Reason must rule the happy person. And if reason rules, then it cares about what is truly good, not just about the appearance of virtue".[17] But Haidt maintains that Socrates goes wrong because he assumes a false view of the role of reason in human life. "Reason is not fit to rule; it was designed to seek justification, not truth", where justification means pursuing "socially strategic goals, such as guarding our reputations and convincing other people to support us". Haidt bolsters his claim about the actual role of reason with an array of psychological experiments cumulatively showing that "Glaucon was right: people care a great deal more about appearance and reputation than about reality".[18]

For example, when people who have been promised cash for carrying out a task are (deliberately) overpaid, only 20 percent point out the mistake. But if they are asked if they received the right amount, 60 percent say they were overpaid. Presumably this is because, if someone later points out the mistake, in the first case they have plausible deniability ("I didn't notice!"), whereas in the second case they don't. People are more likely to do the right thing when there's a good chance that wrongdoing will be found out. (This result is, of course, already apparent from everyday experience.)

Plato, however, would hardly be surprised to learn that people typically don't use reason to seek truth and instead prefer appearance. His cave allegory (in the *Republic*) vividly expresses the very point Haidt is trying to make. The allegory compares us to prisoners in a cave condemned to view only shadows of images of real things. And his metaphor in the *Phaedrus* of a charioteer (reason) desperately trying to control two horses, one of which is struggling to go its own way (representing our irrational desires), makes the same point as Haidt's own image of a rider trying to control an elephant. In fact, Plato's image is more subtle. While one horse (corresponding to Haidt's elephant) represents desires that work against reason, the other represents desires that support reason. Unlike Haidt's, Plato's image catches the truth that, to be effective, reason requires cooperation from our desires.

Haidt also thinks his psychological studies count against Plato because they show that our decisions are usually strongly affected by what he calls "gut feelings"—our immediate, unreasoned intuitions. Plato, according to Haidt, has no place for such intuitive reactions, but thinks moral decisions should be based only on disengaged reasoning. Haidt's own, purportedly more nuanced, view rejects both Plato's excessive rationalism and the polar opposite view that we have no alternative to a life dominated by our gut feelings. Haidt allows that "we should not expect individuals to produce good, open-minded, truth-seeking reasoning, particularly when self-interest or reputational concerns are in play". But he sees hope in the social dimension: "if you put individuals together in the right way . . . , you can create a group that ends up producing good reasoning as an emergent product of the social system".[19]

But Haidt's view is by no means alien to Plato, who saw truth arising only from the right sort of discussion among inquirers accountable to one another. Nor would Plato object to Haidt's claim that ethics is based on *intuition*—direct moral judgments—rather than *reasoning*.

In fact, Plato's account is superior to Haidt's because it shows how intuitions function in moral reasoning. First, Plato emphasizes that moral reasoning (what he calls *dianoia*) logically derives conclusions ultimately by appealing to premises that are not supported by logical argument. Logic yields merely hypothetical knowledge (if *p*, then *q*) since it cannot prove the truth of all its premises (as we saw in Chapter 1). It follows that reasoning will reliably yield truth only when it is completed by intuitive knowledge (*noesis*) that justifies the premises from which we reason.

Haidt's intuitions cannot play this role, since they are merely the snap judgments of everyday life determined by genes and social conditioning. Plato's intuitions are intellectual insights into fundamental moral truths. They are not, however, the mere opinions of an individual meditating in isolation. They derive from a long and complex process of physical, emotional, and intellectual formation in a supportive social system. This is what Plato means by the "education" of his philosopher-rulers, which the *Republic* delineates in detail. Haidt rightly sees reasoning as a social process, but he provides it no foundation because his intuitions— the only plausible source of the premises of arguments—remain unreliable snap judgments. Plato sees the need for responsible intellectual engagement with others that can replace Haidt's snap judgments with reliable moral intuitions.

We see, then, that Plato provides a more adequate account of the fundamental distinction between reason and intuition, one that Haidt could use. But Haidt doesn't take Plato—and most other philosophers—seriously because they don't proceed like empirical scientists, testing their ideas through experiments, but instead rely on their personal insights into morality. He even dismisses the work of Immanuel Kant—probably the most important moral philosopher of the modern age—as reflecting a personality in the "autism zone", rather than any deep insight.[20]

Haidt is right—and many philosophers agree—that ethicists should take into account the recent explosion in sophisticated experimental work on morality. But, in contrast to most work in the physical sciences, our everyday experience (and our reflections on that experience) remain important sources of moral knowledge. Haidt's experimental results often seem plausible because they accord with our prescientific experience (as we noted in the case of people being honest when deceit is likely to be detected). And, without such accord, we could well question (following our distinction between *laboratory* and *world*) the relevance of simplified and controlled laboratory experiments to the complexities of unmanaged real life. A scientific psychology of morality cannot detach itself from our moral experiences and, even more, it needs to take into account philosophical elucidations and refinements of those experiences. Here psychology must build on what we've learned from Plato, Aristotle, Hume, Kant, Hegel, and Nietzsche, as well as from the contemporary philosophers who continue their enterprise.

What Is Reasoning For?

While Jonathan Haidt has challenged philosophical views of moral reasoning, other psychologists have raised questions about traditional views of reason in general. Philosophers think of themselves as experts on reasoning. After all, it was Aristotle who invented the science of logic, and the modern development of symbolic logic emerged from the work of philosophers such as Gottlob Frege, Bertrand Russell, and Alfred North Whitehead. But fascinating work by two French cognitive scientists, Dan Sperber and Hugo Mercier, suggests that reason is not, as philosophers generally think, directed toward attaining truth, *but rather toward* winning arguments. *We examine this claim, using the logic of philosophical arguments against skepticism and the philosophical distinction between* knowledge *and* true belief. *Finally, we see how a* pragmatic view of truth, *developed by American philosophers such as William James, John Dewey, and Richard Rorty, can resolve challenges to Sperber and Mercier's account.*

Sperber and Mercier begin from well-established facts about our deep-rooted tendencies to make mistakes in reasoning.[21] We have a very hard time sticking to rules of deductive logic, and we frequently make basic errors in statistical reasoning. Most importantly, we are strongly inclined to "confirmation bias": we focus on data that support a view we hold and ignore data that count against it (a particularly common way of ignoring the Principle of Relevant Evidence).

One classic experiment gives subjects a sequence of three numbers (e.g., 2, 4, 6) and asks them to form a hypothesis about the rule used to produce that sequence. They are then told to test their hypothesis by asking the experimenter whether other sequences fit the rule. Most people ask only about sequences that fit their hypothesis. If they think the rule is that the sequence contains consecutive even numbers, they ask if 8, 10, 12 and 22, 24, 26 fit. A series of "yes" answers convinces them that they are right. But this approach makes it impossible to discover the rule when, for example, it is merely that each number is larger than its predecessor.

It seems, then, that our evolutionary development has not done an especially good job of making us competent reasoners. Sperber and Mercier, however, point out that this is true only if the point of reasoning is to draw true conclusions. Fallacious reasoning, especially reasoning that focuses on what supports our views and ignores what counts against them, is very effective for the purpose of winning arguments with other people. So, they suggest, it makes sense to think that the evolutionary point of human reasoning is to win arguments, not to reach the truth.

This claim opens Sperber and Mercier to standard philosophical arguments against the skepticism that questions whether we have any knowledge at all. If, for example, skeptics assert that there are no truths, the response is that this means that their assertion that there are no truths is not true and so need not be taken seriously. A similar argument might seem to work against Sperber and Mercier: Do they think that the point of their own reasoning in the paper is not truth but winning an argument? If not, then their theory is falsified by their own reasoning. If so, they are merely trying to win an argument, and there's no reason why scientists—who are interested in truth, not just winning arguments—should pay any attention. Sperber and Mercier seem caught in a destructive dilemma, logically damned if they do and damned if they don't.

They resist this conclusion, but empirical psychology doesn't provide the resources necessary to avoid it. But philosophical thinking has led to this dilemma, and a bit more philosophy shows a way out. We need to think more carefully about the distinction between *seeking the truth* and *winning an argument*. The distinction makes sense for cases where someone does not care about knowing the truth and argues only to convince other people of something, whether or not it's true. But suppose my goal is simply to know the truth. How do I go about achieving this knowledge? Plato long ago pointed out that it is not enough just to believe what is true. Suppose I believe that there are an odd number of galaxies in the universe and in fact there are. Still, unless I have adequate support for my belief, I cannot be said to *know* it. It's just an unsupported opinion. Knowing the truth requires not just true belief but also rational justification for the belief.

But how do I justify a belief and so come to know that it's true? There are competing philosophical answers to this question, but one fits particularly well with Sperber and Mercier's approach. This is the view that justification is a matter of being able to *convince other people* that a claim is correct, a view held in various ways by the classic American pragmatists (Peirce, James, and Dewey) and, in recent years by Richard Rorty and Jürgen Habermas.

The key point is that justification—and therefore knowledge of the truth—is a social process. This need not mean that claims are true *because* we come to rational agreement about them. But such agreement, properly arrived at, is the best possible justification of a claim to truth. For example, our best guarantee that stars are gigantic masses of hot gas is that scientists have developed arguments for this claim that almost anyone competent to judge the matter will accept.

This pragmatic view understands truth-seeking as a special case of trying to win an argument: not winning by coercing or tricking people into agreement, but by achieving agreement through honest arguments. The important practical conclusion is that finding the truth does require winning arguments, but not in the sense that my argument defeats yours. Rather, *we* find an argument that defeats all contrary arguments. Sperber and

Mercier move toward this philosophical view when they (like Jonathan Haidt) argue that reasoning is most problematic when carried out by isolated individuals and most effective when carried out in social groups.

The pragmatic philosophy of justification takes the further steps needed to show that Sperber and Mercier's psychological account of reasoning need not fall victim to the claim that it is a self-destructive skepticism. Conversely, the philosophical view gains plausibility from its convergence with the psychological account. This symbiosis is another instructive example of how philosophy and empirical psychology can fruitfully interact.

Depression and the Limits of Psychiatry

We next turn to applied psychology: the practice of psychiatry, focusing on recent debates about depression. Our main resource will be Michel Foucault's historical and philosophical analysis of mental illness. We will also employ a distinction between "normal" as a description *and as an* evaluation.

In 1961, Michel Foucault published his *History of Madness,* an account of the treatment from the Renaissance through the nineteenth century of those judged "mad."[22] Always implicit (and occasionally strongly explicit) in this historical narrative was a critique of contemporary psychiatry. In excavating the origins of modern psychiatric practice, Foucault raised serious questions about its meaning and validity.

Foucault's central critique claims that modern psychiatry, while purporting to be grounded in scientific truths, is primarily a system of moral judgments. "What we call psychiatric practice," he says, "is a certain moral tactic . . . covered over by the myths of positivism." Indeed, what psychiatry presents as the "liberation of the mad" (from mental illness) is in fact a "gigantic moral imprisonment."[23]

Foucault may well be letting his rhetoric outstrip the sober truth, but his essential point demands consideration. Psychiatric practice does seem to be based on implicit assumptions that certain ways of living are better than others, and efforts to treat mental illness can be in fact society's way of controlling what it views as immoral (or otherwise undesirable) behavior. Not that long ago, homosexuals and women who rejected their stereotypical roles were judged "mentally ill", and there's no guarantee that today's psychiatry is free of similarly dubious judgments.

Consider a prominent recent example. Much current psychiatric practice follows the *Diagnostic and Statistical Manual of Mental Disorders* (DSM). Its most recent (fifth) edition makes important revisions in the definition of depression, eliminating a long-standing "bereavement exclusion" in the guidelines for diagnosing a "major depressive disorder."[24] People grieving for the deaths of loved ones may exhibit the same sorts of symptoms (e.g., sadness, sleeplessness, loss of interest in daily activities) that characterize major depression. For many years the DSM specified that, since grieving is a *normal* response to bereavement, such symptoms are not an adequate basis for diagnosing major depression. The new edition removes this exclusion. The new definition of depression provoked a controversy that provides insight into how philosophical issues relate to the practice of psychiatry.

The dispute over the bereavement exclusion centers on the significance of "normal". Although the term can signify merely what is usual or average, in discussions of mental illness it most often has evaluative rather than descriptive force. We need, therefore, to distinguish between "normal" as a *descriptive* term and as an *evaluative* term. Proponents of the exclusion are not merely saying that depressive symptoms often occur in the bereaved; they are saying that such symptoms are appropriate (or fitting) for the bereaved and so do not require psychiatric treatment.

Opponents of the exclusion have appealed to empirical studies that compare cases of normal bereavement to cases of major depression. They offer evidence that normal bereavement and major depression can present substantially the same symptoms, and conclude that there is no basis for treating them differently. This logic is faulty, confusing the descriptive and the evaluative sense of "normal". Even if the symptoms are exactly the same, proponents of the exclusion can still argue that they are appropriate for someone mourning a loved one, but not otherwise. The suffering may be the same, but suffering from the death of a loved one may still have a value that suffering from other causes does not. No amount of empirical information about the nature and degree of suffering can, by itself, tell us whether someone ought to experience it, rather than take a pill to make it go away.

Foucault is right, then: psychiatric practice makes essential use of moral (and other evaluative) judgments. Why is this dangerous? Because, first of all, psychiatrists as such have no special knowledge about how people should live. They can, from their clinical experience, offer crucial information about the likely psychological consequences of living in various ways (for sexual pleasure, for one's children, for a political cause). But they have no special insight into what sorts of consequences make for a good human life. It is, therefore, dangerous to make them privileged judges of what syndromes should be labeled "mental illnesses".

This is especially so because, like most professionals, psychiatrists are ready to think that just about everyone needs their services. (As the psychologist Abraham Maslow said, "If all you have is a hammer, everything looks like a nail"). Another factor is the pressure the pharmaceutical industry puts on psychiatrists to expand the use of psychotropic drugs. The result has been the often criticized "medicalization" of what had previously been accepted as normal behavior—for example, shyness, the inability of little boys to sit still in school, and milder forms of anxiety.

Of course, some mental conditions—suicidal depression, severe psychosis—obviously require treatment, and for these, psychiatrists are needed. But when there is significant ethical disagreement about treating a given condition, psychiatrists, trained as physicians, may often have a purely medical viewpoint that is not especially suited to judging moral issues.

For cases like the bereavement exclusion, the DSM should give equal weight to the judgments of those who understand the medical view but who also have a broader perspective. For example, humanistic psychology (in the tradition of Maslow, Carl Rogers, and Rollo May) would view bereavement not as a set of symptoms but as a way of living in the world, with its meaning varying for different personalities and in different social contexts. Specialists in medical ethics would complement the heavily empirical focus of psychiatry with the explicitly normative concerns of rigorously developed ethical systems such as utilitarianism, Kantianism, and virtue ethics.

Another important perspective could come from a new but rapidly developing field, philosophy of psychiatry, which analyzes the concepts and methodologies of psychiatric practice. Philosophers of psychiatry have raised fundamental objections to the DSM's assumption that a diagnosis can be made solely from clinical descriptions of symptoms, with little or no attention to the underlying causes of the symptoms. Given these objections, dropping the bereavement exclusion—a rare appeal to the cause of symptoms—is especially problematic.

Finally, as we also saw in Haidt's psychology of morality, we should take into account first-person lived experiences in addition to scientific observations. We need to listen to those who have experienced severe bereavement, as well as to relatives and friends who have suffered with them. As Foucault might have said, the psyche is too important to be left to the psychiatrists.

Despite some of Foucault's rhetoric, the proper conclusion is not that psychiatry has no role to play. As Foucault later said, the point of his critique of psychiatry (and of the human sciences in general) was "not that everything is bad but that everything is dangerous." Philosophical reflection is a crucial guard against the dangers of psychiatry.

THE PHYSICS OF NOTHINGNESS

One of the deepest questions of philosophy is whether something can come from nothing. As we will see in Chapter 4, it is fundamental for arguments about God's existence, and in the twentieth century, the German philosopher Martin Heidegger took it as the essential question for understanding what it means for anything to be. Recently, a prominent astrophysicist, Lawrence Krauss, has maintained that physics can do a better job of answering this question than philosophy can. We will investigate how widely held philosophical views about what "nothing" means might be used to object to this claim. The ideas of twentieth-century French philosopher Henri Bergson and of eighteenth-century Scottish philosopher David Hume call into question the very meaning of this sort of talk about nothingness.

Stephen Hawking's claim that philosophy is "dead" because philosophers haven't kept up with science is not the only recent example of bad blood between physicists and philosophers. Lawrence Krauss, an expert on cosmology, has insisted that "philosophy and theology are incapable of addressing by themselves the truly fundamental questions that perplex us about our existence."[25] David Albert, a distinguished philosopher of science, dismissively reviewed Krauss's book: "all there is to say about this [Krauss's claim that the universe may have come from nothing], as far as I can see, is that Krauss is dead wrong and his religious and philosophical critics are absolutely right."[26] Krauss—ignoring Albert's Ph.D. in theoretical physics—retorted in an interview that Albert is a "moronic philosopher".[27]

If we back away from the combative rhetoric, we can see a more positive picture. Despite some nasty asides, Krauss doesn't deny that philosophers may have something to contribute to our understanding of "fundamental questions" (his "by themselves" in the above quotation is a typical qualification). And almost all philosophers of science—certainly Albert—would agree that an intimate knowledge of science is essential for their discipline. As we will see, there are philosophical distinctions and arguments that complement physicists' efforts to come to terms with nothingness.

There is a long tradition of philosophers' arguing for the existence of God on the grounds that the material (physical) universe as a whole requires an immaterial explanation. Otherwise, they maintain, the universe would have to originate from nothing, and it's not possible that something come from nothing. One response to the argument is that the universe may have always existed and so never came into being, but the Big Bang, well established by contemporary cosmology, is often thought to exclude this possibility.

Krauss is unimpressed by this line of argument, since, he says, its force depends on the meaning of "nothing" and, in the context of cosmology, this meaning in turn depends on what sense science can make of the term. For example, one plausible scientific meaning for "nothing" is "empty space": space with no elementary particles in it. But quantum mechanics, the long-established framework for understanding elementary particles, shows that they can emerge from empty space and so seems to show that the universe (that is, elementary particles and so the things they make up) *could* come from nothing.

But, Krauss admits, particles can emerge from empty space because empty space, despite its name, does contain fields (called "virtual fields") that fluctuate and "spontaneously" produce particles. A philosopher may well urge that these virtual fields, are the "something" from which the particles come. All right, says Krauss, but there is the further possibility that the long-sought quantum theory of gravity, uniting quantum mechanics and general relativity, will allow for the spontaneous production of empty space itself, simply by virtue of the theory's laws. Then we would have everything—space, fields, and particles—coming from nothing.

But, the philosopher asks, what about the theory's laws? They are something, not nothing—and where do they come from? Well, says Krauss—one can imagine him trying to be patient—there's another promising theoretical approach that plausibly posits a "multiverse": a possibly infinite collection of self-contained, non-interacting universes, each with its own laws of nature. In fact, it might well be that the multiverse contains universes with every possible set of laws. We have the laws we do simply because of the particular universe we're in. But the philosopher, of course, can argue that the multiverse itself had to come from somewhere.

At every turn, the philosopher concludes, the physicist's

account presupposes the existence of something (particles, fields, laws, a multiverse—whatever). In no case, then, does something really come from nothing.

But this may be a case of the philosopher's winning the battle yet losing the war. There is an absolute use of "nothing" that excludes literally everything that exists. In one sense, Krauss is obstinately ignoring this use. But he could readily cite philosophers who find this absolute use—and the corresponding principle that something cannot come from nothing—unintelligible, impossible to understand. Henri Bergson, for example, argued that when we claim something doesn't exist, it must be because something else exists in a way that excludes it. There is no one sitting in this chair because everyone is somewhere else. There has never been an American president under the age of thirty-five because the Constitution forbids it.

If Bergson is right, the idea of a state in which nothing at all exists is unintelligible; it violates the condition that nonexistence is always a function of what exists. We need to distinguish our ordinary use of "nothing" as relative (to what exists) from an unintelligible use of "nothing" as an absolute (a state in which absolutely nothing exists). If we do this, we will realize that the question *Can something come from nothing?* is meaningless if it takes "nothing" as an absolute. But if what "nothing" means depends on context, cosmology may be able to tell us what, in the context of the universe as a whole, "nothing" means.

We may have our doubts about Bergson's argument. But even if the claim survives philosophical critiques of its intelligibility, there are still objections to applying "something cannot come from nothing" to the universe as a whole. David Hume, for example, argued that it is only from experience that we know that individual things don't just spring into existence (saying that they do so is not a logical contradiction, so it is not strictly impossible). Since we have no experience of the universe coming into existence, we have no reason to say that if it has come to be, it must have a cause.

While Krauss could appeal to philosophy to strengthen his case against "something cannot come from nothing", he opens himself to philosophical criticism by assuming that scientific experiment is, as he puts it, the "ultimate arbiter of truth" about the world. The success of science gives us every reason to continue to pursue its experimental method in search of further truths. But science itself is incapable of establishing that all truths about the world are discoverable by its methods.

Since science deals only with what can be known, directly or indirectly, by sense experience, it cannot answer the question of whether there is anything—for example, consciousness, morality, beauty, or God—that is not entirely knowable by sense experience. To show that there is nothing beyond sense experience, we would need philosophical arguments, not scientific experiments. Krauss, then, may be right that only science can tell us what there is. But, without philosophy, his claim can only be a matter of faith, not knowledge.

IN EVERY CASE we have looked at, the scientific challenge to philosophy ultimately rests on philosophical assumptions. The claim that consciousness is only a state or process of the brain is based on a philosophical conviction that materialism must be true. Interpreting experiments exploring human choices requires philosophical assumptions about the meaning of freedom. A psychology of happiness must take into account the various ways philosophers have understood and evaluated happiness. Jonathan Haidt's moral psychology needs philosophical reflection to confirm and develop his experiments. A psychological account of reasoning risks falling into a self-refuting skepticism without a proper philosophical analysis. Psychiatric practice is based on moral assumptions that require philosophical scrutiny. Even the claim that science, particularly physics, alone can give a complete account of reality is itself a philosophical claim.

Scientists understandably want to address fundamental human issues, and their data and theories can contribute to the discussion. But to the extent that science moves in this direction, it encounters questions of meaning and values that its empirical methods cannot answer. Scientists are intelligent people and can make some progress on such questions on their own. But if they ignore philosophy's long and fruitful history of clarifying these questions and articulating the range of possible answers, they will waste much time following lines that philosophers have already explored. A science interested in basic issues of meaning and value should return to its original symbiotic relationship with philosophy.

In the end, some questions are ultimately philosophical, and we cannot answer them simply by appealing to empirical science. Our next chapter offers an extended illustration of this principle for the case of religious belief, while also showing that religious claims can be subject to empirical criticism.

4

THE NEW ATHEISTS

We now turn to a philosophical question of great interest to many non-philosophers: Does God exist? The negative answer—put forward by the "new atheists" led by evolutionary biologist Richard Dawkins, Sam Harris, the late Christopher Hitchens, and Daniel Dennett (the only academic philosopher in the group)—has found a dedicated and vocal following among the educated public. The consensus among new atheists is that the case for the existence of God has been discredited to the point that atheism is the only rational position, at least for any reasonable person who takes a fair look at the question. Here we primarily examine Richard Dawkins's case against theism (with a look at Sam Harris on the problem of evil).

This chapter and the next take up a higher level of philosophical thinking, showing how we can employ a large toolkit of philosophical concepts and arguments to reach conclusions about a single issue. The discussion will inevitably be more difficult, but it will also be more satisfying than the instant refutations and slam-dunk proofs that are the standard (though specious) tools of both sides in most popular debates about religion.

Dawkins's Critique of Theistic Arguments

Our first concern will be Dawkins's efforts to refute standard arguments for theism. These efforts suffer from a variety of logical mistakes. His critique of the cosmological argument *confuses an* implication *with a* presupposition, *while his critique of the ontological argument makes an illegitimate move from* distaste *for a conclusion to its* invalidity. *His critique of arguments from religious experience ignores the distinction between when we* can *explain* an experience as illusory *and when we* should *explain* an experience as illusory.

In Chapter 2, we discussed the question *Can something come from nothing?* The *cosmological argument,* one of the most popular theistic arguments, is an effort to support a negative answer to this question. Here's an elementary formulation of the argument:

1. There is something that is caused.
2. Whatever is caused must be caused by a cause other than itself.
3. If every cause is caused, then there is an endless series (an infinite regress) of causes.
4. An infinite regress of causes is impossible.
5. Therefore, there is an uncaused cause (i.e., the first cause: the cause of the series of causes that are themselves caused).

Dawkins thinks the argument is readily refuted: the theistic argument makes "the entirely unwarranted assumption that God himself is immune to the regress."[1] In other words, there is no answer to the intelligent child who, when told that God made everything, asks, who made God?

But, contrary to Dawkins, the argument does not assume that God is "immune to the regress"—that is, has no cause other than himself. Rather, it states premises (1)–(4), from which it logically follows (5) that there is an uncaused cause (God). But none of these premises state (or assume) that God has no cause. Dawkins's criticism works only if we make the elementary logical mistake of thinking that, because the argument's premises *imply* its conclusion, it has *presupposed* the conclusion. (Here recall our definition of a sound argument in Chapter 1.) That doesn't mean the argument is compelling—we'll see below that it isn't, even in a more sophisticated form. But Dawkins's comment isn't even the beginning of a cogent critique.

Dawkins's treatment of the famous ontological argument, first developed by St. Anselm of Canterbury in the eleventh century, is even less satisfactory. He correctly states the central idea that God, understood as a perfect being, would have to exist, since "a being that doesn't exist in the real world is, by that very fact, less than perfect". But he then goes on to express the argument as a playground taunt: "a really really perfect thing would have to be better than a silly old imaginary thing. So I've proved that God exists. Nur Nurny Nur Nur".[2]

Dawkins's critique of the argument goes little beyond the emotional reaction of his mocking formulation: "The very idea that grand conclusions could follow from such logomachist trickery offends me aesthetically" and "isn't it too good to be true that a grand truth about the cosmos should follow from a mere word game?".[3] How can our *distaste* (or puzzlement or outrage) at the conclusion of an argument substitute for a cogent account of why it is logically *invalid* or *unsound*?

But here Dawkins's critic also needs to be more careful. There *are* arguments that we rightly reject just because their conclusions strike us as absurd. Dawkins himself gives the case of Zeno's paradoxes, a set of arguments concluding that motion is impossible. Zeno argued, for example, that even Achilles, the swiftest soldier in the Greek army at Troy, can never catch a tortoise who has a headstart in a race. This, he said, is because in the time it takes Achilles to reach where the tortoise was, the tortoise will have moved a bit further on. It's not easy to say exactly what's wrong with this argument without getting into higher mathematics, but it's reasonable to conclude that there's something wrong with the argument simply because its conclusion (that a faster runner can never catch up with a slower runner) is obviously, absurdly false. Isn't the same true of Anselm's argument?

No. Its conclusion is that God exists—a claim that is controversial but not, like Zeno's conclusion, in direct contradiction to what we see every day. To carry out Dawkins's comparison of Anselm's argument with Zeno's, he would have to say that he knows, without evaluating Anselm's or any other theistic argument, that God obviously doesn't exist. This is not a criticism but a gratuitous assertion that the argument's conclusion is false.*

As a final example, consider Dawkins's critique of theistic arguments from personal religious experience, where he focuses on visions or voices of God or other supernatural entities such as angels and the Blessed Virgin. He rejects the *veridicality* of such experiences (the truth of what they present) in view of "the formidable power of the brain's simulation software". This software, he says, "is well capable of constructing 'visions' and 'visitations' of the upmost veridical power", even if they are false.[4] Almost all of his discussion consists in giving examples of hallu-

---

* Dawkins does briefly allude to important philosophical critiques of the ontological argument by, for example, Kant and Norman Malcolm, based on the idea that the argument falsely assumes that existence is a perfection. But he gives no reason for thinking that this assumption might be false and doesn't mention recent responses (by philosophers such as Charles Hartshorne and, especially, Alvin Plantinga) that have revived philosophical interest in the argument.

cinations and other deceptive experiences and explaining how the brain is able to produce them.

Here we need to formulate Dawkins's argument more fully than he does. His claim is that we shouldn't think that religious experiences are veridical because the brain's "simulation software" is capable of producing them whether or not what they present is in fact true. But does the mere fact that an experience can be produced by simulation software show that the experience is not veridical? The question should give us pause, since almost any experience at all, including my experience of writing this sentence and your experience of reading it, could also be simulations occurring only in the brain. As Descartes famously argued and neuroscience confirms, any experience that seems to be of the world outside my mind could in fact be a dream or some other sort of illusion or hallucination. If the possibility of simulation is enough to cast doubt on an experience, then we need to doubt almost all of our experiences. Dawkins's rejection of religious experiences holds up only if he is willing to doubt almost all of our experiences.*

Dawkins's critique of religious experience goes wrong by starting from the question, Can *we explain this experience as illusory*? He should instead ask, *Is there a specific reason to think that we* should *explain this experience as illusory*? To make his case, he would have to reflect philosophically on the conditions that make it appropriate to dismiss an experience as illusory, and then show that all religious experiences meet those conditions. There is an extensive epistemological literature—often very critical of religion—on how to evaluate the veracity of religious experiences.[5] Dawkins's argument needs to engage this literature.

---

* I say "almost all experiences," since many epistemologists would say that some experiences (for example, of my own existence, of my seeming to see a tree) will be veridical no matter how they are produced.

Another problem is that Dawkins doesn't take into account a much more common, though much less dramatic, form of religious experience. Many believers report experiences—often frequent—that they describe as a vivid (nonvisual and non-auditory) sense of the presence of a divine being. William James, in his classic discussion of religious experience, cites the following as one of many reports:

> There was not a mere consciousness of something there, but fused in the central happiness of it, a startling awareness of some ineffable good. Not vague either, not like the emotional effect of some poem, or scene, or blossom, or music, but the sure knowledge of the close presence of a sort of mighty person, and after it went, the memory persisted as the one perception of reality. Everything else might be a dream, but not that.[6]

Even if there is a strong case against accepting reports of dramatic apparitions and visions, this case would not automatically apply to these more ordinary experiences.

DAWKINS'S ATHEISTIC ARGUMENTS

We turn to a discussion of Dawkins's major arguments against the existence of God: the no-arguments argument, *his* evolutionary argument, *and his* complexity argument.

The no-arguments argument maintains that we ought to deny God's existence because there are no good arguments for his existence. To test this claim, we will try to construct a good cosmological argument *by formulating and criticizing a series of* principles of causality. *Here we will use crucial distinctions between* what needs explaining *and* what does not need explaining *and between the* contingent *and the* necessary. *We will see that the cosmological argument needs a principle for* avoiding an infinite regress of causes. *Here we will need to distinguish between a principle that* says an infinite regress is impossible *and the (preferable) principle that says* an infinite regress itself requires an explanation.

Assessing the force of the argument—and therefore of the no-arguments argument—will depend on a crucial distinction between what a rational person must believe *and what a rational person* can believe.

The No-Arguments Argument for Atheism

Although Dawkins's critiques of theistic arguments are remarkably weak, he and most new atheists are convinced that they need make no special case for their position, but need only point out that theists offer no good arguments for their position. I call this *the no-arguments argument* for atheism.

Many atheists are fond of claiming that the case against God is the same as the case against Santa Claus, the Easter Bunny, or the Tooth Fairy: there are no good reasons for believing in any of them. At least at first blush, it seems odd to compare the argumentative case for God with that for Santa Claus et al. There are, after all, well-known arguments for God's existence, formulated by respected philosophers, that intelligent and informed people have found convincing. No one much over the age of six thinks there is a remotely plausible argument for the existence of Santa Claus.

Of course, the mere existence of theistic arguments doesn't refute the no-arguments argument. More careful examinations than Dawkins offers may still show that all such arguments are worthless. I myself think that there's no argument that decisively establishes that God exists. But, I will argue, this doesn't support the no-arguments argument. To see why, let's dig deeper into the cosmological argument, which, I claim, can be formulated in a way that refutes the no-arguments argument.

The Cosmological Argument

The idea of a cosmological argument is to move from certain known effects to God as their cause. To construct such an argument, we need a *principle of causality*: a statement of which sorts of things need causes to explain them. The simplest such principle would be: *everything has a cause.* But this is too strong a claim, since if everything has a cause, then God will have a cause and so be dependent on something else, which would, therefore, have a better claim to be God. A cosmological argument will work only if we have a causal principle that will not apply to God. (This is the way serious versions of the cosmological argument respond to the "Who made God?" objection.) So we need to look for an improved principle.

Here's a philosophical line of thought that seems like it might do the job. We are always looking for explanations. Why did my car break down? Why did the apple tree bloom early this year? Why do my children do so poorly on standardized math tests? Much of science is the relentless extension of this quest for explanations. Sometimes we find an explanation by referring to things we already know about. My car broke down because I haven't changed the oil for three years; the tree bloomed early because we had an exceptionally warm spring; my children do poorly because they don't study enough. But sometimes seeking an explanation leads to a discovery: perhaps my car broke down because a computer chip I didn't even know about failed; or the tree bloomed early because of an increase in local radiation levels; or my children do poorly because they lack a special "math" gene.

A cosmological argument is an effort to carry the search for an explanation as far as it can go, to see if we can discover not just an explanation of some single thing but an explanation of everything—for, we might say, the world (*kosmos* in Greek) as a whole. Let's call this an *ultimate explanation*. We want, therefore, an argument that will show that God is the ultimate explanation. Perhaps, then, the causal principle we need is that *there must be an ultimate explanation (provided by an ultimate cause).*

Now, however, we need to think more carefully about what an ultimate explanation would explain. We've said it's an explanation of everything, but just what does this mean? Something that needs explanation is, by definition, not self-explanatory. It needs to be explained by something other than itself. As we've seen, if we sought an explanation of literally *everything*, then there would be nothing available to provide the explanation.

If there is to be an ultimate explanation, then, it must be something that itself requires no explanation but explains everything else. The world that the cosmological argument is trying to explain must not be *everything* but *everything that needs an explanation*. But what things require explanation?

One plausible answer is that we must explain those things that do exist but *might not exist*, things that, to use the traditional technical term, are *contingent*. Almost everything in our daily experience is contingent: my cell phone might never have been manufactured; the Earth might not have a moon; Germany might not have won the 2014 World Cup; I myself might have never been born. (In fact, I cited Germany's winning the World Cup as an example before the final game was played, knowing that I might have to replace Germany with the Netherlands.)

Correspondingly, for the cosmological argument to work,

the explanation of everything contingent must be something that is *not contingent*; namely, something that not only exists but also cannot *not* exist; it must, that is, be *necessary*. If it weren't necessary, it would be contingent and so itself in need of explanation. (Notice that what is necessary is not contingent, and vice versa.) Simply put, the God the cosmological argument wants to prove exists has to be a necessary, not a contingent, being.

Here, then, we move to a still better principle of causality: that *every contingent thing requires a cause.* But we still need to be careful. Most contingent things can be explained by other contingent things. The world (the totality of contingent things) is a complex explanatory system. One possibility would seem to be that the world itself could provide all the explanations that we could reasonably ask for. In particular, each contingent thing might be explained by another contingent thing. For example, larger-scale objects, from grains of sand to galaxies, might be explained by the molecules that make them up, with molecules being explained by atoms, atoms by electrons and protons, and these by quarks. If this makes sense, the cosmological argument can't get off the ground because, as we've seen, its God is a necessary being that's needed to explain what contingent things can't.

But can we actually make sense of the idea that each contingent thing is explained (caused) by another contingent thing? In other words, could there be a chain of contingent causes, each in turn explaining another contingent thing? To vary our example, recall the oft-repeated story of Bertrand Russell's alleged encounter with someone who insisted that the Earth was a flat plate supported on the back of an elephant. What, Russell asked, supports the elephant? A large tortoise, was the reply. But what, said Russell—going in for the kill—supports the tortoise? The reply: It's tortoises all the way down.

But can it really be tortoises all the way down? No, at least not if there are only a finite (limited) number of tortoises. Then we would face two equally bad alternatives. First, there might be a tortoise that wasn't supported by anything—a clear violation of our principle of causality. Second, there might be a *circle* of tortoises: one tortoise supporting a second tortoise, but that second tortoise somehow also supporting the first. This would require the absurdity of each of these tortoises supporting itself (or at least a supporting circle of tortoises that itself has no support).

Returning to physics from amphibian biology, if the chain of contingent explainers ended with quarks, they would either have no explanation or would have to explain themselves. Neither of these two cases makes sense. The first violates the principle that every contingent thing has a cause. The second amounts to saying that there is something that explains the existence of its own explanation—which would mean that it somehow preceded itself. Therefore, for contingent things to explain everything, there must be an infinite chain (regress) of contingent things, each explaining the existence of some other contingent thing.

What does this mean for our effort to construct a cosmological argument? It means that our argument must deny that there is an *infinite regress* of contingent things that explains everything that needs explaining. Otherwise, there's no need for a necessary God.

This is a crucial stage in our search for a cosmological argument. We have a plausible principle of causality: any contingent being needs a cause. We now see that we need another premise: that *an infinite regress of contingent things cannot explain everything that needs explaining.*

But we still need one further step, because there are two ways a cosmological argument can deny an infinite regress of contingent explainers. First, we could simply *deny that there could be such an infinite regress*. This seems plausible if we think that an infinite chain of explainers never really explains anything but merely defers the explanations forever. If molecules explain rocks, atoms explain molecules, and so on without end, then have we really even explained rocks? If an infinite regress leaves each of its members with no explanation, its existence would violate our principle of causality.

But this way of thinking loses its force once we realize that an explainer does not cease to explain just because it itself has an explanation. I can explain my headache by noting that I recently had a concussion, even though the concussion is itself explained by my banging my head on a car trunk lid, which is explained in turn by the fact that I was drunk.

Given this, we can rightly claim that each item in an infinite series of explained explainers is explained by the immediately preceding item. In that way, every item in the series is explained. If every item in a series has an explanation, why do we need a separate explanation of the series as a whole? For example, if I can explain why each of twenty people is attending a party, I don't need a further explanation of why all twenty are there. On reflection, a cosmological argument that denies that there can be an infinite regress of explainers does not seem promising.

But a second way of eliminating an infinite regress may do the job. We can agree that there might be an infinite series of contingent explainers but still maintain that *such an infinite series itself needs an explanation*. We might, in effect, grant that there could be an infinite series of tortoises, each supporting the other—and the whole chain supporting the Earth—but still insist that there must be some explanation for why all those tortoises exist. That is, our argument will require that an infinite regress of contingent things must *itself* have an explanation. This gives us the two key premises of our cosmological argument: a principle of causality and a principle for excluding an infinite regress.

Now we can formulate our argument:

1. There are contingent beings.
2. The existence of any contingent being has an explanation.
3. Such an explanation must be provided by either a necessary being or by an infinite regress of contingent beings.
4. An explanation by means of an infinite regress of contingent beings is itself in need of an explanation by a necessary being.
5. Therefore, there is a necessary being that explains the existence of contingent beings.

This argument is logically valid; that is, if the premises are true, then the conclusion is true. Premise (1) is obvious—almost everything we know of is able not to exist. Premise (3), as we've seen, has no plausible alternatives: without an infinite regress, the explanation of contingent beings by contingent beings will either be circular or terminate with an unexplained contingent being. The success of the argument, then, depends on the truth of premise (2)—our principle of causality—and premise (4)—our principle that excludes an infinite regress.

Premise (2) would perhaps be questionable if it had to be understood as including the entire world. In that case you could argue that the world is the collection of all contingent things and so does not require a separate explanation as long as each member of the collection can be explained. But in our argument the premise need only apply to individual contingent beings, not collections of them, and our experience massively supports the claim that any individual contingent being does have an explanation. For example, think once more of the list of contingent things I mentioned above. There must be some explanation for why my cell phone was made, why the Earth has a moon, why Germany won the World Cup, and why I was born.*

Our argument, then, seems to depend only on establishing premise (4): that an infinite chain (regress) of contingent explainers would itself require explanation by a necessary (non-contingent) being.

But why should we think that the existence of such a regress has an explanation? In contrast to premise (2), our principle of causality, we have no direct experience to support the claim, since we have no experience of an infinite regress, just as we can never count all the numbers. We can point to the fact that in science we always seek further levels of explanation, but our practice of looking for explanations does not guarantee that they must be there to be found.

Nonetheless, an infinite chain of contingent things is still a (complex) contingent thing, so why shouldn't it need an explanation? Also, as we've seen, there's good reason to think that any finite chain has an explanation. What reason is there for thinking that going to infinity somehow gets rid of the need to explain contingency? None of these considerations is decisive proof that premise (4) is true. But there's no reason to say that you would be irrational if, after thorough reflection, you found such considerations convincing. Remember what we concluded in Chapter 1 regarding ethical and political convictions: even if there's no proof, it can be rational to maintain what—after looking at

---

* It is sometimes suggested that quantum theory allows for unexplained events. But the laws of quantum physics explain the events they apply to—it's just that the explanation is *statistical* (allowing a range of events, with different probabilities) not, like Newtonian physics, *deterministic* (allowing just one event).

all the evidence and arguments—still seems obvious to you. Of course, a parallel line of thought shows that it is also rational for those who don't find this obvious to reject the premise. It's a premise about which reasonable people can reasonably disagree.

Failure of the No-Arguments Argument

The result at which we have arrived for the cosmological argument typifies many seriously developed philosophical arguments for God's existence. There are, in particular, arguments (based on classical versions by Aquinas, Averroes, and Leibniz) that use a variety of causal principles. Also, Plantinga's formulation of an ontological argument requires only the premise that God's existence is possible (although possible in a suitably strong sense, which leaves room for disagreement).

There are, then, theistic arguments that are logically valid and depend on one or two premises that are not obviously or demonstrably false and have a certain intuitive appeal. Some people may, on reflection, rationally accept the premises and therefore the conclusion. But there is no rational requirement to accept the premises, and it can be equally rational to deny them.

I imagine that some readers will feel our detailed discussion of the cosmological argument has little relevance to actual religious belief. Who, they may say, depends on such logical esoterica to justify their commitment? But I would remind such readers that the point of our discussion was not to show how believers justify their belief in God. It was to answer atheists who claim that their denial of God is justified because there is no serious case for theism. It is the atheist, not the believer, who provokes this discussion.

I emphasize this point because many atheists, like Dawkins, dismiss theistic arguments as obvious nonstarters, and ignore their subtlety and complexity. Of course, there's no general obligation for believers or nonbelievers to enter into this philosophical tangle. But those who make much of the failure of theistic arguments need to support their claims with a detailed analysis of what's available.

So, finally, what about the no-arguments argument? It goes like this:

1. There are no good arguments for God's existence.
2. If there are no good arguments for a claim, then, if we are rational, we should deny it.

Conclusion: If we are rational, we should deny that God exists.

But our discussion of the cosmological argument has just shown that both premise (1) and the argument's conclusion are false. There *are* good (if not decisive) arguments for theism, and a person *can* rationally believe that God exists. So the argument is not sound.

In sum, there are what we might label *credible* but not *conclusive* arguments for God's existence, and these undermine the no-arguments argument for atheism. Therefore, to make his case for atheism, Dawkins does need an argument against the existence of God. As it turns out, Dawkins has such an argument, based on the theory of evolution.

DAWKINS'S EVOLUTIONARY ARGUMENT FOR ATHEISM

The evolutionary argument deploys scientific explanations such as Darwinian natural selection to refute the existence of God. We will see that Dawkins's formulation of this argument is invalid: its conclusion is that "God exists" is false, whereas at best its premises show that "God exists" is not proven by one theistic argument (the design argument). *However, applying the* Principle of Charity, *we will see that we can use two premises of Dawkins's evolutionary argument to construct a better atheistic argument: the* complexity argument.

Dawkins begins at the same point as one of the most appealing arguments for God's existence: the vast improbability of merely chance events (e.g., the blowing of the wind in a junkyard) producing a highly complex object (e.g., a jet airplane). The theistic argument points to the similarity of organs such as the eye to mechanisms—like watches—designed for a particular purpose, and argues that they require a designer. Other forms of the argument claim that the universe itself is a complex mechanism that requires a designer. All of these arguments start from the apparent design (purpose or teleology) we find when we examine the universe.

Like proponents of the argument from design, Dawkins accepts the need to explain "how the complex, improbable appearance of design in the universe arises".[7] But, Dawkins claims, design arguments presuppose that the only possible explanations for complexity are chance (which explains nothing that is highly improbable) and design by an intelligence. He points out a third possibility: the gradual development of the complex from the simple, with Darwin's theory of evolution by natural selection as the prime example. Dawkins bases his argument on this third explanatory possibility and claims to show that "God almost certainly does not exist".[8]

The argument, as Dawkins summarizes it, goes like this:

1. There is need for an explanation of the apparent design of the universe.
2. The universe is highly complex.

3. An intelligent designer of the universe would be even more highly complex.
4. A complex designer would itself require an explanation.
5. Therefore, an intelligent designer will not provide an explanation of the universe's complexity.
6. On the other hand, the (individually) simple processes of natural selection (along with similar processes—as yet not fully understood—for nonliving things) can explain the apparent design of the universe.
7. Therefore, an intelligent designer (God) almost certainly does not exist.[9]

As stated, the argument is not logically valid. Its first four premises do logically imply (5), that an intelligent designer will not explain the universe's complexity. Premise (6) adds that evolutionary principles such as natural selection can explain this complexity. But all this shows is that evolution explains the complexity of the universe and an intelligent designer doesn't. This would refute the claim of the design argument that we need to posit God as the designer of the universe, but that doesn't mean that God doesn't exist. You can't show that God *doesn't exist* by showing that *a particular argument* (the design argument) *doesn't prove his existence.* Even if Dawkins's evolutionary argument is correct, it doesn't, for example, show that the cosmological argument is unsound; God may still be the necessary cause of the existence of contingent things. At best, Dawkins has refuted one argument for theism; he has not shown that God does not exist.

THE COMPLEXITY ARGUMENT

But Dawkins's presentation of his case as a single argument does not do him full justice. It's better (invoking the Principle of

Charity) to regard him as implicitly combining two related but distinct arguments. The first is the critique of the design argument we have just discussed. But we can use his premises (3) and (4) to construct a better argument against God's existence.

> *The complexity argument brings to the fore the fundamental distinction between two conceptions of God: the* anthropomorphic *and the* metaphysical. *The argument disproves the existence of an anthropomorphic God—one whose perfections are "superized" versions of human perfections. But it does not disprove the existence of the God of traditional theistic metaphysics, characterized as* immaterial, simple, *and* necessary. *Such a God transcends human categories and cannot be the object of scientific inquiry.*
>
> *Although the possibility of a metaphysical God blocks the complexity argument, it still poses a fundamental challenge to theism by forcing it to abandon the more accessible anthropomorphic conception and to defend the intelligibility of the metaphysical conception.*

The *complexity argument* starts from the idea that any being capable of designing and maintaining something as complex as the universe would itself have to be highly complex and so require an explanation. David Hume made a similar point over two centuries earlier: "a mental world or universe of ideas requires a cause as much as does a material world or universe of objects; and, if similar in its arrangement, must require a similar cause".[10] Using Dawkins's language, we can develop Hume's suggestion into a full-fledged argument:

1. If God exists, he must be both the intelligent designer of the universe and a being that explains the universe but is not itself in need of explanation.

2. An intelligent designer of the universe would be a highly complex being.

3. A highly complex being would itself require explanation.

4. Therefore, there cannot exist a being that is both the intelligent designer of the universe and the ultimate explanation of the universe.

5 Therefore, God does not exist.

This argument is logically valid: if the premises are true, so is its conclusion. If sound (if its premises are true), the argument proves that there is no God in the traditional sense of an intelligence that is the ultimate explanation of the universe—one that explains but is not explained by anything else.

Any traditional theist would have to accept premise (1), since it merely states central doctrines of the Jewish, Christian, and Muslim religions. Premises (2) and (3) (corresponding to premises (3) and (4) of Dawkins's original argument) seem quite plausible. But they contradict the *metaphysical* conception of God held by the great Western monotheist thinkers (for example, Augustine, Aquinas, Maimonides, and Avicenna). For them, God is a perfect being, but this perfection is not *anthropomorphic*: an extrapolation to infinity of human perfections. Rather, God's perfection is of a radically different sort.

He is, first of all, *immaterial* and so not composed of parts extended in space or in time. This point would undermine Dawkins's assumption that God would have to be complex, since his definition of complexity is in terms of the parts of a material thing. Moreover, his evidence that an intelligent designer would be highly complex is derived from examples of human and animal intelligence, which depend on a material brain.

Further, traditional philosophical accounts of God argue that his perfection requires that he be supremely *unified* and *simple.* This means that what we speak of as his knowledge, power, goodness, etc. are not strictly separate perfections but rather our halting way of expressing the depth and richness of the perfection that is identical with his being. God doesn't just *have* his knowledge, power, and goodness; he *is* his knowledge, power, and goodness. They are identical with his very being—and so identical with one another (whatever that may mean).

Finally, the traditional view is that God's existence is *not contingent.* He is not a being that might or might not have been realized; his existence is *necessary.* As we saw in our discussion of the cosmological argument, if God is a necessary being, it makes no sense to say, as Dawkins does, that God's existence would require explanation by some external cause.

Of course, the fact that there is another way of viewing God does not show that Dawkins is wrong. But unless he can show that this alternative view can be disregarded, there remains a serious question as to whether his premises (2) and (3) are correct. The Principle of Charity requires a serious engagement with the alternative view.

Such an engagement is no trivial matter. The idea that God is radically different from other beings has been developed with immense detail and subtlety in the grand tradition of metaphysics, beginning with Plato and Aristotle, continuing through the philosophical theologians of the Middle Ages (Augustine, Anselm, Aquinas, Scotus) to the early modern rationalists (Descartes, Spinoza, Leibniz) and the German idealists (Fichte, Schelling, Hegel), and flourishing today in the work of contemporary analytic metaphysicians such as Richard Swinburne and Alvin Plantinga. (We will return to the problems these metaphysical views face in Chapter 5.)

Dawkins, unfortunately, has almost nothing to say about these conceptions of the divine nature. He sometimes claims that subtle discussions of philosophical theologians are irrelevant to his argument because they all presuppose the existence of God, and so beg the question against his atheistic argument. This is false. Traditional discussions of God's nature (e.g., by Aquinas) often follow on arguments claiming to have proved that God exists. But these discussions do not assume that God exists. The question they ask is: What would be the nature of God, *if he does exist?* Similarly, contemporary physicists can discuss the nature of the multiverse suggested by some cosmologists without assuming that the multiverse exists.

New atheists sometimes say that we can reject such discussions as nothing more than a tangle of obscure speculations flowing from muddled, inconclusive thinking. But if this is so, it requires showing. The bare fact that a claim is hard to understand or seems obviously wrong, at first glance, does not show that there is nothing to it. To those unfamiliar with the theory of natural selection, the idea that a complicated structure such as the human eye could somehow develop from a series of random mutations may seem incomprehensible or incorrect. This does not mean that we can reject the theory without looking at it in detail.

Some atheists would short-circuit such metaphysical discussions by maintaining that there can be no beings other than ones knowable by sense experience (that, in other words, everything is physical). But—repeating a point we've made previously—how could this claim itself be known from sense experience, which can tell us only about what is knowable by sense experience? For anything else, sense experience is mute—it can't even say that it does not exist or is not possible. In the same way, our sense of sight alone cannot tell us whether there are or could be things that are invisible.

This point applies in spades here, where the question is

whether God could be a being *radically different* from those we know from sense experience. How could such a question be decided by sense experience? From sense experience we could only draw conclusions about the kinds of beings that can be known by sense experience, whereas our question is whether there are other kinds of beings.

Dawkins himself suggests another way for atheists to avoid the issue of God's nature. He argues that, regardless of how different we think God is, if he has causal effects on the material world, his existence must be detectable by empirical methods. As he puts it, "a universe with a supernaturally intelligent creator is a very different kind of universe from one without". From this he concludes, "the presence or absence of a super-intelligence is unequivocally a scientific question".[11] From this it would seem to follow that if science does not find any evidence of God's existence, he does not, in all probability, exist.

But Dawkins offers no features *detectable by science* that must distinguish a universe with God from one without. Suppose, for example, that the Big Bang is a radically spontaneous eruption of a material universe into existence, with no creative agent. There is no reason that such a universe could not be empirically identical to a universe created by an immaterial God. Therefore, scientific evidence cannot undermine the claim that God has created the universe.*

There is, then, no way for a proponent of the complexity argument to avoid examining traditional metaphysical accounts of the divine nature. Dawkins's argument from complexity fails

---

* Science will become relevant if theists argue for God's existence by appealing to miracles—special divine interventions into the world after its creation. The claim that, say, a cure is due to God can be questioned by scientific evidence that the cure could have come about naturally. But you can claim that miracles occur without basing your belief in God on that claim. Many religious people judge certain events as miraculous precisely because they independently believe that there's a God who could do such things.

because he has not engaged and neutralized the metaphysical arguments for thinking of God as simple and necessary. Since he ignores these arguments, he has not shown that "the God Hypothesis is almost certainly not true".

But the metaphysics of God's nature is a two-edged sword. The complexity argument makes a good case that God cannot be an extrapolation, a "superized" version of the kind of intelligent beings we know. Such a creator would be highly complex and so, as the argument shows, could not be the ultimate (unexplained by anything else) explanation of the world's design.

Therefore, theists cannot plausibly understand God as a supersized human: the anthropomorphic conception of God in human form. They must instead try to understand him as a radically different sort of being: immaterial, necessarily existing and, perhaps, entirely simple. As we shall see in Chapter 5, there are serious challenges to thinking of God this way, and theists have to come to terms with them if they want to meet the challenge of atheism.

In fact, the problem of God's nature looms larger for theists than for atheists. The atheists must deal with it if they want to use the complexity argument to refute theism. But they have alternatives—particularly, as we shall soon see, the argument from evil. Theists have no plausible response to the complexity argument unless they show how to make sense of a God that is radically different from the anthropomorphic God of popular religion.

THE PROBLEM OF EVIL

Our tour of new atheist ideas concludes with the atheistic argument from evil, sketching a response based on a distinction between necessary evils *and* unnecessary evils, *as well as a distinction between* human knowledge *and* divine omniscience. *These distinctions support in principle a response to the problem of evil, but once again this leaves the theist with the problem of making sense of the radical gap between God and us.*

Neither the no-arguments argument nor the complexity argument has refuted theism—although the latter puts pressure on theists to make sense of the divine nature. But what about the oldest and most affecting of all arguments for atheism, the problem of evil? The new atheists add little to traditional formulations of this problem, but they do provide clear and representative statements of the issue. Here we look at Sam Harris's version in his book *Letter to a Christian Nation*.[12] Our discussion will be brief, merely stating the argument and suggesting the basic line of a theistic response. In Chapter 5 we will drill down further into the significance of the argument.

Harris begins by citing undeniable examples of evils: torture-rape-murders of children, the massive destruction of human life by tsunamis and hurricanes. He then notes that Christians believe, even when such things are happening to them and their families, that "an all-powerful and all-loving God is watching over" them. "Are they", Harris asks, "right to believe this? Is it *good* that they believe this?" His answer is no, and, he says, "the entirety of atheism is contained in this response". More fully: "An atheist is simply a person who believes that [those who are certain God exists] should be obliged to present evidence for his existence—and, indeed, for his benevolence, given the relentless destruction of innocent human beings we witness in the world each day".[13] Lacking any independent evidence for the existence of an all-good, all-powerful God, atheism follows from the classical reasoning of Epicurus: "If God exists, either he can do nothing to stop the most egregious calamities, or He does not care to. God, therefore, is either impotent or evil".[14]

Here's a way to make the argument vivid. Suppose there is a doctor who knows a simple cure for malignant brain tumors. If such a doctor were in the room with a child dying from such a tumor and were not a moral monster, we expect that she would bring about the cure. Accordingly, if someone maintains that there is a well-intentioned doctor in the child's room who knows how to cure her cancer, we would rightly demand strong evidence for such a claim, since we already have strong evidence that the claim is false from the very fact that the child has not been cured.

But if theism is true, there will be someone in the room capable of curing the child. God, in his omnipotence, can exercise his power anywhere and anytime he chooses. If the child dies, this means that there is no being with both the power and the will to intervene—that is, there is no God.

As Harris notes, theists sometimes suggest that "God cannot be judged by human standards of morality".[15] But he rightly rejects this suggestion. If God is good in some sense quite distinct from what we mean by "good", then there is no reason to praise, rely on, or be consoled by his goodness. Such divine "goodness" would not respond to the questions and longings that lead people to religion. The Christian God must agree with our judgment that human suffering is a great evil, one to be eliminated to the greatest extent possible.

But the theist still has a response. Not every evil should be eliminated. Suppose my child was undergoing a moderate amount of suffering from an illness. Ordinarily, I would want to eliminate the evil of this suffering. But further suppose that I knew this suffering would, in the long run, make my child a far better person, less selfish and more considerate of others. Then I'd have good reason to allow the suffering. This shows that eliminating an evil may produce greater evils or may eliminate goods that outweigh the evil. Given that God is omniscient, it's reasonable to think that he knows a great deal more about the long-term effects of particular evils and may allow them for the sake of making the world a better place overall.

You may object that this line of thought applies only to those—like us—who have limited power, who cannot do everything and must choose between, say, putting out a fire and blocking a flood. But God is omnipotent; his power has no limits. So he should never have to allow any evil for the sake of greater good. He can prevent my child's suffering and also help the child become a better person.

But the response is that even omnipotence has one limitation: it cannot bring about what is logically impossible. It cannot, for example, make me bear pain magnificently (which might be a great good) and, at the same time, not feel any pain. A much cited example is human freedom. God could, of course, control our actions or intervene to prevent their evil consequences. But logically, can he do this if he wants us to have the good of meaningful freedom? It would seem impossible, even for God, to make us genuinely free and still exclude any evil that we might do.* We need, then, to distinguish *necessary evils*—those which even God cannot eliminate without making the world worse— from *unnecessary evils*, which God can and will eliminate.

Given this distinction, it may be that God does not eliminate evils that we would, not because he does not see them as evil but because he knows a lot more than we do about the goods that exist in the universe and the evils that are logically necessary to have them. We need to take account of the distinction between God's *omniscience* and our greatly *limited knowledge*.[16]

---

* This is controversial. Compatibilists, for example, might claim that God could cause our choices in a way that still allows them to be free. My general point is just that theists may plausibly suggest that there are *some* evils that God permits for the sake of goods that otherwise couldn't exist.

Harris might reply that, although it's possible this is the reason God doesn't prevent the evils of our world, there's no reason to think that it's actually the case. What evidence does the Christian have that all the world's evils are necessary for offsetting goods? But it is Harris who is arguing that evil makes God's existence highly unlikely. Given the hypothesis of necessary evils, the fact of evil does not show that God doesn't exist. Further, since our knowledge is extremely limited, we have no firm idea of how likely or unlikely this hypothesis is in itself. It follows that evil makes God's existence unlikely only if some evils are not necessary, and we are totally uncertain whether this is so. The conclusion is that the existence of evil gives us no good reason to think that God does not exist.

There's much more to be said about evil, and we will return to the topic. However, defusing the argument from evil in this way introduces important constraints on how believers can think about God. As with the defense against Dawkins's complexity argument for atheism, God becomes more mysterious and less comprehensible in human terms. We will further explore this problem in Chapter 5.

CONCLUSION

Religious believers may be able to deflect the criticisms of the new atheists. But the deflection is not without consequences for what they believe. First, they must abandon naïve views of God—they must stop thinking of his perfections as supersized versions of human perfections and regarding his interventions in the world as on par with those of any greatly powerful, non-divine being (e.g., a highly advanced space alien). The naïve view is, moreover, inconsistent with the mainstream theological doctrines of God formulated by Augustine, Aquinas, and many others. These doctrines present God as radically different from creatures, particularly in his utter simplicity and necessary existence.

But the naïve view pervades many popular beliefs and practices, and believers need to think hard about how (if at all) they can reconcile the traditional metaphysics of God with what religion means to many people. (Here Chapter 1's Principle of Self-Understanding is relevant.) Also, as we will soon see, there are serious intellectual challenges to the mainstream theological doctrines. Similarly, coming to terms with the problem of evil requires realizing the enormous difference that God's omniscience makes for his view of what the good of the universe requires.

None of these issues provides a decisive refutation of theism that would put it in the intellectual position of belief in the Easter Bunny or the Tooth Fairy. But any intellectually serious belief will have to work with the constraints required to respond to the challenges. The next chapter takes on these challenges.

5

RELIGIOUS AGNOSTICISM

Chapter 4 argued that theists can effectively respond to the criticisms of the new atheists, but that the responses raise further difficulties. Our discussion of these difficulties centers on the divine attributes—the essential features of a divine being. We begin with some philosophical issues that arise when we try to understand the attributes of simplicity and necessity. The problems with simplicity emerge from the distinction between a substance and its properties, as well as the connection of simplicity to unchangeability. Necessity seems to make sense for abstract entities like numbers, but there seems to be a big gap between such entities and concrete realities such as persons.

We then consider a response to the problem of evil. Here the discussion returns to the attribute of omniscience and also raises questions about the religious adequacy of the traditional characterization of God as all good, all knowing, and all powerful.

Our conclusion after all this discussion is that there is a decisive case for neither atheism nor theism. This suggests that agnosticism may be an attractive position. We distinguish various ways of "practicing" agnosticism and note that theistic religions have agnostic elements. Negative theology and Thomas

Aquinas's view that talk of God must use analogous language
are discussed.

*Next we turn to the positive case for belief, starting with a sur-
vey of autobiographical essays by philosophers that give a sense
of what in fact underlies the commitments of reflective religious
believers. This leads to a major distinction among three aspects
of religion:* religion as a way of life, religion as a mode of
understanding, *and* religion as a body of knowledge. *I
argue that there is a viable form of belief that accepts a way of
life and a related mode of understanding, but does not claim to
know. This is what I call* religious agnosticism. *Finally, we
return to the idea of* convictions *in a comparison of religious
and political commitments.*

Richard Dawkins's strongest argument for atheism was that we
cannot reconcile God's complexity with his total independence.
Two of the traditional divine attributes (properties describing
God's total perfection), his simplicity and his necessity, suggest responses to this objection. God, it is said, must be simple
because complexity (having parts or divisions) is an imperfec-
tion: a being with parts would be destroyed if the parts separated. This excludes Dawkins's assumption that God is complex.
And, if God is necessary, then his existence requires no causal
explanation, which excludes Dawkins's conclusion that God
would have to depend on some other being. But even believers
have found it difficult to understand a divine nature that is simple and necessarily existent.

GOD'S SIMPLICITY AND NECESSITY

Simplicity is a particularly difficult hurdle, one at which even
traditional theists have balked. Plantinga, for example, offers

a powerful criticism based on the philosophical distinction between a *substance* and its *properties*.[1] A substance is an independently existing thing, say, a basketball; its properties are the various qualities that the basketball has but that cannot exist separately from it—for example the ball's color and roundness. Plantinga argues that if God lacks all complexity, there are no distinctions among any of his properties: his goodness, power, knowledge, etc. are all exactly the same. So God has only one property—let's call it Superness.

This is hard enough to grasp, but the situation is even worse. We can't even say that God *has* Superness, since this would imply a distinction between *God* (as the person who has Superness) and *the property of Superness*. To be totally simple, God has to be *identical* with his Superness. But that means that God would just be a property. This makes no sense, since a property (think of the redness of a rose or the coolness of water) is not a concrete thing that can exist in its own right—if it did, it would be a substance. As we've seen, a property exists only as an aspect of something else; it depends on the thing that has the property. But, as we've also seen, God can't depend on anything else. So it makes no sense to say that God is a property.

Notice also that simplicity implies *unchangeability*. If a thing can change, we must distinguish its *actuality* (what it is now) from its *potentiality* (what it may become), which means that it's not entirely simple. But how could an unchangeable God love us, since he would be indifferent to—unchanging in the face of—anything that happens to us? It is also hard to grasp how an unchangeable God could cause things to happen in a changing world.

For these reasons, it is very difficult to see how God could be simple. The idea of necessary existence is a bit more tractable. It seems to make sense when we think about mathematics. It's necessarily true that 3 is greater than 2, but that couldn't be true if there were no numbers—so don't 2 and 3 have to necessarily exist? This position has attracted many philosophers (and mathematicians) since Plato first proposed it, and, although the view remains controversial, it at least seems like something for which we might make a case. But abstract entities like numbers are one thing; a person, which God is supposed to be, is something else. It's not clear that we can make sense of a person—even a divine one—that necessarily exists.

Dawkins's argument, then, does not establish atheism, but it does force reflective believers toward a sophisticated metaphysical conception of God. Such a conception may not even make sense, and is in any case hard to reconcile with the personal God of scripture and religious experience.

EVIL AND OMNISCIENCE

We have seen in Chapter 4 how believers can defeat the claim that God's existence is inconsistent with the existence of evil. But the philosophical escape from the problem of evil is not a clean one. We can appeal to our ignorance of what God knows, and perhaps avoid the apparent contradiction of a world created by an all-good God that still contains evils. But this appeal restricts what many theists would like to say about God, particularly claims about "what God would want".

To take a recent example, Una Kroll, one of the first Anglican women priests, wrote in defense of a proposal to ordain women bishops in the Anglican Church, arguing that the proposal would be an "example of how it is possible to live in a community that is based on mutual love and respect despite profound differences". She then clinches her point by saying: "that, I believe, is what God wants us to learn to do".[2]

It may well seem to us that God would want us to learn to live in communities based on love and respect among people who have deep differences—but no more than it would seem that God would want to save innocent children from dying of cancer. Once the appeal is made to the gap between God's knowledge and ours, we cannot move from what we *think* God would want to what he *does* want.

Similarly, there is no real guidance in the frequent suggestion that we should make difficult decisions by asking ourselves "What would Jesus do?". If, as traditional theology has it, Jesus is God, then the only answer can be: "Jesus would do what an omniscient God would do; and, given our ignorance, we have no idea what that might be."

My point here is not that, as some have claimed, God is beyond the basic principles of morality. But the application of such principles will depend on specific facts about the situation in which we are acting. "Thou shalt not kill" does not typically forbid my shooting at a target for practice, but it does if I know there is someone near the target that I might hit. Precisely because God knows so much more than we do, we can have no idea how his superior knowledge will affect his actions, even if he acts according to moral principles he shares with us.

Further, even if God is not "beyond morality", his omniscience does allow for the possibility that his knowledge of moral principles is far superior to ours and may even at times contradict what we think we know about morality. Of course, we remain obliged to act according to what we honestly see as correct moral principles. But there is no way to know that these principles reflect God's perfect knowledge of morality. Here we might want to say that God would never let us be deceived about essential moral principles, but such a response ignores our lesson about the gap between God's knowledge and ours.

Coming to terms with the problem of evil requires one more turn of the screw for the theist. The great theistic religions respond to deep human hopes, most importantly our hope to be ultimately safe (saved, as Christians say) in a world of peril. This is not to say there's nothing to religion beyond this hope, only that a worldview without it will not be religiously fulfilling. Our salvation may depend on our free choice (for example, to accept divine grace), but given the right choices, salvation is assured.

God, then, must be the sure source of that salvation. He must be good in the sense of being fully committed to working for our salvation (given any free cooperation needed from us) and powerful to the extent of assuring that no external circumstances (factors outside his and our wills) will interfere with our salvation. These are what we might call the *conditions of religious adequacy* for a concept of God.

It might seem that the traditional definition of God as all powerful, all knowing, and all good meets these conditions— but it doesn't. First of all, the "all properties" are not necessary to guarantee our salvation. God could be totally committed to saving us, even if he lacked appropriate moral attitudes toward other beings. Similarly, he might lack power over forces that are irrelevant to human salvation.

More importantly, the traditional divine properties are not sufficient to guarantee our salvation. An all-powerful being would be able to do whatever is needed to save us. But God's omniscience, I will argue, could present an obstacle to our salvation.

Here we come back to our response to the problem of evil. The only viable answer to the question *How could an all-good and all-powerful God allow the evils of our world?* is that such a God may have knowledge beyond our understanding. As Hume suggested, the problem of evil is solved only by an appeal to our ignorance.

In particular, theists must admit that an all-good being, even one with maximal power, may have to allow considerable local evils for the sake of the overall good of the universe. But we have no way of knowing whether we humans might ourselves be the victims of this necessity. We do not, for example, know whether there is or will be some other, far more advanced, species for whose sake God will allow us to be annihilated or suffer endlessly.

Of course, an all-good God would do everything possible to minimize the evil done to us, but we have no way of knowing what that minimum looks like. Some have suggested that when God allows suffering it must ultimately be for the benefit of the sufferer. But what basis do we have for thinking that this is the way God, in his omniscience, sees it? One of the most popular responses to the problem of evil, the free-will defense, emphasizes that the freedom of moral agents may be an immense good, worth God's tolerating horrendous wrongdoing. Doing evil and learning from the consequences may be an essential part of the "soul-making" that leads me to greater moral perfection. Could Augustine have become a saint without the sins of his youth? Similarly, we also have no way of knowing whether destroying our happiness is an unavoidable step in the soul-making of a super-race whose eventual achievements would make our ultimate loss acceptable to God.

My conclusion is that, given standard ways of responding to the problem of evil, even knowing that there is an all-good and all-powerful God does not guarantee our hope that we will be saved. There may be higher goals to which a good God will sacrifice us.

Although, then, the problem of evil does not make an effective case for atheism, it does require theists to reject conceptions of God that put him on a moral plane with humans. Just as refuting Dawkins's complexity argument requires thinking of God as radically different from humans on the metaphysical level, so disarming the problem of evil requires thinking of God as radically different from humans on the ethical level. These differences may even lead us to raise questions about whether our faith can guarantee the ultimate security that it promises.

AGNOSTICISM?

We have seen that there is no decisive case for either atheism or theism. This suggests agnosticism—the claim that we don't know whether or not God exists—as an attractive option. Agnosticism can express itself in a variety of ways. You may think that it is not possible to know if God exists and so give up thinking about the question, or you may continue your search for an answer, perhaps with something like religious fervor. Even if you conclude that there's no way of getting beyond agnosticism, you may take quite different attitudes toward theistic religions. In the spirit of Alexander Kinglake, the nineteenth-century historian who proposed that every church should post a sign saying, "Important if true", you may treat religions with indifference since there's no reason to believe they're true. This sort of attitude may be practically equivalent to atheism. But you could think religion important even if it may not be true. You could find it a source of moral guidance, soul-making practices, and intellectual understanding, and therefore even take part in the life of a religious community.

We should also keep in mind that theistic religions can themselves contain strong elements of agnosticism. We've seen how metaphysical conceptions of God raise thorny problems about how to understand our talk of him, and there are no uncontroversial solutions to these problems. Beyond this, even the most orthodox theologians—for example, Thomas Aquinas—emphasize the incomprehensibility of God as an essential counter to anthropomorphic conceptions. This leads to "negative theology", which denies positive assertions about God. We assert that God is good, but insist that any meaning we have for "good" will not adequately characterize God. Therefore, we must say that—in any sense we can understand—God also is *not* good.

Our description of God as good is, as Aquinas has it, "analogous": it does not have the literal sense of our ordinary uses of the term. Nor is this notion of analogy like ordinary cases where I say, for example, "My love is like a rose". Here I can specify the properties my love shares with a rose—beauty, delicacy, freshness—and the properties she does not share—having thorns and needing plant food. For God this is not so. We cannot say that any of the properties we associate with goodness literally apply to God. *Anything* we say about God misrepresents him (although we can't say just how). Even when I say that God exists, "exists" can't mean what it means when I say that I, or my dog, or the galaxy I live in exists.

Of course, this is not the same as saying we can't know that God exists, and Aquinas and other theologians make elaborate efforts to show that there is some meaning in their talk of God. But in their assertions about God there is always a nervous undertone of denial, a constant "yes—but" that has a lot in common with agnosticism. Nor is this uncertainty about God limited to rarefied intellectual analyses. It has deep biblical roots; for example, God rebukes Moses for asking who he should say God is ("I am who I am"), and the mystics insist on God's ineffability (the failure of any language to express their experience of the divine).

At the end of this chapter I'll return to the idea of *religious agnosticism,* but first I want to discuss what sort of positive case there might be for religious belief. We've already seen a case for belief, via our cosmological argument, which can in principle support a minimal theism. But most believers have no serious access to (or interest in) such complex arguments. And, in any case, the actual religions that believers practice assert doctrines that go far beyond the bare claim that God exists. What reasons do they have for their beliefs?

WHY DO PHILOSOPHERS BELIEVE?

There is a long tradition—not so vital today—of Christian apologetics. Apologists begin with philosophical arguments for the existence of God, then go on to argue on historical grounds that Jesus Christ existed and that the Gospels accurately recount his life and teachings. They further argue that, since Jesus claimed to be the Son of God and proved it by rising from the dead, we should accept the truth of what he says in the Gospels. The final step is to show that Jesus' teachings support the beliefs and practices of the apologist's preferred Christian church.

Even if there weren't serious problems with every step in this line of argument, we could be certain that it is not what grounds the faith of most believers. But then what does? There are many believers who are intelligent, informed, and reflective about their beliefs. What sort of reasons do they have? The best answers I've found are in two books published about twenty years ago in which philosophers who are religious believers (mostly Christians) try to explain how and why they believe.[3] Although every story is different, there are some widely shared features that help us see how smart and educated people with a strong commitment to rational reflection in fact become or remain religious believers. Here's a survey of what these accounts suggest as the main factors leading to belief.

An Attractive Way of Life

Believers are, first of all, attracted to religion as a way of life. Sometimes this is a matter of having been born into a certain religious community and always finding it comfortable and rewarding. David Shatz, an expert on Jewish philosophy at Yeshiva University, was raised as an orthodox Jew and has remained content with that way of life. "My commitment", he says, "is not rooted in the (naïve) notion that reason vindicates my beliefs. It is rooted rather in what Judaism provides me with: intellectual excitement, feeling, caring for others, inspiration, and a total perspective that is evocative and affecting".[4]

In other cases, nonbelievers gradually move into a religious community. The move often begins with encountering believers whom they respect and admire. Basil Mitchell (a philosopher of religion at Oxford until his death) notes that when he began teaching at Oxford, "I met for the first time Christian thinkers who were imaginative and articulate and also philosophically sophisticated".[5] Here, "in the company of committed Anglicans, I felt entirely and immediately at home".[6] There is also almost always a sense of satisfaction with participation in a religious community (liturgy, fellowship). An important step for Peter van Inwagen (a specialist in metaphysics at Notre Dame) was simply learning that "I like going to church and that an unconscious fear of churchgoing was no longer a barrier between me and the church".[7]

The late William Alston (who worked on epistemology and philosophy of religion) offers a fuller account. In his mid-fifties, after fifteen years of "secular life" and while visiting at Oxford, he began going to church and found the wonderful music a means of "communication with the divine".[8] Back at Princeton, he kept up churchgoing but didn't "make an intellectual assent to Christian doctrines". Still, his new openness to religion was having an effect: "I began, for the first time in my life, to get a glimmer of what love means". He went to a new parish and found a pastor who was "a living example of what spirituality can be". He next joined a "low-key" Episcopal charismatic group* and came to see that "these people were really in touch with God as a more or less continual presence in their lives". So he now had "a whole bevy of role models for the Christian life". He joined a "hard-core" charismatic group, received the "gift of tongues" and came to "a new and more vivid sense of the presence of the Spirit", which never entirely deserted him. In time he drifted away from charismatic religion but by this point he was fully and permanently a Christian.[9]

Religious Experiences

Alston goes on to say that what finally brought him to faith was that he found in the Christian community an "experience of the love of God and the presence of the Spirit".[10] "It was like having one's eyes opened to an aspect of the environment to which one had previously been blind". Life within this community involved, he says, growing in understanding by studying and thinking about Scripture and theological tradition, prayer and contemplation, reception of sacraments, Christian fellowship, and living a life of love.

There are also religious "experiences of transcendence", though hardly ever visions or visitations.† These experiences vary in specificity, intensity, and frequency, but always amount to

---

* Charismatic Christians emphasize personal religious experiences and dramatic expressions of faith such as prophecy and speaking in tongues.
† We discussed such an experience, cited by William James, in Chapter 4.

at least a strong sense that there is "more" to the universe than a materialist account allows. Alvin Plantinga recalls an event that took place while he was a freshman at Harvard and dealing with "doubts and ambivalences" about his religious faith:

> Suddenly it was as if the heavens opened; I heard, so it seemed, music of overwhelming power and grandeur and sweetness; there was light of unimaginable splendor and beauty; it seemed I could see into heaven itself; and I suddenly saw or perhaps felt with great clarity and persuasion and conviction that the Lord was really there and was all I had thought. The effect of this experience lingered for a long time; I was still caught up in arguments about the existence of God, but they often seemed to me merely academic, of "little existential concern", as if one were to argue about whether there has really been a past . . . or whether there really were other people.[11]

Plantinga reports many similar, though usually not as intense, experiences of what he calls "the presence of God" that occurred "in the mountains, at prayer, in church, when reading the Bible, listening to music, seeing the beauty of the sunshine on the leaves of a tree or on a blade of grass, being in the woods on a snowy night".[12]

Metaphysical and Historical Arguments

Philosophical believers also often, though by no means always, find reasons for God's existence in metaphysical arguments. William Wainwright, a specialist in the philosophy of religion, admits to a "skeptical temperament" that has led him to question all metaphysical positions. But, he says, his considered view is that "classical theistic metaphysics survives criticism at least

as well as, and probably better than, its competitors".[13] He does
not say that classical theism (in particular, the theism of Christianity) is more likely to be true than not; but he does think
it is more probable than any other metaphysical view. Further,
he suggests that "when plausible explanations are available . . .
it is reasonable to adopt *some* explanation rather than none".[14]
Nonetheless, he retains a "sense of the wretched insufficiency
of our reasoning about anything except the most mundane
matters" and particularly about the deepest questions, about
which—especially given Marxist, Freudian, and even Christian
bases for distrusting our reasoning about fundamentals—it is
hard to avoid suspecting that "even our best formulations are
only 'straw' ".[15]

But Wainwright's skepticism also works in the opposite direction: he is inclined to question the demands of what we might
call a "narrow rationality" that ignores faith and feeling: "My
congenital skepticism couldn't help but make me suspect that
I might be duped if I *didn't* trust what James called my *believing
tendencies.* In other words, I have never been able to repress the
suspicion that (as he says) the 'heart' may be 'our deepest organ
of communication' with reality".[16]

Richard Swinburne has, in his philosophical work, gone far
down the path of apologetics, from proofs of God's existence
through historical arguments for the truth of Christian revelation. But he makes it clear that he was a believer before he had
serious arguments for his belief: "My intellectual development
has been largely a matter of systematizing and justifying what I
believed in a very vague way forty years ago. Although my views
on lesser matters have changed, my worldview has not".[17] He
does, however, think that responsible belief requires reasons:
"The practice of religion . . . does indeed involve giving your
life generously for a supremely worthy purpose. But it needs

to be shown that the purpose is indeed worthy . . . ; and that involves showing that the Christian theological system . . . has some reasonable chance of being true".[18] He does not, however, claim that his apologetic efforts provide a decisive proof of his religious belief: "I am less than absolutely confident that [the central claims of Christian faith] are true. . . . But I judge that there is a significant balance of evidence in favor".[19]

Failures of Non-Belief

Most philosophers do insist on plausible responses to important objections to their beliefs, so it's not surprising that philosophical believers often publish discussions of the problem of evil and other objections to theism. But not every difficulty must be removed. As Terence Penelhum, a philosopher of religion, puts it, a philosophical believer does not have to have answers to all objections to his faith: "he does not have to suppose that all the difficulties . . . are resolved; only that some of them can be and have been, and that the rest are not altogether intractable".[20]

Philosophical believers also typically emphasize the questionable materialist or naturalist commitments of most forms of atheism, which they see as simply assuming that such views can make sense of realities such as consciousness and objective moral values. Alvin Plantinga has even developed an argument that naturalism, combined with the theory of evolution, logically implies skepticism (doubt about our ability to know anything).[21] Philosophers are also often pushed toward religion by what they see as the arrogance and complacency of academic nonbelievers. Van Inwagen is particularly disdainful: "I know I was becoming more and more repelled by the 'great secular consensus'. . . . What made it so repulsive to me can be summed up in the schoolyard *cri de coeur*: 'They think they're so smart!' I was simply revolted by the malevolent, self-satisfied stupidity of the attacks on Christianity that proceeded from that consensus".[22]

What Sort of Case is There for Belief?

Even for philosophers, religion is first of all attractive as a way of living. They find it fulfilling to go to church, follow a moral code, read scripture, and so on. Theistic arguments seem to have at best an ancillary role in philosophers' religious beliefs. Nonetheless, there is a strong intellectual component. Believing philosophers are satisfied that they can answer objections to their faith, and they see major difficulties with views such as materialism that would support nonbelief. They often also have religious experiences that at least intimate a transcendent reality that some nonbelievers facilely reject as delusional. Combining these points, believing philosophers conclude that their religion makes coherent sense of the world as a whole, providing an understanding they find unmatched by either agnosticism or atheism. This understanding is the intellectual complement of the moral attraction of a religious way of life. Indeed, explaining the goodness and power of this life is not the least merit of this understanding.

At this point we need to introduce a crucial philosophical distinction between *understanding* and *knowledge.* Here I'm giving knowledge a strong sense: to know that a religion is true would require an historical/metaphysical account of God's existence, nature, and intervention in history that justifies the religion's doctrinal claims. Understanding, by contrast, means a fruitful way of thinking about things, without implying that this way of thinking provides reliable knowledge of what actually exists and has happened in the world.

Can believing philosophers rightly claim to know that their

religion is true? The only elements in these testimonials that might support claims to know are experiences of the divine, metaphysical arguments for God's existence, and historical arguments for God's presence and action in our world. The experiences are common among believers and not readily dismissed, but they are not sufficiently wide and deep to provide certainty akin to, say, sensory perceptions. Certainly the religious experiences of most believers are nowhere near specific enough to support traditional claims about the nature of God (is he just very powerful or actually omnipotent?) or his plans for us (what sort of life—if any—can we expect after death?). The metaphysical and historical arguments play a role only for a few believers—most notably Swinburne—but even then they at best make a plausible case. They do not provide compelling arguments that God exists, that Christ rose from the dead, or that there is a heaven where we will be happy forever. Overall, it's hard to see that even the most acute philosophical believers have robust knowledge that the doctrines of their specific religion are literally true.

BELIEF WITHOUT KNOWLEDGE

Summing up, it seems that religious belief involves three distinct aspects. There is a *religious way of life*, *religious understanding*, and *religious knowledge*. A religious way of life offers a moral orientation within a community that many believers testify makes their lives better. Religious understanding offers a way of making sense of the world as a whole and of our lives in particular. Religious knowledge offers a historical/metaphysical account of supernatural realities that, if true, show the operation of a benevolent power in the universe.

Many believers are entirely justified in believing that their lives in a specific religious community—or in accord with a specific religious tradition—are of great moral value. They are not justified, however, if they think that the lives they live are the only ones that might have been morally fulfilling for them, or that they are the only or best lives of moral fulfillment for everyone. The claim cannot be exclusive.

Many believers are also justified in holding that their religious viewpoints provide a viable understanding of the main features (cognitive, moral, aesthetic) of our lives, that they offer a coherent and fruitful way of thinking about everything that needs thinking about. As above, however, there is no justification for a claim of exclusivity.

Finally, the claim to religious knowledge is not, as the new atheists maintain, risible, on a par with the claim that the Tooth Fairy and Santa Claus exist. But the sort of "evidence" for it—metaphysical arguments from believable but disputable premises, intermittent and fairly vague religious experiences, historical arguments from very limited data—does not meet ordinary (common-sense or scientific) standards for establishing a body of knowledge. It seems to me that agnosticism—even if sympathetic and open to something more positive—is the best judgment about claims of religious knowledge.

AN AGNOSTIC'S RELIGION

Nonbelievers—and even many believers—often assume that without a grounding in religious knowledge, there is no foothold for fruitful religious understanding. But is this really so? Is it perhaps possible to have understanding without knowledge? Here some reflections on the limits of science, our paradigm of knowledge, will be helpful.

Physical science may ultimately give us a complete account

of reality. It may, that is, give us causal laws that allow us to pre-dict (up to the limits of any quantum or similar uncertainty) everything that happens in the universe. This would allow us to entirely explain the universe as a causal system. But there are aspects of our experience (consciousness, personality, moral obligation, beauty) that may not be parts of the causal system. They may, in terms of the distinction we employed in talking about freedom in Chapter 3, be not observable *facts* but *meanings*.

This is obvious for moral and aesthetic meanings; even a complete account of the causal production of an action will not tell us that it is good or beautiful. The same is true of linguistic meanings. We might be able to predict the exact physical config-uration of the writing in a text that will be composed a million years from now in a language entirely unknown to us. Looking at this configuration, we would still not be able to understand the text.

Similarly, although we do not presently have anything like a complete causal account of consciousness, we have a fairly good idea of what such an account would look like from a *third-person objective perspective*, taking the brain as a physical system. But (to invoke another distinction from Chapter 3) we have almost no idea of how to incorporate into such an account the *first-person subjective perspective* of our concrete experiences: what it is like (from the inside) to see a color, hear a symphony, love a friend, or hate an enemy.

At a minimum, we currently do not have an adequate causal account of such experiences. Nor can we know that such an account is forthcoming. Atheists who ground their position in materialism may believe that such an account will someday emerge, but that belief is no more knowledge than is a religious claim that God exists as the ultimate causal power of the universe.

It doesn't follow, however, that we have no ways of understanding our first-person experiences. Not only our everyday lives but also our art, literature, history and philosophy contribute to such understanding. To say that apart from the best current results of, say, neuroscience we have no understanding of these experiences is absurd.

Every mode of understanding has its own *ontology*, a world of entities in terms of which it expresses its understanding. The ontology of fundamental physics includes quarks and other elementary particles; that of biology, cells and species; that of Freudian psychology, the drives of the id and the censorship of the superego; that of sociology, families, tribes, and institutions. There are those who argue that only the ontology of fundamental physics describes the world as it really is; ultimately there is nothing but whirls of elementary particle. But even if that is so, talk of beetles, the Oedipus complex, and the United Nations can help us understand in ways that fundamental physics doesn't. Similarly, literature, with its fictional ontologies, understands sexuality through narratives about Don Juan, Emma Bovary, and Molly Bloom—even if none of these entities have a place in the final account of reality. Turning to religion, it is possible to understand evil by talking about original sin, the beauty of the world by talking about divine creation, and the meaning of happiness by talking about heaven.

The mistake of many who reject religious ontologies out of hand is to think that they have no value if they don't express knowledge of the world's causal mechanisms. The mistake of many believers is to think that understanding through these ontologies shows that they do express such knowledge.

As in the case of morality, there is no exclusive or infallible mode of understanding, religious or otherwise. Religions should, and increasingly do, accept other modes of understanding and try to integrate them with their own. Expressions of religion in art and poetry have always done just this. (Think, for example, of John Donne's images of military, political, and sexual conquest in "Batter My Heart, Three-Person'd God".)

Nonbelievers who express serious interest in and appreciation of religions are thinking of them as modes of living and of understanding. Both they and the believers who welcome their attention should keep in mind that this says nothing at all about claims to religious knowledge.

Knowledge, if it exists, adds a major dimension to religious commitment. But a fruitful way of life and of understanding, even without knowledge, is a tremendous gift, and religious knowledge claims are hard to support. We should make room for those who embrace a religion as a source of moral guidance and understanding but remain agnostic about the religion's knowledge claims. We should, for example, allow that a good Christian may doubt the literal truth of the Trinity and the Resurrection. I wager, in fact, that many professed Christians are not at all sure about the truth of these doctrines—and other believers have similar doubts. They are, quite properly, religious agnostics.

CONCLUSION: RELIGION AND POLITICS

These reflections on religious belief suggest that religious claims have an epistemological status similar to that of political beliefs, as discussed in Chapter 1. Both are ultimately based on convictions that are not established by arguments from more fundamental beliefs. This, however, does not mean that religious (or political) convictions are irrational. Not everything can be established by logical proof, but, as we have seen, *rationality* is not the same as *logicality*. If a conviction makes good sense of the world as I've experienced it, if I've subjected it to critical scrutiny in light of the strongest objections available, and if, following the Principle of Charity, I've given careful and fair consideration to alternate ways of thinking, then I am rationally entitled to maintain the conviction.

I've argued that convictions about the causes that make the world run as it does should not be maintained if scientific inquiry does not support them. If so, we should restrict convictions to claims about meanings and values, not knowledge in the narrow sense. This applies to both politics and religion. It's just as wrong to make empirically ungrounded assumptions about the likely effects of unregulated markets on the U.S. economy as it is to make empirically ungrounded religious assumptions about the interventions of an anthropomorphic god in your life. On the other hand, a religious conviction that you should seek union with God may be as helpful for understanding your life as a political conviction that you should work for the triumph of capitalism (or toward a socialist revolution) may be for understanding current history.

Similarly, the problem of disagreement works out in parallel ways in politics and religion. Even in the face of disagreement from epistemic peers, I have a right (even a duty) to maintain a belief that is essential for my personal integrity. But this right implies a duty to scrutinize closely which of my beliefs are in fact convictions, with a fundamental place in my self-identity. Nor is it pointless to argue with those who embrace quite different religious convictions. As we saw in Chapter 4, such arguments can lead to major clarifications and even modifications in my own convictions.

Finally, we should note the role of philosophical analysis and argument regarding religious and political beliefs. What we've seen in this chapter about religion, we've also seen in Chapter

1 about politics: Philosophy has a warehouse of conceptual and logical tools that are essential for grasping the epistemological status of our convictions, explicating their consequences, and coming to terms with intellectual challenges. To this extent, reflective believers need to appeal to the authority of philosophical experts to understand and defend their beliefs. But religious and political convictions—even those held by philosophers—need not be (and seldom are) derived from philosophical arguments. Philosophy is a major *resource* for but not a *source* of our convictions.

Chapter 1 looked at politics as an example of how philosophical principles of argument can improve the quality of our public discussions. The last four chapters have shown how philosophy can help with discussions of science and of religion. The next two chapters will return to politics, showing how philosophy can help us think and talk about value questions at the center of our public lives.

6

HAPPINESS, WORK, AND CAPITALISM

W*e start with a philosophical account of* happiness *in terms of four elements:* luck, work, pleasure, *and* love. *Pleasure has a peripheral role. Work, on the other hand, is a major part of happiness and must be understood in terms of an Aristotelian distinction between* instrumental activity *(valuable only as a means to something else) and* activity valuable for its own sake *(which requires what Aristotle calls* leisure).

It would seem that capitalism, left to itself, subordinates happiness to profit and so needs regulation to make it work for the happiness of society. We review philosophical criticism of this conclusion based on the liberal principle of the rights of individuals *(in particular, to their own concepts of happiness) and on a distinction between* primary goods *and* basic goods.

In accord with the Principle of Charity, *we will look closely at Milton Friedman's defense of capitalist profit, arguing that this defense still allows for substantial regulation of the capitalist system. This leads to the concept of* public capitalism.

Finally, a paradox of democratic reform *arises, according to which public support for a reform of capitalism would*

require that the reform already be implemented. This leads to the
suggestion that to reform capitalism, education *is needed to*
pave the way for legislation.

Critics of capitalism denounce its assumption that "greed is good". Proponents allow that it may work, as the eighteenth-century writer Bernard Mandeville put it, through "private vices", but that the ultimate result is the "public good" of happiness for society as a whole. Marxists and other radicals maintain that capitalism is in fact an enemy of happiness, and this notion also has support from a different quarter:

> Working men have been surrendered, isolated and help-less, to the hard-heartedness of employers and the greed of unchecked competition . . . . so that a small number of very rich men have been able to lay upon the teeming masses of the labouring poor a yoke little better than that of slavery.[1]

In contemporary American policy discussions, there is little room for serious critiques of capitalism. We accept the capitalist economy as the essential generator of the prosperity we think is a necessary condition of happiness—if not the whole of happiness. We debate whether to increase or decrease regulation of specific businesses for specific purposes, but seldom if ever reflect on the general function and value of the capitalist system itself. In doing so we ignore the fundamental question of capitalism's true relation to our happiness.

In this chapter, I present a philosophical framework for an assessment of capitalism. As in the case of religion, although I will not hesitate to express my own views, my main purpose is to provide readers with the conceptual resources to begin thinking about the morality of our economic system. I will not raise the further issue of comparing capitalism to alternative arrangements such as socialism. My aim is just the first step of leading us to a deeper level of critical reflection on the capitalist system.

In a capitalist economy, privately owned businesses produce and sell goods and services in a "free market"; that is, a market in which supply and demand, rather than public policy, determine what businesses produce and how much they charge. Under capitalism, most of us get the money to buy things by working for businesses or, less frequently, by profiting from investments in them. Capitalism is widely held to be the best system for providing the goods and services we need to lead happy lives. To evaluate the system, we need to look at the two distinctively human elements involved in it: the *work* that keeps the system operating and the *happiness* the system is said to help us achieve.

HAPPINESS

As we saw in Chapter 3, efforts to study happiness as a purely objective phenomenon have severe limitations. Here, following philosophers from Plato and Aristotle on, I will present a view of happiness that fits with our lived experiences of striving for and sometimes achieving it.

Happiness, I suggest, involves four things, and the first one is mostly a matter of luck. You must be sufficiently free of suffering—physical and mental—for happiness even to be possible. Suffering can be noble and build character, but it can also reduce us to a state where there's nothing beyond our pain, nothing to make the pain meaningful. Of course, we can manage an occasional bout of extreme suffering in an otherwise happy life, but at a certain level sustained suffering wipes out happiness.

There are ethical views that confuse happiness with ways of coping with unhappiness. Some versions of Stoicism, for example, recommend adjusting your desires to what's in your power. If, for example, you can't avoid pain, then don't make avoiding it your goal; learn to accept it. But you can accept only so much pain; beyond a certain point it becomes overwhelming and destroys happiness. The Stoic has a good strategy for mitigating some pain but not for ensuring a happy life. Similarly, some religions provide hope for future happiness that may reconcile us to present suffering. But—apart from questions about the basis of the hope—being reconciled to severe pain is not equivalent to being happy. To avoid the worst that life can bring, you need to be lucky.

Here etymology points in the right direction: good luck ("hap" is luck in Old Norse—cf. "happenstance") is essential in a happy life. For a second element, we can look to Voltaire's philosophical tale, *Candide.* Most of its chapters show the hero, Candide, and his companions living through a horrific series of catastrophes: earthquake, violent storms, torture, rape, war. It all seems absurdly unrealistic—how could so few people suffer so much?—until we realize that Voltaire is merely condensing into a few lives the massive sufferings that the human race endures. (You have to read the story to understand how Voltaire is able to make it a comic romp.)

In the final chapter, the characters escape their suffering and form a stable community in rural Turkey. But now boredom poisons their existence, and they almost long for the painful adventures of their past. After consulting some local wise men, Candide realizes that what they need is work. Everyone takes up some task that contributes to the community's welfare, and all are happy. Candide concludes with the famous maxim: "We must cultivate our garden."

Fulfilling work, then, is a second requirement for happiness. But we can't work just for ourselves. We are distinct persons, but to survive and thrive we need a community; therefore, we can't separate our happiness from that of other people. I must do something that both satisfies me as an individual and that I regard as producing significant good for others. Of course, unless I have the luck of being born rich, my work must also generate enough income to provide me the minimal goods without which happiness is not even possible. The challenge is to find satisfying work with an adequate income.

A third feature of happiness is what the ancient Greeks called the proper "use of pleasure" (see Michel Foucault's *History of Sexuality* Volumes 2 and 3). We often think of pleasure as just gratification of our physical senses, but there are also emotional and mental pleasures—joys of art and society—that many find far more important than, say, food and sex. All of these various pleasures are important aspects of happiness. They typically come to us fairly randomly as we move through life and are a delightful supplement to the more diffuse and less intense satisfactions of our work.

The danger—particularly for a rich society—is privileging pleasure in the pursuit of a happy life. This is done explicitly in some versions of utilitarian ethics, which regards happiness as simply the maximal accumulation of pleasurable experiences. But can we really believe that happiness consists in nothing but a series of pleasurable states? Not really. The late Harvard philosopher Robert Nozick makes this essential point in his thought experiment about an "experience-machine".[2]

Suppose neuroscientists develop a device that would allow you to have any subjective experiences you like—a great romantic love, writing a brilliant novel, saving your nation from destruction. You could even program an entire life filled with the most enjoyable experiences possible. But plugging into such a machine would not give you a happy life. How could you be happy if you had never actually done anything, never accomplished a humanly important goal? If (even though you didn't know this) you had spent your life merely sitting in a laboratory enjoying a succession of pleasant feelings?

On the other hand, pleasure does appear to be one important element of happiness. Imagine the inverse of Nozick's experience-machine: a device that does not interfere with my achieving great things in the real world, but deactivates the pleasure centers of the brain so that I never subjectively enjoy anything I do. Would we say the result was a happy life?

Nevertheless, pleasure can play only a subordinate role in a happy life. Pleasures themselves often induce a desire for their repetition and intensification. Without moderation from a reflective mind, they can marginalize the work at the core of true happiness. A pathology of pleasures is often signaled by an obsession with not "missing out" on particularly attractive pleasures and strong disappointment when a highly anticipated experience does not meet expectations. (The long-cellared bottle of Lafite '61 turns out to be past its peak; there's a cold rain the entire week of your twenty-fifth-anniversary trip to Venice.) The best strategy to avoid "hedonic corruption" of happiness is to welcome wholeheartedly the pleasures that come our way but not let their explicit pursuit dominate our lives. Of course, the same applies to the money that is often needed to buy pleasure.

Finally, and often most importantly, there is the happiness of human love, where my happiness arises from and contributes to the happiness of my spouse, my children, my friends—even perhaps of all humankind. Such love can take us beyond the domain of mere happiness into the world of personal moral and religious values. It can even lead to sacrificing my happiness for another's. Love is the culmination of happiness, but, importantly, it opens us to human goods beyond mere happiness, which is why I will have little more to say about it here.

WORK

Discussing happiness has already led us to work, which, I have argued, is the central component of our happiness. In some ways, this is a generally shared view. We applaud people for their work ethic, judge our economy by its productivity, and even have a national holiday honoring work.

But there's an underlying ambivalence. We celebrate Labor Day by not working; the Book of Genesis is often read as saying that work is punishment for Adam's sin; and many of us count the days to our next vacation and see a contented retirement as a central reason for working. We're ambivalent about work because in our capitalist system it means work for pay (wage labor), not work for its own sake. It is what philosophers call an *instrumental activity*, something valuable not in itself but for what we can use it to achieve. For most of us, a paying job is still utterly essential—as the unemployed know all too well. But, in our economic system, most of us see our work as a means to something else; it makes a living, but it doesn't make a life.

What, then, is work for? In his *Nicomachean Ethics*, Aristotle has a striking answer: "we work to have leisure, on which happiness depends."[3] This may at first seem absurd. How can we be happy doing nothing, however sweetly (*dolce far niente*)? Doesn't idleness lead to boredom, the life-destroying ennui portrayed in so many novels, at least since *Madame Bovary*?

Everything depends on how we understand *leisure*. Is it mere idleness, simply doing nothing? Then a life of leisure is at best boring (a lesson of *Candide*) and at worst terrifying (leaving us, as Pascal says, with nothing to distract from the thought of death). No, the leisure Aristotle has in mind is *activity valuable for its own sake* (as opposed to what we've called *instrumental activity*, valuable only as a means to some other end). This of course is what I meant by "work" when I said that it was the central component of happiness. But we will need to distinguish this "Aristotelian work" from the instrumental work that fuels the engine of capitalism.

We can pass by for now the question of what activities are truly enjoyable for their own sake—perhaps love, adventure, art, scientific research, or philosophical contemplation? The point is that engaging in such activities—and sharing them with others—is at the heart of a happy life. They alone are valuable in themselves. In any case, Aristotelian work (leisure, properly understood) should be our primary goal.

Bertrand Russell, in his classic essay, "In Praise of Idleness", agrees.[4] Using "work" in its instrumental sense, he says, "A great deal of harm is being done in the modern world by belief in the virtuousness of work". Instead, "the road to happiness and prosperity lies in an organized diminution of work." Before the technological breakthroughs of the last two centuries, leisure could be only "the prerogative of small privileged classes," supported by slave labor or a near equivalent. But this is no longer necessary: "The morality of work is the morality of slaves, and the modern world has no need of slavery."

Using Adam Smith's famous example of a pin factory, Russell makes the solution seem simple:

> Suppose that, at a given moment, a certain number of people are engaged in the manufacture of pins. They make as

many pins as the world needs, working (say) eight hours a day. Someone makes an invention by which the same number of men can make twice as many pins: pins are already so cheap that hardly any more will be bought at a lower price. In a sensible world, everybody concerned in the manufacturing of pins would take to working four hours instead of eight, and everything else would go on as before.

We are, Russell thinks, kept from a world of leisure only by a perversely lingering prejudice in favor of the self-contradictory idea that instrumental work is worth doing for its own sake.

But Russell's proposal ignores something. He assumes that the only reason to continue working eight hours a day would be to make more pins, which we don't need. In capitalism, however, the idea would be to make better pins (or perhaps something even better than pins), thereby improving the quality of our lives.

Suppose that in 1932, when Russell wrote his essay, we had followed his advice and converted all gains in productivity into increased leisure. Antibiotics, jet airplanes, and digital computers were then just glimmers on the horizon. Creative thinkers, enjoying their Aristotelian leisure, might have spun out speculative designs for such inventions. But without a substantial increase in instrumental work, businesses would never have been able to make them realities and produce them in quantity. Russell's point is well taken, but we need to ask: When and how do we limit (in amount or quality) our production of goods in order to make room for more leisure?

In the language of capitalist productivity, *How much is enough?*[5] This is not an easy question, but since our happiness requires a significant amount of leisure as opposed to instrumental work, it seems we must put some limits on material production.

Problems with Capitalism

Here is where we need to think critically about capitalism. It is essentially a system for producing things to sell for as much profit as possible. If products sell because they contribute to human happiness, that's well and good, but in the end it doesn't matter why they sell. The system works at least as well if a product sells because people are falsely convinced that it promotes happiness. In fact, it's often easier to convince people to buy something that's inferior than it is to make something that's superior. This is why stores are filled with products that cater to fads and insecurities instead of to real human needs.

It makes sense to increase leisure—and make life more worthwhile—by producing only what makes for happier lives. But under capitalism, for most of us, work takes up the bulk of our time and energy. As a result, many of us find what we do valuable mainly as a means of earning money to buy material necessities. Even worse, capitalism's inherent, incessant demand to increase production leads to a culture dominated by advertising, insisting that we need more and more material goods. So even when we could take more time off and enjoy what we have, we instead work more and harder to reach ever higher levels of luxury. The result is that the more successful among us eat at fancy restaurants, live in expensive houses, wear designer clothing, and travel to exotic places—often, however, not having the time to really enjoy what they have. We all, of course, agree that there is a limit beyond which further material goods would make little difference to genuine happiness. But almost all of us think we are well below that limit.

Capitalism, then, seems to work against our happiness from two directions. The amount of instrumental work it demands leaves us little time for work that's valuable for its own sake, and it pushes us to want things we think will make us happy even though they won't. Capitalism thus seems more an obstacle than a means to our happiness. This suggests that we should either replace it with an economic system better able to give us what we need to be happy or, at least, regulate it so that it works less for profit and more for what we really need.

A LIBERAL OBJECTION

But, supporters of capitalism may say, aren't you forgetting that the whole point of capitalism is freedom to choose? You've put forward an elitist ideal of happiness: leisure to write poetry, listen to symphonies, have deep conversations with friends—all things allegedly above the "lower" satisfactions of having a job that pays enough to meet your basic needs and also buy the attractive things you see advertised. Maybe people who aren't overeducated value-snobs actually *are* happy with what capitalism provides.

In fact, this populist criticism of our approach has some impressive intellectual support. Political philosophy in the liberal tradition*—particularly the work of John Rawls—objects to identifying any particular conception of happiness as the norm for a society. According to Rawls (and other liberals including Richard Rorty, Amartya Sen, and Martha Nussbaum), the fundamental idea of a democratic society is that people should be allowed to form and pursue *their own* conceptions of happiness. We may think that leisure for fulfilling work is at the heart of happiness—and maybe this is even true. But, these liberal thinkers maintain, we have no right to place this truth (if it is

---

* Here "liberalism" means a political philosophy that emphasizes individual freedom. In the contemporary division of liberals and conservatives, both sides incorporate different aspects of this emphasis.

one) at the center our society. People must be free to choose for themselves. Anything else opens the door to an authoritarian—perhaps even totalitarian—society.

Liberals do agree that society must provide what Rawls calls *primary goods*: those that are essential to anyone's happiness. Examples of primary goods are "civic and political liberties, income and wealth, access to public office and 'the social bases of respect' ".[6] They are necessary conditions for, as Rawls puts it, "forming a rational plan of life" and so must be desired by all rational agents. Rawls distinguishes between these primary goods and *basic goods*, which define a particular conception of what's involved in a happy life.

In the liberal view, every society must provide the primary goods without which no one would have a meaningful chance at pursuing happiness. But society should not take a position on what basic goods people should pursue, because *autonomy*—the right of people to choose their own conceptions of the good life—is an overarching value. Basic goods specify the content of a happy life. The primary goods merely tell us what we need in order to choose and work for *any* particular conception of a happy life. As liberals see it, the need for autonomy restricts government to promoting primary goods, while remaining neutral regarding basic goods and the conceptions of happiness they specify. The government can properly help me get adequate food and housing, but it shouldn't encourage me to attend classical rather than pop concerts or prefer organic produce to fast food.

From this liberal standpoint, there are two strong reasons to support capitalism. Its unrivaled productive power maximizes the wealth needed to meet our material needs (a primary good), and its free market allows us to pursue whatever basic goods allow us to reach happiness as we conceive it.

But this liberal argument presupposes that capitalism actually does promote individual freedom. Taking a job usually means devoting much of your time and energy not to what you want but to what your employer wants. Apart from work duties, employers even try to mold employees' thought and values. You'll make better tennis shoes or sell more life insurance if you believe in the product—and even the way of life—your bosses are selling. Think of the freedoms guaranteed in the Bill of Rights. People often resist the slightest government restrictions on free expression and privacy, but our employers tell us how to dress, fire us if we challenge their ideas, and spy on us to see if we're stealing or slacking off. Beyond the workplace, we swim in an ocean of advertising, almost all of it trying to make us want what the seller wants us to want.

The capitalist system presents itself as the servant of free choice. It claims to produce whatever consumers desire to the extent that they desire it, and it pays us salaries that allow us to buy what we desire. But these claims are disingenuous. Capitalist enterprises seek to maximize profit above all, a goal that typically requires us to do work we aren't interested in so we can buy things we've been conditioned to want. Profits will be highest when workers' lives consist entirely of the instrumental work that maximizes production and the consumption that maximizes profit. As a result, capitalist businesses work against the freedom and happiness of the workers they employ.

This conflict explains the failure of John Maynard Keynes's prediction in 1930: that within the next century, the capitalist system would be able to meet all our material needs with the average employee working about fifteen hours per week. This, he thought, would allow ample leisure time for people to pursue a happy life. Keynes was right about the productive power of capitalism but wrong about the decrease in instrumental work, which has gone down by only about 20 percent since 1930 and shows no signs of further decreases.[7] Keynes failed to appreciate how successful capitalism would be in molding people to find their happiness in the material goods from which it makes its profits. We have little leisure because we need to earn enough to buy what we think will make us happy. If we agree that capitalism is a threat to our freedom, we should return to the idea that we must either eliminate or severely restrict its drive to maximize profits.

But are we perhaps underestimating the case in favor of capitalism? It's time for another application of the Principle of Charity.

Rethinking Capitalism

After the Great Depression, the New Deal, and the remarkable surge of postwar prosperity, it seemed that the United States was well on its way to a quasi-socialism that would subject the capitalist economic system to strong governmental constraints. Since the election of Ronald Reagan in 1980, a countermovement toward unfettered (laissez-faire) capitalism had become a major political force. This political movement received support from a number of conservative intellectuals. One of the most important was Milton Friedman, perhaps the most lucid and persuasive of those arguing that capitalist enterprises best served society by maximizing their profits. Thus far we have been constructing the case for restraining profits. If Friedman can establish his point, we'll need to rethink the account we have been developing about the relation of happiness, work, and capitalism.

We can best appreciate Friedman's case if we start from the fact that a society requires both an economic system to exchange goods and a political system to make laws. Friedman agrees with the liberal idea that the ultimate goal of a society should be the freedom of individuals to pursue happiness as they conceive it. But, he points out, there is a fundamental tension between any political system and individual freedom, since political decisions cannot represent the will of each individual.

In an absolute monarchy, everyone must conform to the will of the monarch; in a democracy, everyone must conform to the will of the majority; and any intermediate system will involve the conformity of one group to the will of another group. But capitalism, Friedman maintains, is a system that allows individuals to decide for themselves. What we buy and sell from one another is up to each of us. To use Friedman's example, a democratic political system that decides what color ties men should wear could result in the requirement that everyone wear the color favored by the majority. Using the capitalist system allows for competition among tie manufacturers that will likely result in a range of colors corresponding to the subjective tastes of different individuals.

It follows that, whenever possible, we should let the economy rather than the government make decisions. In particular, we should involve the government as little as possible in decisions about what people buy or sell. In many cases, people will use economic transactions to maximize their own profit. (This will typically apply to both buyers and sellers, since I buy because I prefer what you are selling to what I pay for it, and you prefer what I pay to what you are selling.) This is what capitalism is made to do: create more value for both parties in the transaction.

Friedman's position derives from his view of what profit really is. We often think of profit as a gain for the business owner to be spent however the owner likes. But Friedman suggests instead seeing profit as simply a resource for further production, meant to continue the process of creating more and more value for society. From this standpoint, diverting profit to any other purpose—either aggrandizing the owner or supporting a charity—is decreasing production and thereby making fewer goods available to satisfy human desires.

Therefore, according to Friedman, in a free economy "there is one and only one social responsibility of business—to use its resources and engage in activities designed to increase its profits". But why should profit be the sole goal of business? Why not allow, encourage, or even require that businesses also attempt to improve society in ways other than producing things that people want to buy? Friedman replies with his own question: "If businessmen do have a social responsibility other than making maximum profits . . . , how are they to know what it is? Can self-selected private individuals decide what the social interest is?" Moreover, if we allow businesses to divert profits to satisfy needs beyond those met by their products, Friedman thinks we are in effect letting them exercise "public functions of taxation, expenditure, and control" that are rightly the domain of public officials.[8]

There is, of course, nothing wrong with private individuals using their personal incomes to make charitable contributions. But Friedman's view is precisely that business profit in itself is not personal income; rather, it is an essential element of the system we use to produce things.[*] Achieving other purposes, even helping people in need, is a decision best left to the political process.

This suggests a response to our critique of capitalism. It may be that what makes for maximum profit is not what makes for

---

[*] In fact, from Friedman's point of view, it would seem that money the owners and managers of a business take for their personal use should be considered an expense that decreases profits and so should be kept to a minimum, like any other wages the business pays. Huge salaries for executives and unnecessarily large dividends are both contrary to the proper practice of capitalism.

happier human lives. But capitalism's social function is not to make people happier; its job is to maximize the production of things that people want to buy. We might say that businesses should try to make people want the right sort of things, the things that will make them really happy. But why should we think that the people who run businesses have any special insight into what people should want? Decisions about that require value judgments about basic goods—something best left to our democratic political institutions.

But suppose we accept Friedman's view of the proper function of the capitalist system. He does not show that maximizing profit is the only goal of capitalism. He merely shows that any further goal must be set by political decisions and not left to the people who run a business. Friedman in fact agrees, as we can see by reading the concluding part of the passage (omitted when I quoted it above) where he says that the only social responsibility of business is "to increase its profits." The full text reads: "there is one and only one social responsibility of business—to use its resources and engage in activities designed to increase its profits *so long as it stays within the rules of the game, which is to say, engages in open and free competition without deception or fraud*".[9]

The italicized qualification acknowledges a key restriction on the maximization of profit. More importantly, it commits Friedman to the principle that there can be restraints on the capitalist system imposed by the society that employs it. This principle was also implicit in Friedman's claim that any business that used its profits for social goods would be usurping the role of the political system.

In Friedman's account, capitalism is not an economic system that operates independent of the political system. It is a creature of that system, one with goals (e.g., of morality and social responsibility) that transcend the profitable exchange of

goods. Therefore, the owners of businesses must accept governmental restrictions on profit-making for the sake of overriding
social values. It would seem to follow, for example, that we may
in principle restrict production to allow the leisure people need
to engage in Aristotelian work.

It might seem that such an activist role for government flies
in the face of Friedman's libertarian insistence on the magic of
Adam Smith's "invisible hand" to produce "public goods from
private vices", without political control. In fact, however, Friedman makes it clear that the invisible hand is attached to the body
politic. Here is how he introduces Smith's famous phrase: "It is
the responsibility of the rest of us to establish a framework of law
such that an individual in pursuing his own interest is, to quote
Adam Smith again, 'led by an invisible hand to promote an end
which was no part of his intention' ".[10] The "invisible hand" operates for the public good only because it is directed by the social
values that our political system enacts through its laws. These
values shape the function of the capitalist economic system.

Friedman himself acknowledges the need for a wide variety
of government interventions to keep capitalism on track. First,
there are interventions necessary simply for markets to be considered genuinely free: laws against deception and fraud, clear
definitions of property, legal enforcement of contracts, and judi-
cial decisions when there are controversies over the interpretation of market rules. Even those most inclined to a laissez-faire
view would be unlikely to reject this role for government.

Friedman, however, goes much further. For example, he
insists that the government needs to control the money supply
and take steps to prevent monopolies that would destroy a free
market. He is also open to government interventions to offset
"neighborhood effects" (what economists often call *externalities*),
which he defines as "cases in which strictly voluntary exchange

is impossible [because] actions of individuals have effects on other individuals for which it is not feasible to charge or recompense them" (compensating for pollution caused by factories is one of Friedman's examples). He further notes the need for government to "supplement . . . private charity and the private family in protecting the irresponsible" (e.g., children and the insane).[11]

We must also remember that when Friedman says businesses should maximize their profit, he means "profit over the long-term", not over every quarter, every year, or presumably any fixed number of years. This makes sense: the greatest profit overall may require long periods of development, during which time profit may be far from maximal. How, then, should we measure a firm's success? Different investors will have different standards, depending on when they want or need to collect their returns. Also, depending on how long a span we consider, certain approaches will be distinctly more profitable than others. A longer perspective will likely call for "socially responsible" practices that eschew short-term profit to build a company's reputation as a "good citizen" while creating the conditions for greater profits. The longer perspective might, for example, take account of a society as a whole over at least the average lifetime of its members at a given time. Adapting this long-term perspective gives a more humane picture of what is meant by "maximizing profit", since a deserved reputation for social responsibility may well be necessary to maximize long-term profits.

Friedman's defense of capitalism allows in principle even interventions most current economic conservatives would disavow. Consider a strongly progressive proposal to eliminate poverty by providing everyone with primary goods such as adequate food, housing, health care, and education. A proponent of such a project might argue:

Given an economy like ours, which is able to produce far more than enough goods to meet everyone's basic human needs, it makes no sense to require people to compete in the market for these goods. Those who lack such goods have little chance of winning them in competition with those who already have them, and the relatively small diminution of everyone else's wealth would be nugatory in comparison with the suffering eliminated. Why not, then, guarantee that everyone willing to work will be paid enough to meet their primary needs?

Although this may sound like a typically "socialist" scheme, it is consistent with Friedman's account of the nature and function of capitalism.* The only questions are whether we judge poverty a serious social evil, think we have the resources to carry out the scheme, and can find a way of implementing the program that will not have off-setting negative effects. The answers to these questions depend on practical judgments quite independent of the basic theoretical considerations behind Friedman's defense of capitalism.

Indeed, Friedman himself proposed a version of this approach: the use of a "negative income tax" to move people out of poverty. Roughly, his idea was to give anyone reporting income below the poverty line a rebate that would bring them at least up to the line. Our current earned income tax credit—supported by both Richard Nixon and Ronald Reagan—is an application of the idea but is restricted to those who are employed. Similarly, working from Friedmanian principles, we

---

* Of course, the scheme is not socialist in the technical sense (state ownership of the means of production), but it would require the sort of government distribution of profits that many think of as socialist.

might limit capitalist production to give our citizens leisure to pursue higher forms of satisfaction.

Friedman offers a plausible defense of the claim that capitalism should be directed to the maximization of profits. But his defense renders capitalism an instrument of a democratic political system that deploys its profit-making for communally agreed-upon ends. As a result, he acknowledges the need for restrictions on profit for the sake of higher social values. This by no means makes him a political progressive (he opposed social security, corporate and graduated income taxes, and federally supported interstate highways and national parks). But his strong differences from progressives derive primarily from divergent views about our economic situation and the indirect effects of various governmental programs.

We see, then, that Friedman's defense of capitalism does not undermine our critique. He agrees with progressives on the role of social values in formulating political policies and on the need, in appropriate circumstances, for government interventions in the economic system. Over the last few decades, most progressives—apart from a small number of radical academics and activists—have come to agree with Friedman's core position on the role of the capitalist economy. They will, therefore, share Friedman's basic convictions about economic policy. Their disagreements will be over factual questions about what "proper regulation" requires in a given situation.

Our recent political impasses over economic issues have arisen because so many conservatives have moved beyond Friedman's position. They object to almost all regulation of business, reject the need for any governmental solutions to social problems, and often appear to insist on judging corporate success in terms of short-term profits. All of these positions deviate from the capitalism Friedman defends. But whereas Friedman offers

a plausible theoretical case for capitalism, there is no intellectually respectable support for current conservatives' more radical
understanding of the system. A move back to Friedman would
not eliminate the substantial differences between conservatives
and liberals, but it would at least allow for a profitable political
discussion of these differences.

What should we conclude from this analysis of Friedman's
case for capitalism? Whether or not we find it compelling, the
case strongly suggests that if we are operating in a capitalist
economy, we will need to subordinate capitalism's power as a
generator of profits to broader considerations of the overall
social good. Apart from such considerations, capitalism is what
our previous discussion assumed it to be: an engine providing
goods essential for our survival but indifferent to the moral
values that give human life meaning. Reflecting on Friedman's
ideas, we can see beyond a picture of capitalism as a soulless,
amoral mechanism with no purpose beyond the satisfaction of
desires. But we can do this only if we make it an integral part of
a moral vision that takes into account goods beyond those that
capitalism can produce.

Christopher McMahon, a political philosopher at the University of California, Santa Barbara, has recently put forward a
conception of *public capitalism*, which views businesses (at least
large corporations) as government agencies and their executives
as public officials—all subordinated to higher-level elected officials.[12] This is one way to place capitalism in a wider social/polit-
ical context while maintaining Friedman's point that business
executives are in no position to set public policy. At the same
time, McMahon runs counter to Friedman's plausible claim that
government officials are seldom well suited to say how to run a
business. I leave open the question of whether we should accept
McMahon's specific understanding of public capitalism, but we

might well adopt the name, understood in a broader sense as a capitalism essentially connected (whatever the precise nature of that connection) to the social values that sustain our community. *Public capitalism* in this sense may well be fully consistent with both Friedman's analysis of capitalism and the account of work and happiness we developed earlier in this chapter.

WHAT TO DO?

Our conclusion so far—to repeat Michel Foucault's useful phrase—is that capitalism, like all power structures "is not bad but dangerous." How best to offset the dangers? First of all, we can pass laws preventing various abuses of capitalism's power (forming monopolies, mistreating workers, employing deceptive business practices). We can also craft legislation, such as Friedman's negative income tax (or an alternative to it), that would prevent the poverty that capitalism left to itself would tolerate.

But it is difficult to see how we could effectively legislate against capitalism's two greatest threats to happiness: its focus on instrumental labor as opposed to leisure and its support of materialistic values. We might, for example, require a maximum work week of significantly less than forty hours as well as impose higher consumption taxes (levied on spending, like sales taxes) and stronger restrictions on advertising.* But here we encounter the *paradox of reforming capitalism*. Such legislation requires citizens' support, which would be available only if the goal were *already achieved*. Such proposals seem utopian fancies given a population that largely subscribes to the work and pleasure ethos of capitalism. The only people who

---

* These are some of the proposals of Robert and Edward Skidelsky in *How Much Is Enough?*.

would support these reforms are the minority that has already renounced this ethos.

A fundamental reform of capitalism must therefore try to change people's basic values. The only effective way of doing this is through education. There is enormous dissatisfaction with our educational system, but there is also considerable respect for the idea that schooling should provide not just vocational training but also liberal education (here understood as an education that forms citizens who have a broad understanding of the possibilities of human life and a critical ability to make informed choices among these possibilities).* Such education should not inculcate any specific vision of the basic goods of human life, but it will develop self-determining agents who can see through the blandishments of the market and insist that it provide what they have independently decided is necessary to have a happy life.

We neither should nor can control the decisions of such agents. They are free not only in the metaphysical sense of controlling their actions but also in the cultural sense of grasping, to some significant extent, the range of options available to them. This latter freedom derives from access to our cultural history's enduring and ever increasing legacy of literary, philosophical, political, religious, and scientific achievements. These achievements underlie the specific institutions and practices that define a person's world, but they also support radical critiques and alternatives to that world. Culture contains the seeds of revolution.

Here I am appealing to the intellectual and moral heritage to which traditional conservatives (in a sense of the term now under threat) have appealed in formulating their conception of

---

* I will develop this line of thought in some detail in Chapter 7.

happiness. But, as noted, it's foolish to think that we can transform the contemporary world by imposing traditional values from above. Rather, the transformation must come from below, forged by the very people it is meant to benefit. The liberal education needed is not that of old-world hereditary elites bringing their long-distilled wisdom to the masses. It is rather inspired by the American new-world ideal of education equally open to everyone and limited only by their ability and persistence. There is a risk that these free citizens' ultimate conclusion will not be the truth we have in mind. Free and informed, they may choose the material illusions of capitalism. But, in a democracy, an ideal of the good life has no force unless the people's will sustains it. Liberally educated consumers—and voters—are our only hope of subordinating capitalism to a humane vision of a happy life.

Conclusion

Although I have suggested a particular philosophical view of capitalism, my primary purpose has been to illustrate how philosophy can clarify political and economic issues, whether or not it leads to a compelling case for one particular view. You may disagree with my account of happiness, for example, but my discussion should at least have shown you the problems with making pleasure the sole source of happiness and suggested a number of other relevant factors, such as luck and work, that you may have overlooked. Similarly, you and I may hold different views about work, but we might both still appreciate the distinction between instrumental work and the work for its own sake that Aristotle calls "leisure", as well as the strengths and weaknesses of Bertrand Russell's call for a radical reduction of the work week.

We should also have come to see the value of Rawls's distinction between primary and basic goods, and have a sense of the tensions—however they should be resolved—between capitalism and freedom. And regardless of our final judgments on Milton Friedman's conception of maximizing profit, we can understand both how it differs from popular slogans like "greed is good" and how his position is arguably closer to progressive economic views than it initially seems—and how this closeness may open the door to more fruitful discussion of public policy. Finally, we should have gained a sense of how the analysis and evaluation of capitalism connects to the apparently distant subject of democratic education, which in fact will be the subject of the next chapter.

7

EDUCATION IN A
CAPITALIST SOCIETY

e begin with a response to Chapter 6's paradox of reforming capitalism, *starting with Philip Kitch-er's argument for the* incompatibility of capitalism and liberal education. *After several objections and replies to this argument, we see that it rests on an unstated* presupposition: *that our society lacks a fundamental commitment to* intellectual culture *for its own sake. Contrary to the common view, I will maintain that such a commitment is implicit in the central role a research faculty plays in our best colleges and universities. This centrality shows that the values of capitalism are not the only ones fundamental in our society and so removes, in principle, the conflict with liberal education. This argument depends on an Aristotelian distinction between* instrumental knowledge *and* knowledge for its own sake. *This distinction also allows us to reflect on why college should be primarily concerned with intellectual culture, not with vocational training.*

But if colleges do not provide vocational training, K–12 schools must. For this to happen, I argue, we will need to staff these schools with elite professionals, drawn from a pool of high achievers similar to that supplying our doctors, lawyers, and university professors.

Capitalism supports inadequate views of education because it treats it as a commodity *in Karl Marx's sense: something produced for sale. In particular, commodification distorts the meaning of* education, *the role of* tests, *and the nature of* teaching. *Education is not especially concerned with passing on knowledge (regarded as a commodity) to students. We should reject a fundamental role for tests, which measure knowledge, in evaluating teachers and schools. Finally, we should understand teaching as an* art *rather than a* science, *and an art that is not likely to profit much from the "science" of teaching so vigorously promoted as the solution to our educational problems. Here we will make use of the distinction of* action *and* event, *along with a philosophical understanding of an action.*

We reach these conclusions by repeated applications of a favorite technique of philosophical argumentation: the uncovering of presuppositions *(assumptions, often unstated or even unrealized, that support conventional views). By questioning the presuppositions that limit our thinking, this technique is particularly effective at introducing new ideas into a stalemated debate.*

The previous chapter concluded with the need for education as a counter to unregulated capitalism. Our system of economic production, left to itself, will push us toward the materialistic desires that its products can most readily satisfy. The system thrives on an economic circle in which we desire the products that will maximize its profits and produce those products to earn the money we need to buy them. The myth of capitalism is that we are in charge of this system because it produces what we freely choose to buy. In fact, a large part of the capitalist enterprise is devoted to forming and manipulating our desires so that they correspond to what will bring the greatest profits.

A PROBLEM

I've proposed liberal education (roughly, the study of scientific and humanistic disciplines for their own sake) as the essential response to the dangers of capitalism. The term *liberal,* coming from the ancient idea of the life of a free person as opposed to a slave, is fitting, since this is education for a life free from the constraints imposed by capitalism. But the idea that education can help us take charge of the capitalist system confronts an obvious and apparently overwhelming obstacle. A major purpose of our schools is producing employees with the skills capitalist enterprises require. How can we expect such schools to provide the counterbalance to capitalism?

Philip Kitcher, a philosopher at Columbia University, provides a powerful formulation of this problem by developing a line of argument from Adam Smith's *The Wealth of Nations.*[1] The argument begins with Smith's insight that capitalism seeks to maximize productivity and does so by the division of labor: having specially trained workers for various aspects of the production process, as on an assembly line. Given this, capitalism needs workers who have learned particular skills, ranging from elementary manual abilities through high levels of engineering and management. But, Kitcher maintains, liberal education has little relation to these skills. Therefore, as far as the capitalist economy is concerned, such education has at best a minor role.

At this point, we might agree that capitalism requires little in the way of liberal education but object that maximizing production is not necessary. We can educate a workforce with skills adequate to meet our economic needs and still provide substantial training in the liberal arts. But Kitcher points out that in today's global economy, an adequate capitalist system must compete with other such economies, many of which *will* maximize their production. A nation with schools that do not produce the most skilled workers possible will not succeed.

One common reply to this line of thought is that liberal education is essential to capitalist productivity. Without the broader intellectual formation it offers, workers will lack the flexibility needed to acquire new skills, perhaps as yet unknown, that the future will require. To use Kitcher's example, giving computer programmers intensive training only in the current most frequently used programming languages will be less useful than such training combined with broader education in logic, mathematics, and computer science.

But this very example highlights the problem with such a defense of liberal education. As Kitcher points out, a broader education in relevant technical areas will be essential for a flexible workforce. But the broadening a liberal education provides— an understanding of the wide possibilities of human life and the critical ability to make informed and well-reasoned choices among these possibilities—is unlikely to provide that sort of flexibility. Capitalism needs us to acquire new technical skills. It does not need us to have a deeper understanding of human possibilities or the ability to make wise choices among them—quite the contrary, if we are to be docile consumers.

There may be a case that liberal education leads to innovations far beyond what technical thinking, focused on specific practical problems, can achieve. That, after all, is the traditional reason for supporting pure scientific research. (We'll return to this question of creativity below.) Yet, Kitcher points out, only a small percentage of students have the potential for breakthrough creativity. Capitalism can obtain the benefits of innovation by training a small group of elite students for pure research in scientific and humanistic disciplines.

Kitcher concludes that capitalism is at odds with the values of liberal education and that, to preserve those values, we need a fundamental change in our economic system. But if, as I suggested in Chapter 6, the values of liberal education are the key to transforming capitalism, the conclusion seems to be that such education is a lost cause. The education we hope will lead people away from capitalist values will have to be subordinated to those values.

Kitcher's argument, however, works only if we assume that capitalism defines our fundamental values; that, in addition to materialistic satisfactions, we as a society do not have a major commitment to the values of pure scientific and humanistic understanding. Without this *presupposition*, it doesn't follow that preserving the values of liberal education requires a fundamental economic change. But the presupposition is open to question. To see why, we need to look at our system of college education.

What Is College For?

We typically answer this question by citing a variety of purposes, of which liberal education is only one. Most other goals— marketable skills, moral and social development, learning how to learn—are tied to the demands of employers. Yes, young people need all of these qualities. But, apart from liberal education, our best colleges—say, the top hundred major research universities and the fifty best four-year colleges, which are our models of undergraduate education—aren't an efficient way to provide them.

These institutions are all built around their faculties: the remarkable array of physicists, biologists, economists, psychologists, philosophers, historians, literary scholars, poets, artists, etc. who do cutting-edge, highly specialized scholarly and creative work. Such scholars may be superb as teachers of pure scientific and humanistic disciplines, but they are far from a cost-effective source of job training. Even if we include liberal education as one goal among many, colleges do not need such high-powered faculties to teach undergraduates. People dedicated entirely to teaching, with no special interest in research but with master's degrees in their subjects, could do an excellent job.

Although our top universities and colleges educate students for various purposes, their core is a research faculty, those who are hired, retained, and promoted primarily for achievements in specialized research. Given the role and the nature of its faculty, the only plausible raison d'être of a college is to nourish a world of *intellectual culture*: a world of ideas dedicated to what we can know scientifically, understand humanistically, or express artistically. In our society, this world is populated mainly by members of college faculties. Law, medicine, and engineering are included to the extent that they are still understood as "learned professions", deploying practical skills that are nonetheless rooted in scientific knowledge or humanistic understanding.

Support for our current system of higher education makes sense, therefore, only if we regard this intellectual culture as essential. Otherwise, we could provide job training and basic social and moral formation for young adults far more efficiently and cheaply. There would be no need to support, at great expense, the highly specialized interests of tenured academics. Colleges and universities have no distinctive purpose if we do not value highly the knowledge and understanding to which their faculties are dedicated.

Many colleges—for example, branches of state universities and some liberal arts colleges—participate in this project to a lesser though still significant extent. Others, like community colleges, have quite different goals, more akin to the job training provided by high schools and trade schools. But recognizing the diverse goals of various colleges does not affect the central role of intellectual culture in our premier institutions of higher education.

There are important questions about the precise value and role of various academic disciplines in our intellectual culture. Some think that literary scholars have been corrupted by politicized intellectual fads, others that philosophers are lost in the minutiae of logical hair-splitting. But it's absurd to say that this culture overall is not of fundamental importance in our society. Could we seriously say that we don't want a society that supports a high level of pure scientific research, art and music, historical understanding, or philosophical reflection? There have been societies that sustained intellectual culture without universities (ancient Greece and Rome are clear examples). But most of our scientific research and almost all work in the humanities takes place in colleges; and increasingly, colleges are where poets, novelists, artists, and musicians are trained and employed. For us, the tie between intellectual culture and university life is so close that separation would destroy both. For better or worse, colleges and universities are our means of advancing and transmitting such human essentials as science, philosophy, history, art, and literature.

Further, centering intellectual culture in colleges has a distinctive advantage. Specialists in intellectual disciplines need contact with intelligent and challenging non-experts. Otherwise, submerged in the complexities of their advanced research, they will lose sight of the general human significance of what they are doing. This is the wisdom of making universities not just research institutions but also centers of undergraduate education.

Of course, a university has functions other than the preservation, development, and transmission of intellectual culture. Students hope to qualify for better jobs, to make friends and find spouses, even to play sports. But none of these functions require the elite faculties at the heart of our colleges. They could all be carried out by vocational schools with dormitories, social events, and athletic facilities. The only justification for our major investment in college professors is transmitting knowledge and appreciation of intellectual culture to the next generation. We could readily eliminate them if the main point of college were not for students to open themselves to new dimensions of knowledge and understanding.

This conclusion, however, conflicts with another common presupposition: that college teachers need to focus on "*making* their subjects interesting" to students by showing how they relate to students' vocational and pop cultural interests. On the contrary, students need to see how academic subjects are *intrinsically* interesting. It is more a matter of students moving beyond their current interests than of teachers fitting their subjects to interests students already have. Good teaching does not make a course's subject more interesting; it initiates students into a fascinating part of intellectual culture—and so makes *them* more interesting.

In Chapter 6 we saw the value of Aristotle's philosophical distinction between *instrumental work* and *work done for its own sake*. Here we need a parallel Aristotelian distinction between *instrumental knowledge* and *knowledge for its own sake*. An education centered in a research university will focus on knowledge for its own sake: knowledge that forms a major part of a fulfilling life.

An obvious objection: If going to college is primarily for nurturing students' intellectual culture, how can we provide the training they need to get good jobs? Our society has a compelling interest in knowledge for its own sake, but well-qualified employees require instrumental knowledge: information and skills of no special value in their own right, but essential as means to providing the goods and services a capitalist society requires. For those interested in careers in traditional "knowledge professions" such as engineering, law, and medicine, universities can simply maintain the standard graduate schools and undergraduate programs designed for them. This makes sense because these professions call for a combination of liberal education and high-level vocational training.

Current thinking about education, however, assumes that college is the natural place to acquire the relevant instrumental knowledge not only for these elite professions but also for the vast majority of good jobs. This leads directly to the presupposition that almost everyone should go to college. But the basis of this presupposition begins to collapse once we ask how college in fact prepares students for the workplace. For most jobs, it merely provides certain basic intellectual skills: the ability to understand complex instructions, to write and speak clearly and cogently, to evaluate options critically. Beyond these basic skills, earning a college degree shows that you have the moral and social qualities that employers need: you have for a period of four years, and with relatively little supervision, deferred to authority, met deadlines, and carried out difficult tasks even if you found them pointless and boring. What better background for most jobs?

Such intellectual and moral/social training, however, does not require studying with experts on Homeric poetry, elementary particle theory, experimental psychology, or the philosophy of Kant. It does not, that is, require the immersion in intellectual culture that a college faculty is designed to provide. So why think that almost everyone should go to college? Because—and here we encounter yet another widely held presupposition about education—we believe that college is the only place for most young people to gain the instrumental knowledge they need for good jobs.

INSTRUMENTAL EDUCATION

This should seem a very odd assumption. Why shouldn't a good elementary and high school education provide the needed instrumental knowledge? Concretely, what is needed, intellectually, to succeed in most of the "good jobs" in our society? Here's one plausible and traditional model: a background in literature, art, science, history and politics adequate to read and comprehend the articles in national media; a grounding in precalculus mathematics; an ability to write well-organized and grammatically sound business memos and blog posts; and an intermediate level of competence in a foreign language.

Students with this sort of education would be excellent candidates for most satisfying and well-paying jobs (sometimes with the addition of an MBA or other specialized master's degree). From the standpoint of employment, high school graduates with such training would not need a college degree unless they wanted to be accountants or engineers, pursue pre-professional programs leading to law or medical school, or train for doctoral work in science or the humanities. Apart from this, the primary reason for going to college is its intellectual culture.

Of course, many high schools today do not provide the needed instrumental education, and we make up this deficit with remedial work in college. This is an enormous waste of resources. In principle, there is no reason why elementary and high schools could not provide the instrumental knowledge employers require. We hear various explanations for this failure: overcrowding, lack of technology, low teacher salaries, and lack of parental involvement. These factors are important, but, apart from the hard work of students themselves, the results of education mostly depend on who is teaching them. The other candidates for explaining failure are relevant only because they make it impossible for students and teachers to do what they ought to do.

But isn't it clear that our K–12 teachers are not able to provide this sort of education? Even many students from the best public schools, which have small classes, lots of computers, well-paid teachers, and concerned parents, enter college far below the level I'm suggesting they should have achieved. The obvious explanation is the stunningly low standards we set for our K–12 teachers. For every other knowledge-based profession—law, medicine, university teaching—we recruit from the top 10–20 percent of our undergraduate students. Not so for K–12 teachers.

There was a time when outstanding women chose elementary and high school teaching because other professions excluded them. Now that these other professions are more open to women, we have come to accept that pre-college teachers will, on the whole (and with admirable exceptions), be our less successful students. We try to work around this fact by emphasizing training, credentials, and external accountability. But in the end, as in other professions, there's no substitute for talent.

I agree that even the best teachers may be ineffective if they have to work with the oversized classes, lack of discipline, and inane bureaucracies that plague so many of our schools. Above all, they may not be able to reach students with lives devastated by poverty. In fact, there is little chance of attracting the best students to teach in schools with such problems. Alleviating these problems has to be part of the effort to attract a better cohort of teachers.

Perhaps the most crippling presupposition in our debates over education is that we cannot draw K–12 teachers from the pool of our highest achievers. Admittedly, few of the best college students choose elementary or high school teaching. The most encouraging data suggest merely that high school teachers may be a bit above average, while elementary school teachers are considerably below average.[2] But why not adopt the same model for elementary and high school teaching that works for other professions?

One objection is that the best students have little interest in teaching. But there is reason to think the opposite. Top doctoral programs, designed for those who want to be university teachers, have far more applicants than they can accept. Further, many excellent students who would find satisfaction in teaching don't apply to graduate school, either because they lack certain specialized research skills or because they do not want to risk the highly competitive job market for college teachers. These students would form a natural pool for non-college teaching if the pay and working conditions were anywhere near those of most universities. There are also many top students who have no interest in the advanced research that is the focus of doctoral programs but who would prefer non-college teaching to less intellectually engaging and less socially useful work.

Another objection is that teaching children and teenagers requires social and emotional abilities—to empathize, to nurture, to discipline—that may not come along with the intellectual qualities of the "best" college students. But there is no reason to think that people who are smart, articulate, and enthusiastic about ideas are in general less likely to have these pedagogical abilities. We need only choose those who have both high intellectual ability and the qualities needed to work successfully with students at a given grade level. Moreover, it's important that teachers be—as they now often are not—credible authority figures. Teachers with the justified self-confidence and prestige of an elite professional will more readily exercise such authority.

A high level of intellectual ability may not be required to understand high school, not to say elementary school, subjects, but with our current low standards it is not uncommon to find teachers who lack even this basic understanding. Moreover, it requires considerable intelligence to respond adequately to the questions and needs of students.

Most importantly, the greatest intellectual challenge of teaching at any level is to present the content effectively. Our current system seems often to assume that K–12 teachers will need the guidance of "experts" on this. There's considerable doubt as to the existence of this alleged expertise. For decades educational theory has produced a series of failed panaceas (new math, whole-language reading, writing across the curriculum, discovery-based learning, group projects, etc.). But, in any case, more intelligent teachers will be both more likely to develop better methods of teaching on their own and be better able to understand and apply any wisdom that may come to them from above.

The final objection will be that, sensible as it might seem, turning K–12 teaching into an elite, highly respected profession is too expensive. Can we seriously expect to compensate the three million people who teach elementary and high school at the level of doctors and lawyers? How can we afford this?

First we need to overcome our self-destructive aversion to raising taxes to pay for what we need. But beyond this, there are several factors that would reduce the cost. We don't need to pay teachers on par with doctors and lawyers. College teaching (apart from the wage slavery of adjuncts) is strongly attractive at far lower pay levels, and K–12 teaching would not require the pay of full professors at elite institutions. Further, in the long run, the model of a faculty of elite professionals to whom we can trust the education of our youth may pay for itself. There would be far less turnover of teachers who aren't up to the job. We would no longer need the current elaborate—and demoralizing—processes of external evaluation and the continual retraining of teachers in accord with outside experts' latest ideas. Nor would we need the extensive and expensive network of non-teaching administrators that oversee these processes.

Further, if we professionalize elementary and high school teachers, we could rely on them to provide the knowledge and skills most people need to qualify for good jobs. College will be for those seeking to enter certain professions (law, medicine, engineering, teaching) and those who want to take part in intellectual culture at levels beyond that required by most jobs. This will mean that we can transfer to K–12 schools the considerable resources that colleges now use to teach students what they should have already learned.

To what extent does this discussion resolve Kitcher's suggestion that capitalism and liberal education are incompatible? In one sense, it does not resolve it at all. If capitalism alone determines a society's fundamental values, intellectual culture will be marginalized. What we have seen is that, *in our society*, the de facto privileged status of universities as centers of intellectual culture shows that our values are not entirely determined by the capitalist system. This is why we can separate education for instrumental knowledge from education for knowledge for its own sake.

A professionalized K–12 faculty can meet the instrumental needs of capitalist enterprises, leaving college for the pursuit of knowledge that makes us happy simply because we have it. Colleges would also provide instrumental knowledge, but only for those training for the knowledge professions that require highly specialized instrumental knowledge along with intellectual culture. This vision leaves colleges primarily devoted to research and teaching in liberal arts and sciences. In this way, college education functions as a counterforce to capitalism's materialistic values.

Perhaps our most surprising conclusion is that the fate of liberal education depends on improving our K–12 education. Colleges would then be freed from the burden of educating for the job market. Absent this improvement, colleges will have to compromise their commitment to intellectual culture to take up the instrumental slack from elementary and high schools. Avoiding this disaster requires remaking K–12 teaching as a profession along the lines of other knowledge professions.

EDUCATION AS A COMMODITY

Even if our commitment to capitalism has not eliminated our strong commitment to liberal education, it supports ways of thinking that can distort what is going on in our classrooms. The system encourages us to presuppose that everything we value is what Marx calls a *commodity*: something that has a measurable value, and that can be produced and transferred impersonally. For example, hooking up (like prostitution) treats sexual pleasure as a commodity, in contrast to the pleasure of two people who actually love one another and for whom sex is literally a matter of "making love". Whatever is commodified can be given an economic value and so bought and sold. But even if no money in fact changes hands, commodification can skew the way we think about matters of human importance.

Education is a primary example. We speak of knowledge as a commodity, saying that the amount of it is growing rapidly and that schools transfer it to students. In Chapter 2, we even saw how economists evaluate teachers by the amount of added value (defined in terms of higher test scores) they have produced. This way of thinking distorts our views of the purpose of *education*, the role of *tests*, and the nature of *teaching*.

Education vs. Knowledge

Teaching is an *action* (something someone does). Philosophers have paid considerable attention to actions, and their reflections provide useful ideas for talking about the action of teaching. An action is something we do, as opposed to things that happen to us (*events*, in the usual philosophical terminology—we used this distinction discussing freedom in Chapter 3). If my head drops as I'm falling asleep in my chair, the dropping is an event, not an action. By contrast, nodding my head in agreement is an action. Going back to Plato and Aristotle, most philosophers who have addressed the topic have concluded that the nature of an action depends on its purpose, the goal (or as philosophers often put it, the *object*) that the intention aims at achieving. The very same physical movement—say, my hand's moving an electric switch—may be intended to turn on a light, startle a thief, or signal the start of a revolution. Different intentions correspond to different objects (in the philosophical sense) and so to different actions.

In the commodity view, teaching is an action that has as its object the transfer of knowledge to a student, either knowing *how* (skills) or knowing *that* (information). If an argument is needed for this view, it seems enough to note that we need tests to measure the results of our teaching. What does a test do if not determine what knowledge (and how much) teaching has imparted? Therefore, the object of teaching is to increase the quantity of a commodity (knowledge) that students have.

But let's think about the many tests we have taken in the course of our education. How well would most of us do on those we aced even a few years ago? Here's a quick quiz:

Discuss the causes of the Thirty Years War.

Mary is twenty years old, which is twice the age Ann was when Mary was the age Ann is now. How old is Ann?

How do Shakespeare's early comedies differ from his late romances?

Give a brief summary of Mendel's Laws.

If the object of teaching is knowledge, then overall its effects seem short-lived. We may know enough to do well on a test at the end of a course, but unless we return regularly to the material, we will forget everything except a few disjointed elements. (To return to the test questions above: it was about religion; you would need to set up an equation; the comedies were supposed to be funny, the romances not so much; something about the genetics of peas).

Of course, almost everyone eventually learns how to read, write, and do basic arithmetic at some level—along with the rudiments of other subjects such as history and geography. But that's because such knowledge is constantly reviewed as we deal with life—texting, paying bills, keeping up with the news—not because we learned it once and for all in third grade.

The same is true of more sophisticated adult knowledge, even in areas in which we specialize. I know a lot about certain philosophers that I studied in college and graduate school, but only the ones that I've repeatedly returned to in my teaching and research. In general, this is the sort of knowledge we retain. But what we studied once and haven't taken up again and again is largely lost. At best the traces of learning serve as signs of an "educated person" (say madeleines and I'll say Proust).

The commodity picture falls far short of what actually goes on when students "learn". There is some knowledge acquired, but in most cases only for the short term. The object of education—especially liberal education—is something that endures, and that object is not usually knowledge.

But if the object of teaching is not knowledge, what is it? In recent years I've taught a seminar to first-year honors students at Notre Dame in which we read a wide range of texts, from Plato and Thucydides to Calvino and Nabokov. We have lively discussions that require a thorough knowledge of a given text, and the students write excellent papers that require close readings of particular passages. But I'm sure the half-life of their detailed knowledge is less than a year. The real goal of my teaching, I've come to believe, is that my students have close encounters with great writing. If the object of my teaching were knowledge, then my efforts would be mostly in vain. My actions are successful only if their object is *helping students have certain experiences*: intellectual, emotional, aesthetic, and even moral experiences of reading, discussing, and writing about classic works.

What's the value of such experiences? They make students aware of new possibilities for intellectual and aesthetic fulfillment—enjoyment or, perhaps better, happiness. They may not enjoy every book we read, but they enjoy some of them and discover that—and how—this sort of thing (Greek philosophy, modernist literature) can bring them happiness. They may never again exploit the possibility, but it remains part of their lives, something that may start to bud again when they see a review of a new translation of Homer or a biography of T. S. Eliot, or when *Tartuffe* or *The Seagull* is playing at a local theater.

College education introduces students to our intellectual culture mainly through a proliferation of such possibilities: the beauty of mathematical discovery, the thrill of scientific understanding, the fascination of historical narrative, the mystery of theological speculation. We should judge teaching first by the enduring excitement it generates, not by the amount of knowledge it passes on. Knowledge—or, better, understanding—may eventually emerge as students sustain and deepen their initial encounters and eventually come to grasp something substantial about Sophocles or Beckett. But such understanding is a later arrival, flaring up in the fullness of time from the sparks good teachers plant in their students' souls.*

The fruits of college teaching, therefore, should be judged by the popularity of museums, theaters, classical concerts, book discussion groups, and publications like *Scientific American*, the *New York Review of Books*, the *Economist*, and the *Atlantic*. These are where our students are most likely to reap the benefits of their educations. And this benefit is less possession of a commodity and more access to a world of probing thought and creative imagination that helps free students from the commodity values of capitalism.

Capitalism is not entirely adverse to this cultural world. Employers often say they want to hire people who think critically and creatively, who can detect tacit but questionable assumptions and develop new ways of understanding issues—all virtues associated with liberal education. But critical and creative

---

* Recall our discussion of understanding as opposed to knowledge in Chapter 5. My language here is meant to show how I interpret the old wisdom: "Teaching is not the filling of a pail but the lighting of a fire."

attitudes go only so far in the business world. The premium is almost always on ingenuity in adapting standard procedures and established values to make profitable but seldom fundamental changes. In film, for example, you'll usually make more money from sequels than from trying to achieve a new artistic paradigm. The model for what works is not the radical thinking of Kuhn's revolutionary science but the problem solving of what he called normal science. Moreover, encouraging revolutionary thinking might lead to embarrassing questions about the capitalist system.

Despite Bell Labs and a few other (increasingly rare) examples, profound conceptual changes typically come from outside the bureaucracies of big corporations or even from entrepreneurs seeking large profits. In general, those seeking relatively short-term practical results are closely constrained by the demands of standard expectations. It's our intellectual culture—physicists and poets, psychologists and musicians, philosophers and visual artists—that generates significant criticism and creativity. Those not tuned in to this culture lack the primary source for new ways of seeing and thinking. Ezra Pound said, "Literature is news that stays news", and the same is true for all great humanistic and scientific achievements.

WHAT ARE TESTS FOR?

Another effect of the commodification of knowledge is the dominant role of testing in our educational system. Tests are very useful to help teachers judge students' progress in a given course, but now single tests such as the SAT and GRE affect a student's entire future. Tests also evaluate teachers themselves and, in fact, the entire educational system. As a result, they are becoming the crux of our educational efforts, the touchstone of whether our schools are successful. They should have a much more limited role.

In 2010, reading scores showed American fifteen-year-olds in the middle of an international pack led by Asian countries, which prompted calls from researchers and educators for immediate action.[3] The following year two sociologists, Richard Arum and Josipa Roksa, published work showing that 45 percent of students, after two years of college, had made no significant gains on a test of critical thinking.[4] From this many concluded that college teachers should raise standards in their courses, requiring more hours of study and assigning longer papers.

But here we need to ask whether the evidence presented responds to concerns we actually have (a kind of negative application of the Principle of Relevant Evidence). One question is whether a given instrument actually tests for the things we want students to know. We very seldom want students simply to do well on a test for its own sake. Tests must require or demonstrate some valuable knowledge or skill, like knowing how to multiply, understanding the Civil War, or thinking critically. It is entirely possible for students to fail tests on such topics and still have the abilities or knowledge we desire. If, for example, a math test required mentally multiplying 392 x 654 in five seconds or a history test required knowing the precise dates of fifty Civil War battles, we would not be concerned that students did poorly.

This problem becomes especially serious when we are testing a complex skill like critical thinking. The test of college students' critical thinking that Arum and Raksa used involved a simulated "performance task" (for instance, weighing evidence to determine if a fictional company should buy a type of airplane that had recently crashed). Do we in fact care whether students can think critically about artificial cases on topics that may be outside their experiences and interests? Perhaps so, but then we need to show that doing well with such cases corresponds to a real-world facility with critical thinking.

In my own teaching, I've noticed that students who have great difficulty arguing cogently about philosophical questions I raise in class nevertheless develop very sophisticated cases for being allowed to turn a paper in late. I've also learned that once they realize the importance of those philosophical questions, the critical skills follow rather quickly.

In any case, as we saw above, there's little reason to think that the long-run outcome of the courses we take is knowledge; rather, our experiences create the possibilities for future understanding of intellectual culture. The primary purpose for a test, then, is to let a teacher know whether students have been adequately engaged with the material, judged by their short-term grasp of it. Standardized tests, given weeks or months after students have worked through lessons, will inevitably show a significant falling off unless (as is likely) teachers waste time reviewing old material rather than leading students to new experiences.

Putting tests at the center of education is therefore fundamentally flawed. It assumes that learning is the passive reception of knowledge viewed as a transmittable commodity. Here we can again employ the distinction between *action* and *event*, this time applying it to the student's learning. If learning is a mere event, poor test scores primarily reflect badly on the teachers, who are the only responsible agents involved. But in fact teachers at best offer the resources students can use to educate themselves; that is, to engage actively in and profit from the experiences teachers make available. Education depends on the joint actions of teacher and student, and the object of these actions is not knowledge. Thinking that education is the transfer of a commodity obscures this truth.

We do, of course, need information about whether particular students have engaged sufficiently with their current courses to move on to more advanced material, as well as comparative information about the relative achievement of different students. But here it would seem that a teacher who has worked with a class for a semester or more would be in the best position to make such judgments. Why should there be any need for additional external evaluation?

There is such a need only if we have reason to distrust the judgment of our teachers. The current insistence on standardized testing in elementary and high school flows from this distrust, and the professionalization of K–12 teaching I urged above would greatly reduce the need for such testing. We would still need consistent standards of achievement and ways of identifying teachers whose evaluations are unfair. But these are matters that we can trust to the professional community itself, just as we trust doctors, lawyers, and university professors to be the primary monitors of their professions.

TEACHING: SCIENCE OR ART?

There exists an influential view that runs counter to the idea that we can trust teachers, at any level, to figure out how to teach and evaluate their students. The main thrust of the argument maintains that a body of empirical knowledge, drawn from cognitive psychology and neuroscience, tells us how the mind learns and should form the basis of classroom practice. So, for example, psychologists Diane Halpern and Milton Hakel say in an influential article that "the study of human cognition is an empirical science with a solid theoretical foundation and research-based applications that we can and should be using in college classrooms." But, they add, "unfortunately, the research literature is usually ignored" and instead "virtually all college faculty . . . teach the way they were taught" with the result that "it would be difficult to design an educational model that is more at odds with the findings of current research about human cognition than the one being used today at most colleges and universities."[5]

Similarly, Derek Bok, a former president of Harvard University, asserts that "the methods [college teachers] use are often poorly designed to achieve their goals."[6] He is particularly critical of the dominant method of lecturing, which, he claims, empirical studies have shown to be remarkably ineffective. Nora Newcombe, a psychologist at Temple University, nicely summarizes the position: "The existing conceptualization of teaching is implicitly to view it as a craft or an art, into which college students can be inducted by courses of general relevance and observation of working artisans. The proposed reconceptualization is to view teaching as an applied science of learning."[7]

The distinction between science (or knowledge) and art (or craft) is as old as philosophy; it's a central theme in the thought of Socrates as reported by both Xenophon and Plato. But from the beginning the distinction has been elusive, particularly because of different understandings of knowledge. Abstract mathematics and metaphysics might be examples of purely theoretical disciplines, sharply separated from practical arts and crafts. But scientific knowledge in the modern sense arises from empirical disciplines that test their theories with experiments that apply them in practice. Such applications involve a considerable amount of artful judgment and technique. Even the most acute and informed theoretician may (and often does) turn out to be an inept experimenter. The lore of physics, for example, is full of anecdotes such as the claim by Wolfgang Pauli, who won a Nobel Prize for his theoretical work in quantum physics, that his mere presence in the laboratory was likely to wreck any experiment.

How, then, are we to distinguish, as Newcombe rightly does, sciences from applied sciences, and both of these from arts? So-called pure science is a matter of testing hypotheses through careful observations, typically in the meticulously constructed environment of a laboratory. Its claims are established by "applying" them, but only in a maximally controlled situation. Applied science, on the other hand, is the effort to use the results of experimental science to produce results in a real, relatively uncontrolled environment, as when engineers build bridges. In contrast to both science and applied science (e.g., engineering), an art or craft works without any significant body of experimentally established laws. It uses an accumulated body of real-world experiences to formulate various techniques and rules of thumb and to develop successful habits of practical judgment, all for the sake of producing desired results.

Given this understanding, it seems clear that teaching is much closer to art than to applied science; it is more like, say, writing a novel than building a bridge. Here we can once again appeal to the distinction of *works here and works there* from Chapter 3. Even supposing that educational psychology has established a significant body of laboratory results, there is—as in all human sciences—seldom an effective way of applying them to the real world; or, if there is, it is extraordinarily difficult to transfer success from one context to another. By contrast, engineers have long-established techniques for applying the laws of physics to building bridges.

Derek Bok recognizes the limitations of research in educational psychology even while urging college professors to let its results inform their teaching. He concedes that "much of the research on education reaches conflicting results or is subject to criticism on methodological grounds." He tries to mitigate this point by noting that "the same is true of empirical work on most questions involving social institutions or human behavior". But generalizing a defect does not remove it.

He also notes that professors may "doubt whether studies . . . in other universities can tell them much about the appropriate methods of instruction for *their* students". To this he replies, "that cannot explain why they show so little interest in conducting serious research about educational practices in their own institutions".[8] But a "study" designed for a particular local context is far short of a contribution to psychology or cognitive science. For example, I may have learned, by trying both methods, that my students have better discussions when they systematically outline a text than when they keep informal reading journals. But I have no reason to think I've discovered a general truth about how to stimulate discussion. I have merely found a method that works better for the sort of students and the sort of material I teach—a standard tactic of teaching as a craft. Similarly, I might figure out how to construct a walkable footbridge over my garden stream without knowing anything about the applied science of bridge building.

Even apart from the deficiencies of educational research and the difficulties of its application, it is hard to see a need for it. The situation is not like that of biological science in relation to medicine. Biomedical research is important for medicine when there are diseases (e.g., smallpox, tuberculosis) that doctors cannot adequately treat. There have not been any subjects that schools have not been able to teach, from basic reading and writing to philosophy and advanced mathematics. Our efforts to teach more students with a wider range of abilities require more good teachers and better teaching conditions, but there's no reason to think that we need techniques other than those that have worked in the past. The call for an applied science of education seems to be mostly a case of a dubious solution looking for a problem.

Finally, suppose that there is a robust science of education that, effectively applied, could significantly improve teaching in a wide range of contexts. There should be no problem showing the superiority of such an approach. Simply set up schools where the teaching follows the correct scientific approach and let everyone see how much better their students are educated. This is how scientifically based medicine has established its superiority to traditional medical practices. In fact, no one has a better idea for an excellent school than staffing it with a faculty adept in the art of teaching and giving them adequate resources for doing what they know how to do. There are instances of "scientific methods" yielding good results, but this is typically because exceptionally good teachers (often teaching highly motivated students) were using the methods. Where are the examples of scientific teaching methods that have been successful in a wide range of contexts in which ordinary teachers use them with ordinary students?

Not everyone who is bright, articulate, enthusiastic, and knows the subject matter well will be a good teacher. Like any art, teaching requires long practice, hard thought, and interactions with other people who are good at it. But there is no reason why teachers should not keep an eye on cognitive science for hints at approaches they might try, just as artists have found helpful ideas from optics and the science of color. Still, good teaching has long been, and will long remain, primarily an art developed by individual teachers from their experiences in the classroom.

As in other cases, the idea that teaching is applied science— in other words, a form of social engineering—arises from a capitalist commodity view. A school is a factory for producing knowledge, and efficient production must be grounded in a science of knowledge (cognition). But teaching is not the transfer of a commodity. It is an art that has and will serve us well, provided teachers are an elite group of knowledge professionals.

In this chapter I've illustrated how philosophical thinking can lead to ideas for dealing with deficiencies in our educational system. The view developed is radical—both in the sense of opposing much current educational thought and practice, as well as challenging the roots of that thought and practice. I acknowledge that it is an ideal not easy to achieve. But philosophical ideals with few short-term prospects have at least the essential function of shaking debates out of their conventional ruts—Plato's *Republic* is the paradigm for this. And these ideals can give glimpses of what will much later become the new accepted wisdom (for example, Plato on gender equality). Of course, as always, my primary goal has not been to insist on the specific view that I defend but to provide an illustration of what the tools of philosophical thinking can bring to discussions of public policy.

Our next two chapters reverse the increasingly more general direction of our discussion in the last four chapters of such broad topics as religion, happiness, capitalism, and education. Focusing on two very specific issues—out of dozens of possibilities—we will see how complex lines of argument put forward by professional philosophers can illuminate disputes about the significance of Andy Warhol's art and the morality of abortion.

8

THINKING ABOUT ART

I s Andy Warhol's Brillo Box *a great work of art, as so many critics think? Here I make particular use of Arthur Danto's seminal work on Warhol and employ important distinctions between* artistic achievement *and* aesthetic achievement; *as well as between* discovering *and* imposing meaning. *These reflections lead to the broader question of whether some works of art are rightly judged to be intrinsically and objectively better (for example, more beautiful) than others.*

In the case of music, we can ask whether classical music is "better" than popular music. We will consider and dismiss the common relativist move that says "it's just a matter of personal taste", arguing that even those who say this in fact deny it in practice (a typical philosophical response to relativism). Given that there are objective standards for evaluating music, we can build an argument that, by those standards, classical music is in general superior to popular music.

This argument, however, presupposes that popular and classical music can be judged by the same standards. The philosopher Bruce Baugh has argued against this presupposition, drawing a distinction between the intellectual standards *appropriate for judging classical music and the* emotional standards *appropriate for rock music. We employ another distinction, between* an artwork's general value *and* its importance to an individual, *which leads to refinements of the claim of the superiority of classical music. Noting a distinction between* aesthetic value *and* moral significance, *we evaluate the claim that great art is a source of moral strength. Finally, Noel Carroll's distinction between* avant-garde art *and* mass art *returns us to the significance of Warhol's* Brillo Box.

THE *BRILLO BOX* AS ART

In 1964 an art gallery exhibited a stack of Brillo boxes Andy Warhol had made. They were not exact replicas of the boxes the manufacturer of the scouring pads used, but most people looking at them in the gallery couldn't tell the difference. I've seen these boxes occasionally in museums—and often in photos—and must admit that they (and most of Warhol's other work) do very little for me.

Many experts on art think I'm missing something. *The New Yorker's* art critic Peter Schjeldahl, for example, calls Warhol a "genius" and a "great artist" and even says that "the gold standard of Warhol exposes every inflated value in other [artistic] currencies."[1] According to Rainer Crone, a professor of art at the University of Munich, "Warhol's technique of mechanical reproduction is one of the most important advancements in artistic techniques of the entire twentieth century, comparable to the invention of the mimetic painting style with its central perspective by artists of the Renaissance in the fourteenth and fifteenth centuries."[2] And the noted art critic and philosopher Arthur Danto says "with the *Brillo Box,* the true character of the philosophical question about the nature of art had been attained" and that, therefore, Andy Warhol is "the nearest thing to a philosophical genius the history of art has produced".[3]

I'm no expert on art, but art is an important part of my life. I don't want to let ignorance keep me from appreciating a great achievement. So I want to think more about the *Brillo Box*. I propose to start with the question, "Are these boxes great works of art?" Trying to answer this single question with tools provided by recent philosophical discussions will lead us to a group of important questions about the value of art and its place in society.

Let's start with two obvious facts. First, many knowledgeable critics regard Warhol's *Brillo Box* as great art. Ordinary Brillo boxes are not great art—no one would pay a hundred thousand dollars for an ordinary Brillo box. Second, as far as their appearance is concerned, there are no significant differences between the two sorts of boxes, artistic and ordinary. (Danto even says "they look exactly like" one another.) If there were a supermarket display of Brillo boxes that included just one of Warhol's boxes, we could not pick it out from the others. It follows that, if a work of art is considered great because of the way it looks, then Warhol's boxes are not great works of art.

We may be inclined to say that a work of art *is* great precisely because of the way it looks—beautiful, sublime, fascinating—and conclude that Warhol's boxes are not great works of art. But perhaps this is a mistake. Appreciation of Warhol's boxes typically emphasizes their effects on viewers rather than their physical appearance. This appreciation takes two different forms.

Warhol's boxes sometimes earn praise for subverting the distinction between mundane objects of everyday life and "art" in a museum. They help us enjoy and appreciate the things that make up our everyday world as much as what we see in museums, and with far less effort. Whereas the joys of traditional art

frequently require an initiation into an esoteric world of historical information and refined taste, Warhol's Pop Art reveals the
joy inherent in what we all readily understand and appreciate.
Roberta Smith, a *New York Times* art critic, gives some detail in
support of this point:

> Warhol deserves a lot of credit. . . . He eliminated a long-
> accepted filter between his various art forms and reality,
> letting the nation's tarnished soul shine through in all its
> cheap, materialistic, radiant, often violent, implicitly erotic
> glory.
>
> He trained his movie camera on real people doing noth-
> ing but staring back at the lens, sleeping, eating or kissing;
> on unscripted actors and nonactors making things up as
> they went along; on the emblematic Empire State Building,
> which he filmed with a stationary camera for some seven
> hours one night. In painting he skimmed images from
> newspapers, enlarged them onto silk-screens and slapped
> them onto canvas, before or after adding splashes of off-
> register color.[4]

Danto sums it up: "Warhol's intuition was that nothing an artist
could do would give us more of what art sought than reality
already gave us".[5]

But we didn't need Warhol's close imitations of ordinary
objects displayed in a gallery to give us the thought that ordinary
objects could be viewed with enjoyment. In everyday experience
we often notice that ordinary objects have the beauty, charm, or
fascination of art works. Such objects have long found a place in
museums' design collections or displays of utensils from ancient
civilizations. In fact, even traditional artistic portrayals of ordinary objects, for example in still lifes, represent the objects in

ways that alert us to their aesthetic qualities. After leaving an art museum, we often see the world with new eyes. Long before Warhol, the line between art objects and ordinary objects was blurred.

A different sort of appreciation of Warhol's work derives from Danto's idea that it has philosophical significance. Richard Dorment, the art critic for the *Daily Telegraph*, makes the case this way:

> [Y]ou can't look at Warhol's *Marilyn* [his famous silkscreen painting] in the same way that you look at a painting by Rembrandt or Titian because Warhol isn't interested in any of the things those artists were—the representation of material reality, the exploration of character, or the creation of pictorial illusion.
>
> Warhol asked different questions about art. How does it differ from any other commodity? What value do we place on originality, invention, rarity, and the uniqueness of the art object?[6]

Warhol's work does pose these questions, but they have long been central issues in the philosophy of art. Ever since Plato, people have offered accounts of what makes something a work of art. And the fact that excellent copies or forgeries can pass for the genuine article naturally leads us to ask why we privilege the originals. Does Warhol deepen or advance this discussion?

Danto himself claims that Warhol does, arguing that only with his *Brillo Box* did we have a work of art that looked exactly like something that wasn't a work of art. It allowed us to pose the question: "Given two objects that look exactly alike, how is it possible for one of them to be a work of art and the other just an ordinary object?" Answering this question, Danto points out, requires realizing that there are no perceptual qualities (nothing we see with our five senses) that make something a work of art. This in turn implies that anything, no matter how it looks, can be a work of art. Danto cautions that this does not mean that everything *is* a work of art. But it raises the fundamental question: What non-perceptual features make a thing a work of art?

This question led to Danto's own work on the definition of art and to his notion of the "artworld", which he characterized as "an atmosphere of artistic theory, a knowledge of the history of art" that exists at a particular time. George Dickie, a leading philosopher of art, used this notion in his influential "institutional theory of art", which holds that something is a work of art if and only if it is proposed or accepted as such by the artists, dealers, patrons, critics, and theorists who are the art world. (Danto himself did not accept this precise characterization of the artworld.)

This philosophical defense of Warhol's greatness contradicts the view that he subverted the distinction between art objects and ordinary objects. It makes art appreciation once again a matter of esoteric knowledge and taste, now focused on subtle philosophical puzzles about the nature of art. Warhol's work (in the artworld context in which he presented it) no doubt occasioned Danto's philosophical question, but any replica of a commonplace object could have done this. In fact Danto admits he could have raised his question by thinking about Marcel Duchamp's famous 1915 exhibition of a urinal he purchased at a plumbing supply store (and titled *Fountain*). But it was Danto, not Warhol, who supplied the intellectual/aesthetic excitement by formulating the question and developing a brilliant answer to it. To the extent that the philosophical questions have artistic value in the context of the contemporary art world, Danto was perhaps a greater artist than Warhol.

It is a mistake to credit to an artwork (or an artist) meanings that primarily arise from our interpretative efforts. There is a fundamental difference between *discovering meaning* in an object and *imposing meaning* on it. A great work of art has embedded in it categories of understanding and appreciation that we uncover in experiencing the work. It is quite another thing to use an object as a framework for displaying categories that we bring to it. While visiting the Tate Modern in London shortly after it opened, I noticed a metal object on a wall and was well on my way to appreciating its interesting textures, honest monochrome color, and ironic similarity to an ordinary pipe fixture—when I suddenly realized that it *was* an ordinary pipe fixture. There is a difference between discovering a gold mine and constructing glittering objects from dross.

In any case, we can agree that Warhol—along with other artists and art critics—had a role in opening up new ways of making art that traditional conceptions of art had excluded. But new modes of artistic creation—commercial design techniques, performances, installations, conceptual art—do not guarantee a new kind or a higher quality of aesthetic experience. It may well be that, following Warhol, Duchamp, and others, anything can be presented as a work of art. It does not follow that anything can produce a satisfying aesthetic experience. A great work—say, Vermeer's *Woman Reading a Letter*—does not circumscribe the sorts of things that can be art, but it displays to a high degree the effect a work of art can have on us. This is what Kant had in mind when he claimed that originally beautiful works of art are *exemplary*, even though that doesn't mean that there can't be other, quite different works, such as Picasso's *Les Demoiselles d'Avignon*, that are also exemplary.

The fact that Warhol helped open up new possibilities of artistic creation makes his work important in the history of art and for that reason of considerable interest. But, as Jerrold Levinson and other philosophers have pointed out, there is an important distinction between a work's *artistic achievement* (such as its positive effect on subsequent work) and its *aesthetic achievement* (its intrinsic value as a source of worthwhile aesthetic experiences).[7] It seems that we should think of Warhol's *Brillo Box* as a great artistic achievement but not a great aesthetic achievement.

This response, however, privileges the aesthetic qualities exemplified by traditional works of what is often called "high art", as opposed to more readily enjoyable but allegedly less profound and edifying works sometimes called "low" or "popular art". Another way of reading Warhol's *Brillo Box* is as a challenge to that privilege. The writer and visual artist Gary Indiana, for example, suggests that Warhol (and Pop Art in general) rejected the traditional "hierarchy of aesthetic pleasures" based on the idea that "some art was ennobling and other art coarsening".[8] In his view, Warhol was in effect saying that his *Brillo Box* (or his various Campbell's soup cans) had as much aesthetic value as works of "high art", such as the "masterpieces" of abstract expressionism (e.g., Jackson Pollock's *Convergence*), which Warhol may have had in mind. His success in the art world effectively leveled the traditional distinction—especially associated with Matthew Arnold's *Culture and Anarchy*—of high and low art.

In this leveling view, *Brillo Box* established a new way of thinking about the quality of art. Previously, an artwork's quality depended on how it looked, with aesthetic success judged by standards of representation, beauty, or emotion. After Warhol, not only could anything be a work of art, but also the standards of artistic success could vary with the artistic context (or artworld) in which the art was produced.

This development led to what we might call the "end of art": not an end to producing works of art, but to any fixed conception of what makes for a successful work of art. This had consequences. On the one hand, avant-garde works (found or mechanically produced objects, blank canvases, erasures of drawings, etc.), often denounced as "not art", would gain artistic status in the appropriate artworld. On the other hand, popular works disdained by elitist critics could be judged of high quality by the standards of an alternative artworld.

This "Warholian" picture corresponds pretty well to the view of many sophisticated art lovers, including scholars and critics. It is not a naive relativism—it does not deny any standards of evaluation beyond what individuals happen to like. But it does relativize evaluations to socially shared contexts.

There are, then, several ways of seeing *Brillo Box* as a great work of art. (1) We can view it as subverting the distinction between art works and ordinary objects (but this amounts to the commonplace thought that there is an aesthetics of the ordinary). (2) We can regard *Brillo Box* as posing an important new question about the nature of art (but this makes Danto, the critic who saw this in the work, a major contributor to its greatness). (3) We can credit *Brillo Box* with helping pave the way to new modes of artistic expression (but this makes it important artistically, not aesthetically). (4) We can say that *Brillo Box* helped create a new artworld characterized by a picture of art that makes standards of aesthetic quality relative to a given artworld.

If we accept (4), then *Brillo Box* is a great work of art: it is recognized as such by the current artworld, which sees *Brillo Box*'s revelation of the Warholian picture as itself a major artistic achievement. But should we accept this picture of art? To answer this question, we need to examine, in typical philosophical fashion, the *presupposition* of the traditional idea that the

Warholian picture rejects: that some art works have greater degrees of intrinsic qualities (like beauty) that, independent of any single artworld, make them better art works.

Raising this question takes us well beyond reflections on Warhol's *Brillo Box* to questions relevant to all works of art. At this point, it's appropriate to widen our range of examples to include music.

IS MOZART BETTER THAN THE BEATLES?

Especially since the 1960s, our democratic society has been uneasy with the idea that traditional "high culture" (symphonies, Shakespeare, Picasso) is superior to popular culture (rap music, TV dramas, magazine advertising). Our media often make a point of blurring the distinction: we find reviews of rock concerts and operas side by side and articles on *Batman* sequels next to discussions of Chekhov plays. Sophisticated academic critics apply the same methods of analysis and appreciation to comic books as they do to Proust. And at all levels, claims of objective artistic superiority are often met with smug assertions that the days of absolute value judgments about art are long gone. Such assertions reflect the dominance of what I've called the Warholian picture.

Such a picture is attractive in a democratic society, since the alleged superiority of high culture has often supported the pretensions of an aristocratic class claiming privileged access to it. For example, Virginia Woolf's classic essay "Middlebrow"—arch, snobbish, and very funny—reserved the appreciation of great art to the "highbrow": a "thoroughbred of the mind" who combines innate taste with sufficient inherited wealth to sustain a life dedicated to art.[9] Lowbrows are working-class people who have neither the taste nor the time for the artistic life. Woolf claimed to admire lowbrows, who do the work highbrows like herself cannot and accept their cultural inferiority. But she expresses only disdain for a third class—the "middlebrows"—who have earned (probably through trade) enough money to purchase the signifiers of a high culture that they could never properly appreciate. Middlebrows pursue "no single object, neither art itself nor life itself, but both mixed indistinguishably, and rather nastily, with money, fame, power, or prestige."

There is no need to tie a defense of high art to Woolf's "snobocracy". We can define the high/low distinction directly in terms of aesthetic quality, without tendentious connections to social status or wealth. (We might also appropriate Woolf's term "middlebrow", using it to refer to those who, admirably, employ the opportunities of a democratic society to reach a level of culture they were not born to.)

But the high/low terminology can be misleading because it suggests that popular art (art accessible to and highly regarded by the majority) is as such inferior to more "difficult" art accessible only to the highly educated. To arrive at a better way of talking about degrees of artistic quality, it will help to reflect on the much abused notion of an artistic "canon".

This term is often taken to mean an elite's essentially arbitrary selection of preferred works, designed more to assert and maintain their social power than to recognize genuine merit. But the word is better used to designate a class of artwork that has been greatly valued over many decades if not centuries. These works are accompanied by highly developed traditions of interpretation and appreciation, which testify to their emotional and conceptual depth.

Such works do often contrast with the more readily accessible works popular in a given period. But popular works have often enough entered the canon, with the writings of Homer, the Greek tragedians, and Dickens as obvious examples. Conversely, there are lesser works by canonical figures—Beethoven's "Wellington's Victory", for example—that are closer to many popular works. Better, then, to contrast *extraordinary art* (the paradigms of excellence included in traditional canons) with *ordinary art* and to view the two as defining a continuum of aesthetic quality, without corresponding distinctions between what is popular and what is not.

Our question is how to justify the validity of such a continuum against claims that artistic value is always somehow relative and not intrinsic. Centuries of unresolved philosophical debate show that there is little hope of refuting someone who insists on a relativist view of art. We should not expect, for example, to provide a definition of beauty (or some other criterion of artistic excellence) that will prove to all doubters that Schubert's *lieder* are objectively superior as art to songs like "I Want to Hold Your Hand." But in practice there is no need for such proof, since hardly anyone really holds a purely relativist view. We may say, "You can't argue about taste", but when it comes to art we care about, we almost always do.

Fans of the Beatles may respond to claims about the superiority of Schubert with a facile relativism—"It just depends on what you like". But they tend to abandon this relativism when arguing, say, the comparative merits of the Beatles and the Rolling Stones. You might maintain that the Beatles were superior to the Stones (or vice versa) because their music is more complex, less derivative, and has greater emotional range and deeper intellectual content. Here you are putting forward objective standards from which you argue for a band's superiority. Arguing from such criteria implicitly rejects the view that artistic evaluations are matters of personal taste. You are giving reasons for your view that you think others ought to accept.

Given the standards fans use to show that their favorites are superior, it would seem that we can show by those same standards that works of extraordinary art are superior to works of ordinary art. If the Beatles are better than the Stones in complexity, originality, emotional impact, and intellectual content, then Mozart's arias are, by those standards, superior to the Beatles' songs. Similarly, a case for the superiority of one blockbuster movie over another would likely invoke standards of dramatic power, penetration into character, and quality of dialogue by which almost all blockbuster movies would pale compared to Sophocles or Shakespeare.*

From this standpoint, we can see why—keeping to the example of music—classical works are in general capable of much higher levels of aesthetic value than popular ones. Compared to a classical composer, someone writing a popular song can typically utilize only a very small range of musical possibilities: a shorter time span, fewer kinds of instruments, a lower level of technical virtuosity, and relatively simple compositional techniques. Correspondingly, classical performers are able to supply composers whatever they need for a given piece; popular performers seriously restrict what composers (often the performers themselves) can ask for. Of course, there are sublime works that require minimal resources. But constant restriction of resources reduces the opportunities for greater achievement (whatever the standards of achievement). Looked at this way, the general superiority of high art seems almost a truism.

Consider once again the Brillo box—not Warhol's work but that of James Harvey, a commercial designer (who was also an

---

* Note that I'm not assuming that the standards invoked in these examples (complexity, originality, etc.) are the best or the only criteria of aesthetic excellence.

abstract expressionist painter). Arthur Danto himself gives us an excellent appreciation of the box's aesthetic value:

> The . . . box is decorated with two wavy zones of red separated by one of white, which flows between them and around the box like a river. The word "Brillo" is printed in proclamatory letters: the consonants in blue, the vowels . . . in red, on the river of white. Red, white, and blue are the colors of patriotism, as the wave is a property of water and of flags. This connects cleanliness and duty, and transforms the sides of the box into a flag of patriotic sanitation. . . . The carton conveys ecstasy and in its own way is a masterpiece of visual rhetoric.[10]

But compare Danto's description of what he calls a "really great work of art", Piero della Francesca's fifteenth-century painting, *Resurrection*:

> This tremendous painting [has] a lower registrar in which a group of soldiers, heavily armed, sleeps besides Christ's sepulcher; and an upper register, in which Christ is shown climbing out of his tomb . . . with what I think is a look of dazed triumph. . . .He and the soldier belong to different perspective systems: one has to raise one's eyes to see Christ. The resurrection takes place in "the dawn's early light." It is, literally and symbolically, a new day . . . and . . . a new era. . . . Christ returns to life as they sleep, completely unaware. He does not even disturb the lid of the sepulcher. . . .The whole complex of idea of death and resurrection, flesh and spirit, a new beginning for humankind, is embodied in a single compelling image. We can see the mystery enacted before our eyes.[11]

Danto's description of Harvey's Brillo box teases out the deft craftsmanship and rhetorical force (perhaps along with a soupçon of irony) that a casual shopper might miss. But his analysis of Piero's painting presents a masterpiece that embodies a profound idea through brilliant representation and powerful symbols. The content expressed and the means used to express it put his painting in a different artistic world than the Brillo box.

There are, in sum, works of stunning intellectual and emotional complexity and depth such as Homer's *Iliad*, the Chartres Cathedral, or Bach's Mass in B minor. Their extraordinary aesthetic value far exceeds that of ordinary art and so should have a privileged importance in our lives.

But putting classical and popular music on a single evaluative continuum assumes that they should be judged by the same standards, that the same qualities make for artistic greatness in different modes of expression. Philosopher Bruce Baugh, focusing on comparisons of rock to classical music, has made an interesting argument that this presupposition is false.

To make his point, he compares the typical classical concert to the typical rock concert. A classical audience sits in silence, applauding only at the end of a piece (and not, as novices learn to their embarrassment, at the end of a movement). They remain motionless: no jumping up, dancing, waving arms—not even the "air conducting" many allow themselves when listening to recordings privately. This, it seems, is music that appeals to the mind. Programs for classical concerts often even provide notes by experts, explaining what the composer is trying to achieve and what to listen for to appreciate that achievement. During the performance, you can see people reading the notes to follow what's going on. Of course, there are those who know enough to appreciate the concert and are listening intently—but others slip into a bored trance or even fall asleep.

By contrast, the music at a rock concert galvanizes the audience. They shout out, sing along, dance. The music has an immediate, visceral impact. The appeal is primarily to the body. As Baugh puts it, rock is "registered in the body core, in the gut, and in the muscles and sinews of the arms and legs, rather than in any intellectual faculty of judgment".[12] As a result, Baugh argues, the criteria for good rock music are far from the intellectualized standards by which we evaluate classical music.

In particular, he cites rhythm, emotional expression, and loudness. Rhythm corresponds to the bodily motion of dance: "A bad rock song is one that tries and fails to inspire the body to dance".* Emotional expression belongs, first, to the vocal soloist, and depends on "the amount of feeling conveyed, and with the nuances of feeling expressed". This is independent of the technical quality of the singer's voice: "Some of the best rock vocalists, from Muddy Waters to Elvis to Lennon to Joplin, are technically quite bad singers", but they have a "virtuosity . . . that connects directly with the body, provoking a visceral response which may be complicated and hard to describe, but easy to recognize for those who have experienced it".[13]

Finally, the loudness of rock is a powerful means of expressing emotion through its power to shake the body. Used just for its own sake, loudness can "become simply exhausting and overwhelming, but used properly, it can add to expressivity. . . . [S]ome passages of rock music must be played loud in order to have the proper effect".[14]

Baugh acknowledges that these "bodily" features have some role in classical music, but insists that, on the whole, "intellec-

---

* But Baugh allows that some excellent rock music doesn't try to incite dancing, emphasizing expressivity over rhythm.

tual" features, particularly *formal* features predominate. "Form" refers to the musical structure of a piece and is well illustrated by standard analyses designed to help listeners understand classical music. Consider, for example, the following from a popular textbook for music appreciation courses:

> The first movement of Beethoven's Fifth Symphony is dense and concentrated. There is not a note or a gesture too many in the whole movement. The exposition begins with a short-short-short-LONG motive that colors almost every measure of the movement. The second theme is announced by a horn call. The theme itself starts quietly and smoothly, but underneath it, on cellos and basses, the initial rhythmic motive quietly makes itself heard. Quickly another climax builds, and the exposition ends with the whole orchestra playing the original motive together. During the development section, the horn call that introduced the second theme is gradually broken down into smaller and smaller elements until only a single chord is echoed quietly between the strings and the woodwinds. Then the recapitulation brings back the music of the movement's first part with crashing force. A short coda brings the movement to a powerful conclusion.[15]

Here, as Baugh suggests, there is little attention to the physical or emotional impact of the music; the focus is on identifying the compositional elements of the piece and how they relate to one another. There's room for such analysis because, as Baugh allows, classical music is often extraordinarily complex on this formal level—far more so, in most cases, than rock or other popular music—and understanding this complexity reveals one aspect of the music's beauty.

But formal structures also support the sorts of "bodily" features—rhythm, volume, emotional expression—that Baugh sees as distinctive of rock. In classical music, moreover, these features are generally far richer and more powerful than in rock music. Individual elements such as a graceful waltz, a stirring march, or a gorgeous melody will have the same sort of direct physical and emotional effect as the corresponding elements of popular pieces. But a classical work can combine and develop these elements to produce emotional reactions far beyond those of popular music.

Here, for example, is a description of Mahler's Fifth Symphony:

> After a piercing horn call, the first movement begins with a funeral march: tough as nails, lean, scrubbed clean of simple pictorial touches. . . . [T]he march gives way to a defiant trio—a terrible outburst of grief; then the cortège returns, followed by the trio, now dragged down to the march's slow, lumbering pace. Near the end there is a new idea, full of yearning, but the trumpet calls the first movement to a close, in utter desolation. The second movement is predominately angry and savage music, with periodic lapses into the quieter, despairing music we have left behind. There is one jarring moment when all the grief and anger spills over into sheer giddiness. The music quickly regains its composure, but seems even more disturbed. Near the end, the trumpets and trombones begin a noble brass chorale, brave and affirmative. For a moment it soars. And then, suddenly, almost inexplicably, it loses steam, falters, and falls flat. It is one of Mahler's cruelest jokes. But Mahler's Fifth ultimately moves from tragedy to triumph, and ultimately, the same brass chorale that fell to defeat in the sec-

ond movement enters and carries the finale to a rollicking conclusion.[16]

An audience transfixed by such music does not shout, dance, or sing along; the content is so rich that it takes all their psychic energy to process what is happening.

We should also keep in mind that the distinction between emotions and intellect involves a great simplification. In reality, emotions are embedded in an intellectual context and thinking in an emotional context. My reaction to a threatening gesture combines a raw feeling of fear with my memories of similar gestures and my beliefs about what they mean. As a result, the admittedly much richer intellectual content of classical music, including both its formal structure and (sometimes) its connection to, say, philosophical or religious ideas, enhances its emotional effects.

There's a simple reason why many sorts of music are popular: their range of expression is restricted to fairly simple emotions with which everyone is familiar. Nowadays, also, popular music appeals largely to adolescent feelings of love, insecurity, and angst and so wins the allegiance of youth, who later continue to appreciate memories of its joys and consolations, listening to radio stations that play only music from "their" decade. It's easy to make this accessible and nostalgic music "the soundtrack of our lives". But the very sources of popularity correspond to the aesthetic limitations of the music.

ART, LOVE, AND MORALITY

So far, then, the idea that there's a hierarchy of artistic values seems vindicated. Nonetheless, it also seems to run counter to the experience of many music lovers, even those highly knowledgeable and sophisticated. Consider, for example, Alex Ross, the distinguished music critic of *The New Yorker*:

> Music is too personal a medium to support an absolute hier-
> archy of values. The best music is music that persuades us
> that there is no other music in the world. This morning,
> for me, it was Sibelius's Fifth; late last night, Dylan's "Sad-
> Eyed Lady of the Lowlands"; tomorrow, it may be something
> entirely new. I can't rank my favorite music any more than
> I can rank my memories. Yet some discerning souls . . . say,
> in effect, "The music you love is trash. Listen instead to our
> great, arty music". . . . They are making little headway with
> the unconverted because they have forgotten to define the
> music as something worth loving. If it is worth loving, it
> must be great; no more need be said.[17]

There is truth in what Ross says—we love works of art for many reasons. The Beatles, for example, attracted people with their catchy melodies, teasing lyrics, cool attitudes, sense of musical adventure, political views, and, by now, the memories they evoke. More generally, the movies, TV shows, and hit songs of the day will attract simply because they connect to what currently seems most vivid and fascinating; they speak to the "way we live now". Many of these reasons are unrelated to the purely aesthetic qualities of the work. The same can be true of extraordinary works of art, which may attract us more as expressions of the artist's personality or as evocations of a fascinating age than for their aesthetic merit.

There is philosophical analysis to support Ross's attitude.[18] It begins with a distinction between something's *value in general* and its *importance for an individual*. Suppose that reading Homer in the original Greek is a poetic experience far superior to reading Homer in a translation. It does not follow that having this experience is important to me. I might quite rightly believe I would not get enough out of such a reading to warrant the enormous effort of learning Homeric Greek, or judge that an equivalent project of reading Shakespeare would be more profitable. I may agree that reading Homer in Greek is more valuable than reading him in translation, but correctly conclude that it's not important for me to do so.

Similarly, someone who lacks the background (or, to use Pierre Bourdieu's term, the "cultural capital") to readily appreciate classical music might find popular music, which is far more accessible, more important in his or her life. Further—and here we converge with Ross's position—even those quite capable of appreciating any sort of classical music may have needs or concerns (from time to time or even always) that make other forms of music more important for them.

This line of thought at least requires us to limit the practical significance of the aesthetic superiority of extraordinary works of art. It does not mean that everyone should make them a part of their lives or even that they are necessary to a fulfilling human life. An elitism that says, "The music you love is trash. Listen instead to our great, arty music", will usually be wrong and in any case unpersuasive. But the danger for many of us is that love of ordinary art is so easy, so comfortable, so reinforced by our environment that we are likely to ignore the less accessible world of extraordinary art, with its even greater aesthetic power. Speaking to fans of ordinary art, the case for extraordinary art should be a matter of getting them to see how much more there is to love.

We can therefore accept Ross's point and, without becoming

snobs, still preserve the aesthetic superiority of extraordinary art. But much more than aesthetic superiority has been claimed for the greatest works.

An impressive tradition, including Plato, Hegel, and Matthew Arnold maintains that great art has not just aesthetic but also moral value. This may be, as Plato suggests, because it improves character, making us, say, braver or more just; or perhaps, as Hegel thought, because it leads to a deeper understanding of the spiritual meaning of life. But it would be hard to exceed Arnold's enthusiasm, at least for poetry: "More and more mankind will discover that we have to turn to poetry to interpret life for us, to console us, to sustain us. Without poetry, our science will appear incomplete; and most of what now passes with us for religion and philosophy will be replaced by poetry".[19] Today, such ideas are unfashionable, often dismissed by noting that there were lovers of Beethoven and Schubert who ran concentration camps, that bloody tyrants were patrons of art, or even that professors of the humanities are not more faithful to their spouses than those in other disciplines. These are usually no more than glib debater's points, but even serious supporters of the human value of art have found them disturbing. The literary critic George Steiner, for example, was shocked by the Nazis "who sang Schubert in the evening and tortured in the morning" and found himself "haunted more and more by the question, "'Why did the humanities not humanize?'", concluding, "I don't have an answer."[20]

Richard Taruskin, a distinguished musicologist, pushes the point even further. Steiner has no answer to the question, he says,

> because the question is wrong. It is all too obvious by now that teaching people that their love of Schubert makes them

better people teaches them nothing but vainglory, and inspires attitudes that are the very opposite of humane. . . . To cast aesthetic preferences as moral choices at the dawn of the twenty-first century is an obscenity.[21]

But Taruskin assumes we are telling people that their ability to love Schubert's extraordinary music is a result of their already being morally superior persons. Rather, I would say, our love of Schubert opens us to experiences that can help us move to a higher moral level. His music is not only a source of enjoyment, but it can also, like all extraordinary art, take us out of ourselves and let us appreciate values (beauty, joy, grandeur) beyond the satisfaction of more mundane desires.

Experiences of extraordinary art can help us transcend the selfish concerns that destroy our moral judgment and corrupt our behavior.* Religion has historically been the primary source of such transcendence, but given modern obstacles to belief, extraordinary art becomes ever more important in our world. (And we should keep in mind the major role great art can play in the development of religious sensibilities.)

But profound moral transformation is a result of loving Schubert's music, not its cause. Nor is it the inevitable result of this love. I may never go beyond the mere enjoyment of extraordinary art, and perhaps even see my access to this enjoyment as a sign of my moral superiority. An opportunity to become better can also be an opportunity to become worse. But if I become worse, it is because I've rejected the good, not that the good was not really good.

---

* In a perceptive discussion of music and morality, Jerrold Levinson suggests that Nazis who enjoyed classical in the evening and tortured the next morning "strike us so forcefully . . . precisely because they are, in fact, exceptional. They violate an empirically grounded regularity of artistic taste comporting with some degree of moral awareness" (*Contemplating Art*, p. 189, note 6).

Extraordinary art, then, is valuable as a source of an especially satisfying form of aesthetic enjoyment that also opens the way to a transforming moral experience of transcendence. (I write this just after hearing a deeply moving performance of Benjamin Britten's *War Requiem*.) This is the justification for giving such art a privileged place in our society.

On a less transcendent level, extraordinary art may present us with ways of thinking, feeling, and living quite different from those we find in our everyday lives. For instance, our attitudes toward love and sex develop from the mores of the culture available to us. For many, this culture is that of mass-market movies, TV, and music. Encountering Shakespeare, Jane Austen, or Proust could elucidate the strengths and weaknesses of our current mores. In particular, the impulse of adolescents to rebel would be much better grounded in the alternative perspectives of extraordinary art than in the conventional and commercialized paths of "rebellion" provided by the very culture they are reacting against.

I conclude then that extraordinary art is superior both aesthetically and morally to ordinary art. Practically, this does not mean that ordinary art cannot have significant aesthetic and moral value; moreover, there are many contexts in which it fits our needs much better than extraordinary art. But extraordinary art should be a strong presence in our society, introduced to everyone through our educational system so that those who might profit from it can gain the cultural capital needed to do so. And we should encourage those who have the cultural capital to make extraordinary art part of their lives. A corollary is that society should provide the support needed to make extraordinary art widely available and accessible to everyone. Surprisingly, the Warholian picture is a great help toward achieving this last goal.

The Avant-garde and Mass Art

We return, therefore, to the picture of art embodied in Warhol's *Brillo Box*. Although the picture has no place for the distinction between ordinary art and extraordinary art, the picture has led to what Noël Carroll calls *mass art* (as distinct from *avant-garde art*).[22] Avant-garde art deliberately provokes the question, *Is this art?*, thereby itself questioning preconceptions its audience might have about the nature of art. Mass art is today the dominant form of popular art: objects produced on a huge scale and readily available to anyone who wants them (movies, TV shows, rap music, YouTube, commercials, product packaging, etc.).

In an ironic way, the distinction between mass and avant-garde art parallels the old distinction between low and high art. Avant-garde art is produced by elites whose esoteric works are often sold for enormous prices but lack the general appeal of mass art. But countering this division is avant-garde artists' own taste for mass art, which they incorporate into their work, often to undermine the supposed privilege of high art. This, in fact, is why *Brillo Box* is a paradigm of avant-garde art: it made the elite (philosophical) point that we can't see any difference between high and low art by successfully presenting a reproduction of a piece of commercial art as a work of high art.

But despite the avant-garde's enthusiasm for mass art, the masses have scant interest in avant-garde art. At best they appreciate pieces that reproduce or imitate mass art (Warhol's boxes and soup cans, Robert Rauschenberg's cartoons) just as they appreciate the real things: not for the works' irony or subtle philosophical points about the nature of art but for their familiarity and accessibility. (It also helps that the works of Warhol and others are often easily recognized as by the artist, allowing a display of sophistication with no real knowledge.) The result is that the contemporary avant-garde has, in its own terms, little impact on the artistic experiences of anyone outside a small circle of aficionados.

But the extraordinary art of the traditional canon has more impact. In fact, given the wide availability of inexpensive books, recorded music, and blockbuster museum exhibits, the more accessible works of extraordinary art have in a sense become part of mass art. But esoteric masterworks languish, especially those of high modernism, which makes extraordinary difficulty one of their distinctive features: witness the continuing tepid receptions of the atonal music of Arnold Schönberg and his followers, over a century since its invention.

At the same time, as mass art grows more entrenched and confident of its audience, it can introduce more of the depth, complexity, and subtlety of traditional extraordinary art. In this way, it both approaches the level of that art and makes the mass audience more capable of appreciating such art. Think, for example, of the almost scholarly attention to detail and analyses of character, plot, and morality sometimes seen in blog discussions of television series such as *The Sopranos*, *The Wire*, and *Breaking Bad*.

While mass art brings both itself and its audience closer to canonical models of extraordinary art, the avant-garde grows more irrelevant to the aesthetic experience of most people. But it remains important in two dimensions. Its relentless experimentation generates new ways of making art that those aiming at traditional aesthetic values draw on; and its insistence that "anything can be art" legitimizes not only its own always more radically original creations but also traditional work that, in a less permissive environment, would be judged derivative and reactionary. Andy Warhol's world turns out not to be the end of traditional extraordinary art but an impetus for its flourishing, even in a world of mass art.

Our next chapter, on a very different topic, will nonetheless provide another example of how the professional work of academic philosophers can aid the thinking of non-specialists about contested issues—indeed about perhaps the most bitterly contested issue: the morality of abortion.

9

Can We Stop Fighting about Abortion?

We start with a distinction between general principles *and* particular cases, *arguing that, even though we disagree about what principles make an abortion moral or not, there is wide agreement that infanticide is immoral and that abortions in the case of rape are not. Starting from this agreement, we unpack three influential philosophical discussions of abortion: Jeff McMahan's argument that the fetus is not a person; Judith Jarvis Thomson's argument that, even if the fetus is a person, some abortions are moral because of a woman's right to control her body; and Don Marquis's argument that abortion is wrong because the fetus has at least the potential for a human life.*

As it turns out, our agreement on the moral status of particular cases of abortion requires all three of the philosophical arguments to retreat from an extreme pro-choice or pro-life position. Combining the defensible parts of these arguments decreases the distance between the opposing views on abortion.

Next, we consider the role of religious beliefs in the abortion debate. Dogmatic avowals of "faith" can, in Richard Rorty's phrase, be "conversation-stoppers". But it's a mistake to claim that matters of public (rather than private) concern should appeal only to premises accepted by all parties. Invoking the concepts of overlapping consensus and immanent criticism, we see how fruitful discussion is possible even without shared premises.

Finally, the crucial distinction between legality and morality shows how disagreement about the morality of abortion need not translate into disagreement about the laws that should govern it.

Polls suggest a sharp division in the United States over abortion, with roughly half of respondents saying they are pro-life and half pro-choice.[1] Debate between the two sides centers on the question, *Is the fetus a person?** Answering this question depends on the deeper question: what is a person?

The strong pro-life view (that there is a human being with the full moral rights of a person from the moment of conception, when the egg is fertilized) argues that a person is a human being in the biological sense of an organism with the DNA programmed to develop into a mature human being. As legal philosopher Robert George and bioethicist Patrick Lee put it: "from the zygote stage [the fertilized egg] onward, the human embryo has within it all of the internal information needed—including chiefly its genetic and epigenetic constitution—and the active disposition to develop itself to the mature stage of a human organism."[2] Given this, they argue that the fetus is a person and, since deliberately killing an innocent person is murder and murder is morally wrong, abortion is morally wrong.

---

* Choosing convenience over scientific precision, I'll use "fetus" to cover every stage of pregnancy, from the fertilized egg to birth.

The strong pro-choice view (that there is no human being with the full moral rights of a person before birth) argues that a person is much more than an organism with human DNA. Such an organism is biologically human, but to be a person is to have a moral status that is not determined biologically. A person, then, is (to cite a standard formulation) "a self-conscious being with some degree of rationality and . . . psychological interconnections between temporal stages".[3]

In these terms, the public debate is unresolvable. There have been centuries of amazingly subtle philosophical debate about what it means to be a person, and, although this debate has provided important insights, it remains far from answering the question. It's foolish to expect that our public debate can answer a question that thinkers such as Plato, Thomas Aquinas, John Locke, and Immanuel Kant have not been able to settle.

The impasse arises because we are trying to find a general principle that will tell us when a particular abortion is morally wrong. As is often the case, disagreement at the general level is unresolvable. But we sometimes can make progress by looking at *particular examples* rather than *general principles*. This, I suggest, is the way to approach abortion. If we turn away from general questions about personhood and rights, we start from our general agreement on two specific points: that abortion is moral in cases of rape and of threat to the mother's life, and that killing an infant after its birth is immoral. Despite an even divide in pro-life/pro-choice identification, overwhelming majorities support abortion to save a mother's life (83 percent) and in the case of rape (75 percent), and virtually everyone rejects infanticide.[4] Working from these areas of agreement on extreme cases, we can develop a position on abortion that should have wide acceptance. Recent philosophical discussions of abortion will be a great help in carrying out this project.

Our discussion will center on three philosophers whose work on abortion has been especially perceptive and influential: Jeff McMahan, Judith Jarvis Thomson, and Don Marquis.

McMahan's Pro-choice Argument: The Rights of the Fetus

Jeff McMahan begins his defense of abortion with an account of the stages preceding birth.[5] First, he says, we have an organism, developing from the union of sperm and ovum but without sufficient structure to support even a capacity for consciousness. Next, when a brain and central nervous system develop to the point of supporting consciousness, there exists an "embodied mind". Eventually the fetus has a conscious existence. But even then, the fetus is not a person in the sense of being aware of itself as continuously existing through time and acting for the sake of future goals. In fact, even a newborn requires further development to be a person in McMahan's sense.

Given this picture, McMahan next asks: When does a being have an interest in continuing to live? If something (e.g., a stone) does not even have a capacity for consciousness, then it cannot have an interest in anything, including its own survival, and cannot be harmed by being destroyed. But McMahan also thinks that survival matters very little, if at all, to a conscious being that has no sense of having a future but lives entirely in each moment with no awareness of living an ongoing life. In general, death can be an evil for a being only to the extent that there are strong conscious connections between its present and its future states. If the being has little or no interest in its future, then its death is of little significance to it.

From here, McMahan moves to a discussion of the morality of abortion. His first point is that for a fetus that does not have a capacity for consciousness, dying is no loss, since there is nothing that matters to it. But even a later fetus, capable of consciousness and perhaps even actually conscious, would have little or no psychological continuity and sense of having a future; it too would lose little or nothing by dying. In general, then, there is no objection in principle to abortion when it would prevent a significant degree of harm (particularly to the mother or the child). He allows that the degree of harm avoided needs to be greater the more the fetus develops, but at no point does abortion become simply wrong no matter what amount of harm it would prevent. For an abortion to be simply wrong, the fetus would have to be a person (in McMahan's sense) with psychological continuity and a sense of and interest in its future. But, he argues, even the fully formed fetus does not satisfy this requirement.

For all its care and subtlety, McMahan's case is, as he acknowledges, open to the objection that it allows infanticide. A newborn infant is no more a person than a full-term fetus. Indeed, as McMahan himself admits, the difference between the two is only "geographical", the fetus still in the womb, the infant outside it. He even points out that a premature newborn may be significantly less developed than a full-term but still unborn fetus.

The least offensive option would seem to be to agree that late-term abortions are immoral, unless to save the mother's life. But McMahan notes a problem with that move. An adult chimpanzee, for example, is at least on the psychological level of a newborn human. Hardly anyone would object to killing a chimp if it were necessary to save a human mother's life (by, for example, using its heart to repair her defective organ). If we are willing to kill a non-human animal on the same developmental level as a human newborn, why should we refrain from killing the newborn? An immediate response is that the newborn has a *potential* to achieve a much higher psychological level than the chimp. But, McMahan points out, a child with a severe mental handicap might not have this capacity, so we are still left with parity between the chimp and at least some children.

We might be inclined to scoff at the inanity of such contorted philosophical discussions. It is, we may think, common sense that human infants are on a different moral level from even the most advanced animals. Therefore, it's wrong to kill a human infant for any purpose, although there are cases where it is all right to kill an animal. McMahan is just confusing a simple point.

But it's not McMahan who is introducing the confusion. The problem is that our common sense is confused. Most of us think it's moral to kill a chimp for a good purpose, but not a human infant. But we also can't specify any feature of the psychological state of a severely mentally handicapped child that makes killing it worse than killing a chimp. We can keep our "common-sense" view that it's wrong to kill the child to save an adult's life, but then we have nothing to say to the animal rights activist who insists that it's equally wrong to kill a chimpanzee for that purpose. We can reply that we prefer humans to chimpanzees, even when there are no morally relevant differences. But how is this different from racists who discriminate in favor of their own race because they prefer it? Here speciesism seems no different from racism.

In any case, the pro-choice view runs into trouble if we need to cite an infant's *potential* to reach a level where killing it would be wrong. For this same appeal applies to the case of an early- or middle-stage fetus. If it's wrong to kill an infant because of its capacity to reach a higher level, why shouldn't we conclude the same thing about the fetus? Resolving the problem posed by non-human animals undermines the case for the morality of many abortions.

For these sorts of reasons, McMahan—and other pro-choice philosophers such as Peter Singer—have argued that it may be better to back away from our absolute condemnation of infanticide. They agree that it would be acceptable only in extraordinary circumstances, but, to be consistent, they must limit late-term abortions to precisely the same extent that they limit infanticide. If, for example, they allow late-term abortions of fetuses with severe mental or physical defects, they must allow the killing of similar infants. In any case, I suspect that most people will see the need to entertain the morality of infanticide as a proof that McMahan's strong pro-choice position is untenable.

THOMSON'S PRO-CHOICE ARGUMENT: THE RIGHTS OF A PREGNANT WOMAN

McMahan's position centered on the fetus's right to life. Many on the pro-choice side maintain that an adequate treatment of abortion requires equal attention to a woman's right to control what happens to her body. In light of the difficulties we've encountered in McMahan's pro-choice argument, this perspective becomes particularly important. McMahan's case for the morality of abortion depended on lowering the level of moral consideration accorded to the fetus. But this made it difficult to make a moral distinction between the fetus and a newborn (or even a higher non-human animal).

Suppose, then, we claim that a woman's right to control her body can take precedence over the fetus's right to life. This approach has two advantages: it may allow us to show that abortion can be moral even if the fetus is a person, and it avoids the problem of infanticide, since the woman's right is relevant only because the fetus is physically connected to her body.

The classic development of this approach is Judith Jarvis Thomson's essay, "A Defense of Abortion".[6] She begins by asking us to consider a bizarre—but, it turns out, quite instructive—scenario:

> You wake up in the morning and find yourself back to back in bed with an unconscious violinist. A famous unconscious violinist. He has been found to have a fatal kidney ailment, and the Society of Music Lovers has canvassed all the available medical records and found that you alone have the right blood type to help. They have therefore kidnapped you, and last night the violinist's circulatory system was plugged into yours, so that your kidneys can be used to extract poisons from his blood as well as your own. The director of the hospital now tells you, "Look, we're sorry the Society of Music Lovers did this to you—we would never have permitted it if we had known. But still, they did it, and the violinist is now plugged into you. To unplug you would be to kill him. But never mind, it's only for nine months. By then he will have recovered from his ailment, and can safely be unplugged from you."

Thomson's question is: Would it be morally wrong for you to unplug the violinist, thereby causing him to die? Her answer, which seems to be the sheerest common sense, is no. "No doubt", she says, "it would be very nice of you if you did [stay plugged into him], a great kindness". But surely you have no obligation to be so kind. You are perfectly in your rights to say that, in this case, your right to control what happens to your body takes precedence over the famous violinist's right to life.

Almost everyone's first response to this example (apart from its wild implausibility) is that it corresponds only to the exceptional case of a pregnancy (as in the case of rape) that was beyond a woman's control. Doesn't this make the example irrelevant for most abortions? Thomson immediately notes this point but maintains that the example nonetheless offers a starting point for thinking about the morality of abortion. If we temporarily suspend our doubts, I think we will find that she is right.

The first thing the violinist example shows is that my having a right to life (as everyone does) and also being innocent (as the violinist and the fetus are) do not imply that it is not right for you to kill me. One reason it might be right to kill me is that I am a threat to your life (even if not deliberately). I might, for example, be attacking you in a psychotic rage. In such a case, you would have a right to kill me to save yourself, even if I were your child. It follows that a pregnancy that seriously threatens the mother's life may be terminated with an abortion.

This is a common view, of course, even among strong opponents of abortion. But what if the fetus is not a threat to the mother's life? If carrying the fetus to term will not kill the mother, doesn't the fetus's right to life outweigh any harm the mother suffers? Once again, the violinist example is instructive. Even though you may be obligated to endure a certain amount of inconvenience to save the violinist, you surely are not obliged to do anything short of death. Indeed, it seems clear you would not be obliged to stay hooked to the violinist for nine months. The right to life does not imply a right to use another's body in any way short of death. Once again, this point is one that most people accept; as we've seen, most of us think that abortion is permissible for a pregnancy that results from rape.

Thomson's analysis has led thus far only to the rather uncontroversial conclusion that abortion is moral in cases of rape and threat to the mother's life. But what about more difficult cases?

Here we need to go beyond Thomson's violinist example and take up the question of a woman's "responsibility" for her pregnancy. Thomson rightly suggests that the issue of responsibility is complex and that judgments will differ from case to case. On the one hand, if a woman does not want to have a child and has used a reliable method of birth control to prevent conception, then, Thomson thinks, she is not responsible and an abortion for a good reason is not immoral.

Of course, much depends on what we take as a good reason. Is it sufficient not to want the irritations and pain of a routine pregnancy, or must there be a stronger reason—if, for example, a particular pregnancy is likely to require extraordinary suffering from nausea or confinement to bed for several months? Further, there are hard questions about how much a woman must have done to prevent conception. Is she responsible if she forgot to take a pill or if she was carried away by a surge of passion?

Thomson insists that, even apart from rape, in some cases there is not sufficient responsibility to obligate the woman to go through with pregnancy. But she also allows the possibility that a woman's responsibility can make an abortion immoral. We can, she says, "establish at most that there are . . . some cases in which abortion is unjust killing. There is room for much discussion and argument as to precisely which, if any". Despite Thomson's hesitation, it seems clear that her line of argument does imply that not all abortions are moral. It would, for example, be immoral if a woman who had intentionally become pregnant decided, in her eighth month, to have an abortion so she could wear a favorite dress to a party.*

Thomson notes that her discussion assumes that the fetus is a person only for the sake of argument. Her point was to show that, even on this assumption, abortion is permissible in at least some cases. Her own view is that, at least in the initial stages, the fetus is obviously not a person, which makes it much easier to defend early abortions. This point, however, does not morally justify late-term abortions of planned pregnancies for trivial reasons.

McMahan and Thomson represent two of the strongest lines of philosophical argument for the morality of abortion: an argument from the nature of the fetus and an argument from the rights of the mother. Neither argument alone shows that all abortions are moral. McMahan, if we accept his view of the nature of the fetus, shows that abortions are moral until the fetus has reached the psychological level of a newborn. But to allow abortions beyond that stage, he needs to accept the morality of infanticide. Thomson, arguing from the rights of the mother, shows that abortions are not all immoral, even if the fetus is a person. But she also has to allow for cases in which an abortion is wrong, either because the woman would suffer very little harm by having the baby or because she was sufficiently responsible for the pregnancy.

It might seem, however, that the two pro-choice arguments complement one another. McMahan shows that all abortions are moral except for late ones, where the fully developed fetus has a right to life equal to that of a newborn. Thomson shows

---

* This is what philosophers call a *counterexample*: a particular case that refutes a universal claim. Extreme—and highly unlikely—counterexamples (like this one) often occur in professional philosophical discussions. They are relevant, as here, to show that a universal claim is not in fact true for all possible cases. But they often do not so much refute an opponent's position as show a need to clarify or refine its formulation.

that even if the fetus has a right to life, that right still can be overridden by the woman's right to control her body. Putting the two arguments together might seem to show that all abortions are morally permissible.

But, as we saw, Thomson has to admit that there are cases in which the mother's right to control her body does not override the fetus's right to life. In these cases (those of a late-term fetus) neither line of argument shows the morality of all abortions. Even combining the two best pro-choice arguments, it still seems that if a woman is sufficiently responsible for her pregnancy and has no extraordinary reason for terminating it, a late-term abortion will always be immoral.

In particular, even after taking account of the pro-choice arguments of McMahan and Thomson, we can still construct the following pro-life argument:

1. Infanticide is always morally wrong.
2. A late-term abortion is morally equivalent to infanticide, unless (a) the mother's life is threatened, or (b) the mother is not sufficiently responsible for the pregnancy.
3. For some late-term abortions, neither (a) nor (b) holds.
4. Therefore, some late-term abortions are immoral.

Conclusion: even the best pro-choice cases can't avoid the conclusion that some abortions are immoral. But, as we shall see, the strong pro-life position encounters a similar problem.

MARQUIS'S PRO-LIFE ARGUMENT: HUMAN POTENTIAL

Making the strong philosophical case against abortion requires finding a feature that gives an unchallengeable right to life and is also present at all stages of fetal development. It's not easy to show that the most obvious feature—being biologically human—confers a moral right to life. Being a person in some strong sense will confer the moral right, but it's hard to show that early-stage fetuses are persons in any such sense.

Don Marquis's "Why Abortion is Immoral" responds to this problem.[7] He begins by putting aside murky questions about persons and rights and simply asks what harm is done by killing someone. To this, he says, there is a straightforward answer: "The loss of one's life deprives one of all the experiences, activities, projects, and enjoyments which would otherwise have constituted one's future." In short, when you take my life, you take away my future. This alone—apart from any deep considerations about the nature and rights of persons—is why (lacking special circumstances such as self-defense) it's wrong to kill someone. There may be other, more profound reasons—perhaps the sanctity of personhood—but this by itself is a good reason for the immorality of murder.

But, we may object, the abortion debate concerns in part whether the fetus is a human being; if we aren't clear on that, how does it help to explain why it's wrong to kill a human? But here's the power of Marquis's proposal: even if the fetus, at an early stage, is not a human being, its future, should it live and thrive, is to be human and to have the sorts of goods that make for a fulfilling human life. Indeed, a recently fertilized egg has a natural path to such a future, a future that will come to be unless something intervenes. The fact that the potential child from conception onward has a human future is a good reason against aborting it at any stage.

Marquis sums up his view nicely: "Since a fetus possesses a property [the potential for a human future], the possession of which in adult human beings is sufficient to make killing an adult human being wrong, abortion is wrong". This might seem to support a near-universal ban on abortion (with exceptions only for cases, such as self-defense, in which we would also allow the killing of adult humans).

But Marquis himself suggests an important limitation. He says that his argument is "subject to the assumption that the moral permissibility of abortion stands or falls on the moral status of the fetus". He is taking account of only the fetus's "right to life", not of any other considerations such as the mother's right to control her body. As we've seen from Thomson's discussion, the mother's right can override the fetus's right to life. Here there is a difference between a typical adult human and a fetus: only the fetus depends for its existence on a physical connection to another person. As Thomson shows, when the mother is not (sufficiently) responsible for this connection and will be seriously harmed by it, an abortion will be permissible. Marquis's argument from the fetus's right to life does not exclude the abortions that Thomson's argument allows.

A further problem: Marquis's argument assumes that there are no gradations in the fetus's right to life in virtue of its human potential. It takes the right to life of a two-week embryo or even of a fertilized egg to be on par with the right to life of an adult. In fact, not even the most committed pro-lifers treat the two as morally equivalent. They do not, for example, take any action to prevent the spontaneous abortions (many so early that they aren't ordinarily detected) that occur in about 30 percent of pregnancies.[8] If 30 percent of young adults (or newborn infants) died for unknown reasons, we would see this as a medical crisis and spend billions on research to prevent these deaths. In the face of an entirely similar problem for early embryos, we do nothing. This suggests that we in fact do not think that early-stage fetuses have a right to life to the same degree as those who have been born. As a result, the rights of the mother are far stronger in comparison, and more early abortions will be morally acceptable.

Once we think through carefully philosophical cases for and against abortion, we see that defensible pro-choice and pro-life positions are much less opposed to each other than our strident public debate suggests. Both should reject an absolute prohibition on abortions, allowing them, first, when there is a serious threat to the mother's health or when she is a victim of rape. Also, the pro-choice position should accept the pro-life view that most late-term abortions would be immoral, and the pro-life position should agree that many early abortions are morally acceptable. As a result, the defining slogans of the two sides ("Abortion is murder" and "A woman always has a right to choose") are both false. There may still be disagreements over specific examples, but the cases for the two positions do not warrant the polarization that characterizes our public debate.

ABORTION AND RELIGIOUS FAITH

I've ignored an obvious feature of our discussions of abortion. Many on the pro-life side reject abortion on religious grounds. God, they think, has made it clear—whether through the Bible or his Church—that abortion is immoral. Isn't it foolish to talk about fruitful, rational discussion of abortion when the strongest voices on one side make a dogmatic assertion that they are not prepared to question through argument?

Many Americans, those who hold that religious commitments have no place in discussions of public policy, will answer, "Yes". One plausible formulation of this idea sees religion as part of what philosopher Richard Rorty called the *private sphere*: what pertains to me as an individual or as a member of a voluntary community of like-minded individuals (e.g., a church). Political life, by contrast, concerns the *public sphere*: what pertains to me as a member of a political community (a city, state, or nation) of individuals with diverse views on issues such as religion. This distinction seems necessary once we recognize the hatred and violence historically associated with religious disputes. We must exclude the passions of religion from our policy debates if we hope to sustain a civil society.

This exclusion of religion from public discussion has historically attracted Americans from two opposed perspectives. Some have found the claims of rival religions all equally absurd and so all equally to be ignored. Others have taken at least their own religious views as true and important, but, fearing the political triumph of conflicting views, have agreed to a truce under which all religious claims are withdrawn from the public sphere. The bitterness of our abortion debate suggests the need for such a truce.

As long as we are talking about specific theological doctrines, most Americans agree that religion has no place in our public life. Few, for example, think that Christian doctrines such as transubstantiation, predestination, Trinitarian theology, or the nature of episcopal authority are legitimate topics of political discussion. Religion enters our public discourse primarily as a voice on moral issues such as abortion.

But should religious viewpoints, even on moral issues, have any role in political debate? Here another consideration is relevant. It would seem that effective arguments require premises that virtually everyone taking part in the discussion accepts. A religious argument based only on, say, the authority of the Bible or the pope would be out of place in a public debate among citizens with every variety of belief and disbelief. To say "My religion says so" may explain why you believe something, but it has no function in a discussion with people who do not accept your religion. Such an appeal to religion is, as Richard Rorty once put it, merely a "conversation-stopper."

But the model of public discussion conducted from a set of premises that all participants do (or should) share is grossly misleading. There is hardly ever such a set of premises. Public discussion is instead a matter of forging "piecemeal" agreements among subgroups of citizens. The eventual consensus about the need to extend full civil rights first to black men and later to women arose from a convergence of quite diverse grounds for this conclusion. Some saw it as justified by the equality of all human beings as children of God, others by self-evident truths about human nature, still others by the overall value for society of equal treatment. There is no reason to think that everyone was convinced by the same arguments. Rather, there was what John Rawls calls an "overlapping consensus", whereby people accept the same conclusion for different and even incompatible reasons.

Further, there is an important role for what Jeffrey Stout, a professor of religion at Princeton, calls "immanent criticism".[9] This occurs when I can show you that your own premises support my conclusions. For example, a secular liberal might find in papal encyclicals a religious critique of capitalism that would convince a conservative Catholic. Coming back to our current topic, the Catholic Church—the most prominent pro-life voice—has long insisted that arguments from reason unaided by revelation establish the immorality of abortion. Criticism of these arguments could go a long way toward undermining Catholic objections to abortion.

The combination of overlapping consensus and immanent criticism could well produce agreement on issues even without generally shared premises. Further, carefully explaining the grounds of my position can help others better understand my views and, perhaps, better respect and appreciate what I am saying, even if they do not agree with my premises. As Rawls points out, democratic discussion should aim not only at agreement on specific disputed issues but also at building solidarity among its citizens, even amid disagreement.[10] Rightly expressed, frank avowals of religious premises can have this effect. It is also possible that an argument from premises I reject may suggest to me a similar line of argument for the conclusion from premises I do accept. For instance, your argument for equality from the fact that we are all children of God may lead me to construct a parallel argument from a purely secular notion of the human family.

Examples like these suggest replacing the model of arguments from shared premises with Stout's model of "conversation" among believers and nonbelievers: "an exchange of views in which the respective parties express their premises in as much detail as they see fit and in whatever idiom they wish, try to make sense of each other's perspectives, and expose their own commitments to the possibility of criticism".[11]

Given the strong case for admitting religious premises into public debates, we can understand why many religious critics object to the secular liberal prohibition against such premises. It is suspiciously convenient when what presents itself as a merely methodological rule for rational discussion turns out to be functionally equivalent to the liberal agnostic's antireligious position.

But insistence on the public rights of religious discourse can equally involve bad faith. A distinctive feature of the modern world is the inability of religious believers to make a convincing public case for their religious claims. In this respect, there is a crucial asymmetry between the position of a secular agnostic who is open-mindedly skeptical and the position of a religious believer. The ultimate "justification" for religious claims is typically a private faith that believers cannot persuasively articulate to those (even other religious believers) who do not share them. This may ground a private right for an individual to believe, but nothing more.

Secular liberals are rightly suspicious that the demand to allow religious premises in a democracy's deliberations is a way of giving faith-based claims a public respectability they do not deserve. To overcome this suspicion, religious believers should use their faith claims in the positive ways sketched above and not as a stubborn means of injecting into the public forum claims for which they are not prepared to argue. Of course, parallel points apply to secular "faiths" such as Marxism and naturalism.

Some religious believers will remain impervious to any rational considerations about abortion (as will, perhaps, some on the pro-choice side, who have a secular faith in the absolute priority of a woman's right to control her body). But as we've seen in Chapter 1, even views based on faith (convictions) can form part of fruitful rational discussions.

Morality and Law

So far we've been thinking about the morality of abortions: whether they are right or wrong. In the last analysis, however, the public debate is about whether abortion should be legal. It's true that "you can't legislate morality"; that is, no law can guarantee moral behavior. There are immoral actions we don't forbid by law, such as unkindness to friends and lying to a spouse. But there are also actions, from murder to shoplifting, that we think should be illegal. In principle, then, there is a distinction between *law* and *morality*, and disagreements about the morality of abortion need not translate into laws for or against it.

If we accept the strong pro-life claim that any abortion is murder—entirely equivalent to the intentional killing of an innocent human being, which no one thinks should be legal—then the legal/moral distinction becomes irrelevant. If abortions were always murder, we should make them illegal. But, as we've seen, many who think that some abortions are morally wrong don't think that all are. Also, we've seen some reason to think that even the strongest opponents of abortion don't treat all embryos as they do newborns. As a result, there should be more flexibility when we're talking about whether abortion should be legal.

We might well agree that morality requires a substantial reason for an abortion, even at an early stage of pregnancy. Wanting not to be less mobile for nine months or not to have to purchase maternity clothes would not be plausible reasons. But how are we to write legislation to enforce such judgments? Even if—against all probability—we were able to formulate some generally acceptable criteria for legal abortions, who would decide in a particular case that they were or were not met?

It seems likely that apart from allowing abortions in cases of rape, serious threat to the mother's health, and severely defective fetuses (and forbidding late abortions except in these cases), we would find it best to leave the decision up to the mother's conscience. Beyond that, we might also try to ensure better decisions by requiring a waiting period and/or consultation with a non-directive but medically and ethically informed counselor.

The above is, of course, only a tentative sketch of where a less dogmatic approach to the legality of abortion might lead. There are many other possibilities, although this one is fairly close to the system that has actually emerged from the *Roe v. Wade* decision. If we agree with the approach I've sketched, the main result of thinking about abortion along the lines developed here will be a consensus that the status quo is acceptable.

This would be no trivial result. Our idea was to find a way past an abortion debate that is defined by extremes that either reject virtually all or accept virtually all abortions. We did this by starting not from interminable quarrels about the nature and rights of persons but from the view, first, that abortions are justified in cases of rape and threat to the mother's health and, second, that infanticide is always wrong. A decision to maintain the status quo, reached from such generally accepted premises, would marginalize the mutually demonizing rancor of the "true believers" and support a stable political consensus.

10

WHAT PHILOSOPHY CAN DO

O f the hundreds of comments readers make on almost every column in The Stone, there will usually be a few who say that philosophy is a useless and boring "ivory-tower" exercise that has nothing relevant to say to non-philosophers. Even a *Times* columnist, the distinguished literary critic Stanley Fish, has said that the academic discipline of philosophy "is a special, insular form of thought and its propositions have weight and value only in the precincts of its game".[1]

The preceding nine chapters are my reply to this charge. Here, in conclusion, I want to reflect explicitly on the nature of the help we can (and cannot) expect from philosophy in our efforts to think about problems of general public concern.

Our discussion moves from doing philosophy *to the meta-level of* reflection on philosophy. *(But this too is a kind of philosophy:* metaphilosophy.*) We begin with the project of* philosophical foundationalism, *often associated with Descartes, which thinks that philosophy can provide decisive answers to the fundamental questions of human life. I reject this view of philos-*

ophy, arguing that in the real world we can't avoid unjustified convictions *about the most important matters. The function of philosophy is not to "solve the world" but to provide* intellectual maintenance *for our convictions, which can be* properly basic beliefs. *Historical examples from Plato, Aquinas, and Descartes illustrate this conception of philosophy.*

Finally, we turn to what philosophy can do for us today, centering the discussion on Wilfrid Sellars's distinction between the manifest image *and the* scientific image. *I argue that philosophy's concern is with perennial questions about* meanings *and* values *within the manifest image, and with the proper understanding of how the two images are related.*

WHAT PHILOSOPHY CAN'T DO

Before we formulate the positive picture, we need to clear the ground by looking at what we *shouldn't* expect from philosophy. I focus on two expectations that philosophers themselves have often fostered. Both readily attract readers of René Descartes, often viewed as the founder of modern philosophy.

Descartes (in his *Discourse on Method* and, more fully, in his *Meditations on First Philosophy*) laments philosophy's failure to make intellectual progress in something like the way he and other seventeenth-century thinkers were beginning to do in mathematics and natural science. He gives the impression that, properly done, philosophy could progressively establish its own distinctive body of knowledge and provide a rigorous basis for all other truths. Doing this would require a two-step method. First, we would marshal a series of skeptical arguments that critically question all our current beliefs, allowing us to discard (at least for the moment) those that can't withstand rigorous critique. This would leave standing only beliefs that are entirely unquestionable and so provide a solid foundation on which to build. Second, we would develop a series of constructive arguments, based on the surviving claims that we can't reasonably doubt, to establish firmly claims the first step had made us doubt.

Whether or not Descartes himself was actually undertaking this project, it is an attractive idea that has drawn many ambitious and optimistic thinkers to philosophy. But a major achievement of philosophy since Descartes has been to discredit both steps of the project.*

Descartes's first step makes sense for beliefs held out of prejudice or ignorance, but the Cartesian method requires looking for objections to even the most obvious everyday beliefs. For example, I believe that there is a material world and other people who experience it as I do. But do I know that any of this is true? Might I merely be dreaming of a world outside my thoughts? And since (at best) I see only other human bodies, what reason do I have to think that there are any minds connected to those bodies? To answer these questions, I would seem to need rigorous philosophical arguments for the existence of the material world and of other minds.

But, of course, I don't actually need any such arguments, if only because I have no practical alternative to believing that the material world and other people exist. As soon as we stop thinking weird philosophical thoughts, we immediately go back to believing what skeptical arguments call into question. And rightly so, since, as David Hume pointed out, we are human beings before we are philosophers. There is nothing at all wrong with accepting such truths; they are in practice unassailable,

---

* In the next section we will see that there is good reason to think that Descartes's actual project was something quite different. But he does suggest the ideal of a philosophy that provides a solid foundation for all truth. I'll refer to the famous method and its goals as "Cartesian" rather than "Descartes's".

even if we can't provide a logical refutation of philosophical objections to them.

The second step in the Cartesian program seems more plausible, at least as it applies to beliefs that are avoidable and may be quite controversial—for example, views on disputed ethical, political, and religious questions. Why should we believe what is neither obviously true nor supported by convincing arguments? But here we need to recall our discussion of disagreement in Chapter 1, where we concluded that the mere fact that a belief remains controversial is not a reason to give it up. Some beliefs, we said, may be so tied to my personal identity and integrity that it makes no sense to abandon them even though I can't prove that those who disagree with me are wrong. As we noted in Chapter 1, such beliefs are convictions on which, as Wittgenstein said, "my spade turns". They are claims more certain than the premises of any arguments that would call them into question.

Various philosophers have recently endorsed Wittgenstein's point for specific cases. Richard Rorty, for example, noted the foolishness of thinking that a fundamental commitment to democracy as a political institution is inappropriate unless we have good arguments against totalitarian rejections of democracy. Americans could be sure that they were right to fight the Nazis, even if they had no decisive proof that the Nazis were wrong. John Rawls similarly held that, in setting rules for a just society, we should begin with basic liberal ideas about what's fair and what isn't. In a quite different vein, Alvin Plantinga argued that a philosophically sophisticated theist, aware of the various intellectual objections to her belief, might ultimately find all the objections unconvincing. If so, what reason could there be for claiming that she was not entitled to her belief in God?

What Hume and many contemporary philosophers are rejecting is what I call the *foundationalist* conception of philosophy.* Rejecting this conception means accepting that we have every right to hold convictions that are not legitimated by philosophical reflection. If philosophy is supposed to be a way of proving what doesn't need any proof, then it is indeed useless.

We need to give up the Cartesian ideal and reconceive the primary function of philosophy. To see what this might mean, consider the following thought experiment. Suppose the project of philosophy in the Cartesian sense—as an intellectual discipline committed to developing a rationally based consensus about the big questions—disappeared or had never existed. What difference would that make? For example, would people still have beliefs about God, freedom, immortality, and morality? Of course. Once humans have reached a certain level of intellectual culture, they will develop religions, codes of behavior, and political systems, along with the beliefs that underlie them. All they would lack would be the peculiar idea (not accepted by even most people in modern Western society) that such beliefs can or ought to be established by arguments of the sort philosophers try to develop. They would take such beliefs as (in Plantinga's terminology) *properly basic*: rightly accepted without argument or evidence.

But a world without foundational philosophy does not mean a world with no thinking about the fundamental beliefs of religion, ethics, politics, etc. Even though properly basic beliefs about such matters do not require prior philosophical justification, they do need *intellectual maintenance*, which itself typically involves philosophical thinking. At a minimum, most people

---

* For those who know some epistemology, I should emphasize that rejecting philosophical foundationalism does not require rejecting foundationalism (as opposed to coherentism, for example) as a general view of how knowledge is justified.

are interested in better understanding their cherished beliefs, deriving logical consequences of these beliefs, and—in an intellectually diverse society—answering challenges from those who disagree. Because of this, a world that has no need for a philosophical grounding of its beliefs will nonetheless profit from the resources that philosophical thought offers.

WHAT PHILOSOPHY HAS DONE

Since the Greeks, philosophical thinking has played a central role in Western societies. We need, however, to distinguish two different ways of understanding this fact. The most common—endorsed by many textbooks and courses—sees the history of philosophy as a perennial enterprise, one in which successive philosophers have discussed a set of core problems, proposing a variety of (generally mutually inconsistent) solutions. For example, undergraduates might study the question of God's existence by reading theistic proofs from Anselm, Aquinas, Descartes, and Pascal, balanced against anti-theistic ideas from Hume, Russell, Jean-Paul Sartre, and J. L. Mackie. Discussions of the mind/body problem typically pair the dualistic views of Plato and Descartes with critiques of dualism from more recent philosophers such as Gilbert Ryle and Daniel Dennett. Students explore the nature of ethical obligations as treated by such figures as Plato, Aristotle, Epictetus, Kant, and Mill, with Nietzsche added as a challenge to morality itself.

The inevitable impression is that of an ahistorical seminar in which great minds argue with one another about the correct solutions to a shared set of fundamental problems. A similar view underlies much current professional philosophy, where philosophers see themselves as defending or rejecting Platonic and Aristotelian positions on the nature of universals, Millian or Kantian positions on ethics, and Cartesian or Humean positions on knowledge.

This approach to philosophy is not entirely a matter of ahistorical illusion. Even some of the most informed and sensitive historians of philosophy make the thinkers they study participants in current debates. But such participation always requires significant abstraction from the convictions and concerns that in fact guided the work of these thinkers.

Plato, for example, lived in a world where mathematics was in the early stages of rigorous development, democracy was an experiment that seemed to have gone badly wrong, poets such as Homer were the established religious authorities, sophists were challenging traditional values, and philosophy was either a kind of proto-natural science or an ethical way of life (or both). Plato embraced mathematics as a model of knowledge; was deeply opposed to the Athenian democracy; broadly endorsed religion and traditional values (while still maintaining a spirit of critical inquiry); and took his friend and mentor, Socrates, as the paradigm of the philosophical life. His philosophy can be properly understood only as an effort to combine these and other elements into a coherent and defensible whole: a project of intellectual maintenance.

We can understand and appreciate this project, but its assumptions and concerns are far removed from ours. Plato developed intellectual tools—conceptual distinctions, modes of argumentation, and, especially, comprehensive *pictures* of reality, knowledge, and values that we still find worthwhile. But his specific formulations and arguments are typically foreign to our own philosophical problems, which arise in a different historical context. This becomes clear when we try to reconstruct his arguments for, say, immortality (in the *Phaedo*) or the superiority of a just life (in the *Republic*). It's not hard to understand why the apparent inadequacy of Plato's arguments is a recurring theme in commentaries on his work. More likely, though, the problem is that our conceptions of what is obvious or plausible are quite different from Plato's, which explains why his problems are not, except at a high level of abstraction, the same as ours.

In terms of the ahistorical seminar model, Plato is a great philosopher but not a good one. He illuminates fundamental distinctions (between appearance and reality, opinion and knowledge, reason and understanding); constructs provocative theories (the theory of Forms, the recollection theory of knowledge); and has a brilliant intellectual imagination (the Cave, the Divided Line, the Charioteer). But his weak arguments (faulty inferences, questionable premises) fall short of solving the perennial questions we (and perhaps he himself) think he should be answering. If, however, we look at Plato's arguments as intellectual maintenance—drawing the consequences and constructing internally consistent defenses of convictions we do not share—then his argumentation may be quite respectable.

To cite just one example, Plato seems to regard Socrates's final argument for the immortality of the soul in the *Phaedo* as conclusive. The basic ideas of the argument are that the soul is the principle that brings life to the body, and that a principle that brings a property (quality) to something cannot itself lose that property. Therefore, since death is the opposite of life, the soul, as the principle that brings life, cannot die. (I leave to readers the exercise of explaining the many ways this argument seems problematic.)

In one of the best analyses of this argument, Dorothea Frede, a leading historian of ancient philosophy, concludes after working through various interpretative problems and objections that the argument can be made sound. To do that, we need to give Plato the assumption that the soul is a substance: a thing with properties of its own, rather than a mere property.[2] (Establishing this claim requires considerable analysis and argument on Frede's part, which we needn't go into here.)

But, Frede maintains, the argument does not succeed because Socrates offers no proof that the soul is a substance rather than a property; that is, he does not show that the body (itself a substance) is alive only because it is united to another substance (the soul) that brings it to life. It remains possible that the soul is merely the body's property of being alive and so will perish when the body does. In short, Plato's dualism—the view that a human being is a union of two substances—is the unjustified premise of his argument for immortality.

For those taking part in the ahistorical seminar, this is the end of the story. Moreover, as Frede points out, Plato himself may well agree, since in other places he insists that a good philosophical argument must always start from a convincing definition of the nature of what we are arguing about. In particular, an argument about the soul must start with a convincing definition of the soul—here, a definition that shows that the soul is a substance. Lacking such a definition, Plato would have to agree that his argument fails.

But if we think of Plato as engaged in the intellectual maintenance of his convictions, then his argument turns out to be quite effective: he has shown how the crucial conclusion that the soul can never die follows from his *conviction* that a living human being is a union of two substances. Even if Plato also aimed at a decisive proof of immortality from premises that no one could question, on this account he at least succeeded in answering the question of immortality on the basis of his own firm convictions.

We find another quite different example in the work of Thomas Aquinas. As a medieval Christian, he held the basic doctrines of the Catholic Church as convictions. But from early on, Christian intellectuals employed ideas from pagan Greek philosophers to clarify, develop, and defend their convictions—the enterprise of "faith seeking understanding" (their version of intellectual maintenance). The translation of Aristotle's works into Latin provided an enormous resource for this enterprise, and Aquinas's theological system was an impressive—and eventually dominant—synthesis of Christian doctrine and Aristotelian philosophy.

Aquinas did accept the first principles of Aristotle's philosophy as self-evident truths. Further, he believed that important parts of the Christian belief system could be decisively established using entirely natural philosophical reasoning from these self-evident truths. In particular, he thought he could philosophically establish God's existence and nature, as well as natural-law morality (which derives ethical principles from our knowledge of human nature). But Aquinas insisted that such philosophical support is not necessary; it is an optional though valuable supplement to faith, which itself provides both the natural and supernatural truths essential to Christianity.

Apart from this optional foundational role for philosophy, Aquinas found in Aristotle a variety of conceptual distinctions and modes of argument that were crucial tools as he developed his defense of Christian faith. Aristotle's distinction between substance and accident, for example, enabled Aquinas to explain how what seem to be bread and wine could in fact be the body and blood of Christ. What Christ essentially was, his substance as God-man, could, as a matter of sheer logical possibility, exhibit the non-essential ("accidental") properties of bread and wine. Such an occurrence is of course contrary to the laws of nature—which place limits on the sorts of properties a given substance can have. But natural laws are not laws of logic, and, for Aquinas, God's omnipotence can miraculously suspend them.

Most of us will see these as desperate contortions to save gratuitous theological dogmas. Aquinas, however, may have thought of them somewhat in the way we think of mathematically consistent formulations of current physics that make no intuitive sense to us. As the philosopher of science Bas van Fraassen has noted, "Do the concepts of the Trinity and the soul, haecceity, universals, prime matter, and potentiality baffle you? They pale beside the unimaginable otherness of closed space-time, event horizons. EPR correlations and bootstrap models".[3] If you think a truth is important enough, you may go to great lengths to defend its intelligibility.

Aristotle's philosophy was useful not only for defending the logical coherence of metaphysical theology but also for enriching Aquinas's understanding of Christian moral teachings. Like Aristotle, Christians saw morality as directed toward happiness, which is achieved by a life of virtue. But Aristotle viewed happiness as a natural state, achieved through life in human society, whereas for Aquinas happiness—although dependent on natural morality in human society—is ultimately a supernatural state of union with God, attainable only by possession of the virtues instilled through divine grace. Aquinas set out to deploy and transform Aristotle's ethical thought to create a Christian vision that integrates the old pagan virtues of justice, courage, self-restraint, and wisdom with the Christian theological virtues of faith, hope, and charity.[4]

Overall, the Aristotelian picture of the world, at least as rethought by Aquinas, provided an intellectually comfortable context for Christian thinking for many centuries.

We may be willing to grant that ancient and medieval philosophers such as Plato and Aquinas were engaged in intellectual maintenance of pre-philosophical convictions. But what about modern philosophers, particularly Descartes? Didn't he, as the familiar story goes, undertake a radical critique of all pre-philosophical beliefs, starting from only those few beliefs that proved impervious to skeptical questioning after bracketing all that he could in any way doubt?

As noted in the previous section, this is an attractive picture, and one strongly suggested by the opening pages of Descartes's *Meditations*, where he tells us that he "realized that it was necessary, once in the course of my life, to overthrow everything completely and start again right from the foundations" and vows to "devote myself sincerely and without reservation to the overthrow of all my opinions".[5]

He then proceeds to question all beliefs derived from sense experience by noting that, for all he knows, he might be dreaming. What he takes to be the material world might be an illusion. This doubt, however, leaves standing his beliefs in the truths of mathematics, which are about ideas, not material bodies. But he then points out that, say, a sufficiently powerful evil demon could deceive him about even the truths of mathematics. This seems to leave him reduced to total skepticism, until Descartes points out that even the demon couldn't deceive him about the fact that he exists: as long as he thinks that he exists, he does, since if he thinks, then he exists (cogito, ergo sum).

From this first, indubitable truth (the cogito), Descartes, it is said, proceeds to reconstruct the essential core of his previous beliefs. He first derives a criterion of truth: anything he sees clearly and distinctly—the way he sees the cogito—must also be true (otherwise, he might be wrong about the cogito). Using this criterion, he establishes truths about causality that he uses to prove that his idea of God (understood as a totally perfect being) must have been produced in him by God himself—the essential point being that an idea requires a cause that has as much reality (in this case, perfection) as its content.

He also argues that since (as he clearly and distinctly sees) his mind is nothing but a thinking thing and his body is nothing but a spatially extended thing, and thought and extension are entirely different, the two can in principle exist separately. As such, immortality (the mind's survival of the body's death) is at least possible. Finally, Descartes argues, he can trust his strong natural inclination to believe that the external material world exists, since a good God would not have given him a nature intrinsically directed to error. With this it seems that Descartes can claim to have reconstructed the core of his earlier beliefs on an absolutely certain basis.

Except that no one believes that he did. Many agree that the cogito is absolutely certain—how could I seriously claim that I don't exist? (Nonetheless, there are important questions as to what this existing "I" is. Is it, for example, an enduring person or just an instantaneous thought?) But beyond that, Descartes's chain of argument breaks at numerous points.

His argument for God's existence requires that we accept murky principles that are open to question as indubitably "clear and distinct". We may grant that any idea has a cause (although there's more reason for doubting this than there is for doubting that the external world exists). But why assume that what causes an idea must have as much reality as its content—e.g., that the idea of a cow must be caused by something with as much reality as a cow? Indeed, how much reality does a cow have? As much as a horse? Does it even make sense to talk about degrees of reality? It seems absurd to claim that such a principle is as clearly and distinctly true as the cogito. The same is true of Descartes's claims that the mind is merely a thinking thing, that the body is merely an extended thing, and that thinking and extension are mutually exclusive. Similarly (recalling our discussion in Chapters 4 and 5), how can Descartes be so sure that an all-good God might not have reasons we can't understand for giving us a nature built to make mistakes?

Generations of commentators have exhausted their ingenuity trying to find cogent ways of making Descartes's case. But at best the arguments are strained, and the reconstructions typically destroy what Descartes seems to regard as the tight logical unity of his *Meditations*. We can maintain the familiar view of the *Meditations* as a brave attempt to provide a rigorous philosophical justification of our core beliefs, but only at the price of recognizing the attempt as an abject failure. How could a brilliant mathematician like Descartes have argued so poorly? And why should we think that so unconvincing a discussion reveals him to be a great philosopher?

The answer, I suggest, is that, contrary to the familiar view, Descartes's main interest is not in providing an unquestionable chain of arguments, beginning with the cogito and rigorously demonstrating the existence of God, the separation of mind and body, and the existence of the external world.[6] He begins instead with a basic conviction about the power of human reason, a conviction that he wants to clarify, develop, and defend against objections.

The conviction is that, contrary to Aristotle and his medieval followers, our knowledge does not derive from sense experience but from direct rational insight, quite independent of the senses. It might seem odd that one of the founders of modern science would emphasize reason over experience. But while science does rely on experience, it's experience in a rationally controlled laboratory setting reformulated with the precision of mathematics. Science is built from experiments, which are rationalizations of our unreliable everyday experience (of which science is a severe critic—remember that our untutored experience leads us to think the Sun moves around the Earth and that colors exist outside our minds). Aristotle, Descartes thought, failed as a scientist because he trusted too much in mere experience. Successful science had to recognize the priority of reason, designing experiments and applying mathematics to the world.

The intellectual ferment of Descartes's time led Michel de Montaigne and many others to a skepticism that questioned whether we really know anything. (Montaigne's motto was "*Que sais-je?*"—What do I know?). In his *Meditations*, Descartes set out to show that refuting skepticism required starting from reason, not from the senses. In his first Meditation, Descartes demonstrates how skeptical objections call into question everything our senses tell us, including the very existence of an external world. But in the second Meditation he concludes that, even supposing the senses are completely unreliable, he still has knowledge of his existence and of the contents of his mind. In later Meditations he goes on to illustrate how trusting reason yields knowledge of God's existence, as well as of the nature of both mind and matter, and even of the existence of the material world.

Descartes believes that once we accept direct rational insight as the basis of our knowledge, we can use this insight to respond to skeptical objections that we could not answer relying on experience alone. This is the only sense in which Descartes tries to "refute skepticism". His project is not to answer a radical skeptical demand to justify reason itself, but rather to show the superiority of his "rationalist" approach to science over the "empiricist" approach of Aristotle and his followers. This is how he defends and develops his fundamental conviction that scientific truth is based on reason, not experience.

We see, then, that even some of the great philosophers of the past can be read in terms of our model of philosophy as intellectual maintenance. Finally, we turn to a general view of what we can expect from philosophy in today's world.

WHAT PHILOSOPHY CAN DO

In our pluralistic society, there is a considerable variety of basic convictions, especially about religion, science, ethics, politics, and art. In a world of such intellectual diversity, we encounter constant challenges to clarify, develop, and defend our convictions —hence the need for intellectual maintenance. Many of the resources for this maintenance come from what philosophers have achieved over the last 2,500 years. Our earlier chapters provide numerous examples of such resources, particularly principles of reasoning and conceptual distinctions.

Intellectual maintenance calls for two things. First, we need to respond to objections that call our convictions into question. The previous chapters provide a variety of illustrations. Believers in an all-good, all-powerful God may need to show the logical consistency of their God and the reality of evil. The philosophy of religion is full of discussions relevant to this question. Or an atheist who thinks all arguments for God's existence are demonstrably fallacious may need a clever philosopher to show what's wrong with a sophisticated version of the cosmological argument or the design argument from fine-tuning. Similarly, someone committed to the aesthetic superiority of certain artistic works may feel challenged by a relativism regarding judgments of taste and need to respond through some reflection on the nature of such judgments. Or those on opposite sides of the abortion debate may need to counter one another's strongest arguments.

A second main aspect of intellectual maintenance is clarifying what our convictions mean or logically entail. Again, our previous discussions provide examples. We have firm convictions about the value of scientific knowledge, but how should we understand the cognitive authority of various scientific disciplines, from physics to economics to educational psychology? What is the meaning of happiness? How can we clarify our ambivalent attitude toward work? Does a conviction that capitalism is a preferable economic system exclude all forms of social welfare? How do we reconcile the vocational demands of the capitalist system with the values of liberal education?

But the role of philosophy is more than a series of disparate interventions to help with isolated intellectual problems. There is a unity to the philosophical project that reflects the distinctive function and value of philosophy in the contemporary world. To my mind, the best way to express this unity and value is to reflect on a crucial philosophical distinction formulated by one of the greatest philosophers of the twentieth century, Wilfrid Sellars. This is the distinction between what Sellars called the *manifest image* and the *scientific image* of humanity.[7]

The manifest image, Sellars says, "contains most of what [we] know about [ourselves] at the properly human level"; it contains familiar things such as "persons, animals, lower forms of life and 'merely material' things, like rivers and stones".[8] We (persons) are central to the image, everything else being the objects of our perception and thought.

From its beginning philosophy has been concerned with the manifest image: "what has been called the perennial tradition in philosophy—*philosophia perennis*—can be construed as the attempt to understand the structure of this image, to know one's way around in it reflectively with no intellectual holds barred".[9] At first, philosophy so understood sought all general knowledge. This is why Aristotle's "philosophy" contained treatises on topics we would now assign to "special sciences" such as physics, biology, psychology, and sociology. These special sciences eventually developed distinctive methodologies, emphasizing empirical observation and testing rather than the logical and conceptual techniques of philosophy, and so became separate disciplines.

Philosophy, however, remained interested in the domains of these special sciences, seeking to understand how their results fit into the overall structure of the manifest framework. Science itself was a feature of the manifest image, and its results modified and refined the content of that image. For example, science discovered that the Sun, not the Earth, was the center of the solar system.

Separated from the special sciences, philosophy focused on just the fundamental questions that did not fall into their domain. To cite just a few: Are our actions free? How is the mind related to the body? Is death the end of our existence? Are there any objective ethical principles to guide our behavior? How can we evaluate various types of political organization? What is knowledge, and how can we best attain it? Is artistic judgment always subjective? None of these questions have been definitively settled, and they still require discussion, if only to provide the best tools for probing our convictions about them.

Eventually, however—particularly with the "new sciences" emerging from the seventeenth century onward—scientists began to discover another world of "theoretical entities" too small for our eyes to see, such as atoms and genes, posited to explain the behavior of familiar manifest objects. This scientific image, Sellars points out, "presents itself as a *rival* image. From its point of view the manifest image . . . is an 'inadequate' but pragmatically useful likeness of a reality which first finds its adequate (in principle) likeness in the scientific image".[10] This is because the new micro-entities are not just additional objects in the manifest image. Scientists explain the behavior of manifest objects by *identifying them* with complexes of micro-entities. The kinetic theory, for example, describes gases as complex arrangements of molecules. Eventually, everything material was found to be composed of various sorts of micro-entities.

The physicist Arthur Eddington nicely expresses the puzzle of the two images in his famous description of the *two tables*— one ordinary, the other scientific—that he is sitting at while writing a lecture:

> One of them has been familiar to me from earliest years. . . . It has extension; it is comparatively permanent; it is coloured; above all it is *substantial*. . . . My scientific table is mostly emptiness. Sparsely scattered in that emptiness are numerous electric charges rushing about with great speed; but their combined bulk amounts to less than a billionth of the bulk of the table itself. . . .There is nothing *substantial* about my second table. It is nearly all empty space.[11]

Eddington illustrates the fundamental question for contemporary philosophical thought: how to understand the relation between the manifest and the scientific images. There is, after all, only one table—and one world. But is it the manifest image or the scientific image that is real? Or is there some way—as Sellars believes—of combining the two images in a philosophical "synoptic vision" of the world?

In any case, Sellars says, "the philosopher is confronted not by one complex many-dimensional picture, the unity of which, such as it is, he must come to appreciate; but by *two* pictures of essentially the same order of complexity, each of which purports to be a complete picture of man-in-the-world, and which, after separate scrutiny, he must fuse into one vision". And the stakes of this confrontation are high: "man is that being which conceives of itself in terms of the manifest image", and therefore "to the extent that the manifest image does not survive in the synoptic view, to that extent man himself would not survive".[12]

Sellars's two images provide a good basis for understanding what philosophy can do in our current intellectual climate. First, philosophy will, as it always has, discuss fundamental questions arising from the manifest image. These are dealt with by what Sellars calls *perennial philosophy*—wrestling with questions about, for example, the origin of the universe, the foundations of morality, and the limits of human knowledge.* But philosophy will also confront what are today the particularly urgent questions of how to relate the manifest and the scientific images.

There are (as we noted above) two opposing, but equally tempting, approaches that promise an easy answer to these questions. We might claim that the manifest image alone is real, with the scientific image just an abstract model providing useful ways of predicting the behavior of manifest entities. Or we might, conversely, maintain that only the scientific image is real, with the distinctive features of the manifest image (colors and other sense qualities, subjective experiences, values, etc.) mere appearances, in principle replaceable by complexes of scientific theoretical entities.

But if we take the first option, how can we understand the stunning explanatory and predictive success of this model without treating it realistically? If gases behave exactly as if they were collections of molecules, then why aren't they collections of molecules? On the other hand, if we take the second option, aren't

---

* As we've noted above, seeing strong continuity in this perennial discussion requires a fairly high level of abstraction from the specific historical concerns of any given philosopher.

we, as Sellars suggests, eliminating everything—experience, values—that makes us the human beings that we are?

An adequate account of the relation between the manifest and scientific images promises to be the major agenda for philosophy in the twenty-first century, so I can hardly propose to provide that here. But there is at least a compelling case for thinking that science alone, without the cooperation of philosophy, cannot supply the account.

The questions that need to be answered to reconcile the two images are expressed in the concepts of the manifest image. We can answer the question, "Is a human being identical with a complex of atoms?" only if we know what we mean by "human being". And to define "human" from the beginning in purely scientific terms begs the question by simply assuming that we can dispense with the manifest image altogether. Once we have an adequate understanding of what a human being is in terms of the manifest image, we may be able to show that, so understood, a human being is nothing but a complex of atoms. In other words, the question, "Is a human being a complex of atoms?" must be posed from *within* the manifest image. We are pointing to a human being we are experiencing through our ordinary (manifest-image) perceptual abilities and asking whether *it* could be a complex of atoms.

Our discussion in Chapter 3 of neurological attempts to determine whether we are free also highlights this point. A neuroscientific account may show that an apparently free movement of my wrist was causally determined by brain events preceding the motion. But no neuroscientific account alone could show that this cause excludes freedom in the sense that we understand it in the manifest image. That would require a philosophical understanding of the *meaning* of freedom that is not available in the scientific image.

Philosophy is often derided because it tries to answer important questions by thinking about them. The implication is that such questions should be pursued by *looking* (observations, experiments) instead of by *thinking* (e.g., the understanding of concepts). But such an implication ignores the fact that, even for questions that require looking, we must first understand what the questions mean in order to know where to look and what to look for. You can't see a computer if you have no idea of what it means to be a computer—you'll see only a hunk of metal and glass (and that only if you have some idea of what metal and glass are). Further, the existence of mathematics as a pure (non-empirical) discipline shows that there are important truths available simply by thinking. Why should we suppose that it's only mathematical concepts that have this feature?

In any case, a concern with concepts (meanings) is therefore an essential part of any fruitful intellectual enterprise. Within the narrow limits of a specific scientific discipline, the requisite conceptual understanding may be readily available—we presumably don't need a philosophical analysis of what a gas or a liquid is. But once science takes on ideas that have deep and complex roots in our manifest-image thinking—concepts like space, time, causality, or freedom—then the resources of philosophy's reflection on these concepts becomes relevant. This is a point well illustrated by the history of relativity and quantum theory, where both philosophers such as Hans Reichenbach and philosophically informed scientists such as Niels Bohr have made important contributions to our understanding of basic physical concepts.

Most importantly, we need to keep in mind that the descriptive and explanatory accounts the sciences offer tell us nothing essential about the *normative* dimension of the manifest image. Unless we are prepared to give up all normative judgments (including the judgment that we *should* give up such judgments!), we must allow a need for non-empirical (philosophical) discussions of such judgments. A proponent of evolutionary ethics may claim that ethical principles are really just the expression of basic desires or dispositions that have proven adaptive for our species. But no amount of empirical evidence can establish that this definition accords with what we in fact are talking about when we formulate ethical principles. If the evolutionary definition is to be sustained, it needs the support of a philosophical understanding of what an ethical principle is *for us.*

The success of science—where its methods are appropriate— can tempt us to apply it everywhere. Here, however, we need to remember the old joke about the man who dropped his keys behind his house but was looking for them underneath his front porch lamp because the light was better there.

Sellars points out that any truth about the meaning of a term is normative in the broad sense that it tells us how the term *ought to be used* (or how the corresponding concept *requires* us to think). Given that wide notion of normativity, he suggests that philosophy can be understood as the discipline concerned with all manner of basic normative issues, scrutinizing all questions of what we ought to do, from the use of language to the making of ethical and aesthetic judgments.

Further, he maintains that this normative dimension of the manifest image is precisely what is essential to it and cannot be replaced by the scientific image: "the irreducibility of the personal is the irreducibility of the 'ought' to the 'is' ".[13] And, as we saw, the human person is the center to which all aspects of the manifest image are essentially related.

But corresponding to the manifest image's authority over normative questions, Sellars asserts the authority of the scientific image over all questions about the causes that drive the operation of the world, and therefore about what there is. In this way, the manifest image's "conceptual framework of persons is not something that needs to be *reconciled with* the scientific image, but rather something to *be joined* to it. Thus, to complete the scientific image we need to enrich it *not* with more ways of saying what is the case, but with the language of community and individual intentions"—the language in which we express the shared norms that, above all, make us human beings.[14] In other words, Sellars's "synoptic vision" combines the *ontology* of the scientific image with the *norms* of the manifest image.

We may have our doubts about this particular way of relating the two images, wondering, for example, if the distinction of what is (ontology) and what ought to be (normativity) can be drawn as sharply as Sellars does. But by any plausible account, we need philosophy to understand both ourselves and our world. Moreover, philosophy, if it is to see humanity whole, must itself develop in interaction with other humanistic modes of understanding, such as history, literature, and art. Moreover, as our discussion in Chapter 3 has shown, much that is done in what are called the "human sciences" in fact contributes to the humanistic project of understanding the manifest image. In view of this, philosophy needs to keep as close a contact with these disciplines as it does with the traditional humanities.

What, finally, can philosophy do? Relatively little, as an isolated discipline. But isolation—though sometimes encouraged by the contemporary call for specialization—is contrary to philosophy's long tradition of engagement with all modes of knowing. Moreover, once we reject philosophical foundationalism, this engagement is not a matter of judging and regulating the work of other disciplines in their own domains. Rather, philosophy's role is to coordinate and integrate the results of all disciplines (including itself) in an effort to understand, in Sellars's phrase, "how things in the broadest possible sense of the term hang together in the broadest possible sense of the term".[15] In the context of our modern, science-oriented world, this means conceiving of contemporary philosophy as a three-pronged enterprise: continuing philosophy's historical project of understanding the manifest image through reflection on the perennial themes of philosophy; formulating what modern science has achieved that is relevant to our manifest understanding of ourselves as human beings; and constructing the best combined vision of the two images, resulting in a complete picture of what it means to be a human being in a scientific world.

Given our rejection of philosophical foundationalism, we should not expect philosophy to provide decisive answers to fundamental questions about the manifest and scientific images. But each of us can expect it to provide resources for understanding, defending, and even revising our basic convictions about these questions. Understood this way, philosophy is essential to our identity and our integrity as human beings.

FOR FURTHER THOUGHT

Chapter 1

There's an excellent set of articles on logic and reasoning in Stephen M. Cahn, ed., *Exploring Philosophy: An Introductory Anthology*, 5th edition (Oxford: Oxford University Press), part 2. I also recommend Cahn's anthology as a good source of accessible texts (historical and contemporary) on major philosophical questions.

For a good anthology of the philosophical literature on disagreement, see Richard Feldman and Ted A. Warfield, eds., *Disagreement* (Oxford: Oxford University Press, 2010).

There are recurring exchanges between Paul Krugman and John Taylor in their blog posts (Krugman's at krugman.blogs.nytimes.com; Taylor's at economicsone.com).

Chapter 2

For a basic overview of the philosophy of science, read Samir Okasha, *Philosophy of Science: A Very Short Introduction* (Oxford: Oxford Unversity Press, 2002). Peter Godfrey-Smith, *Theory and Reality: An Introduction to the Philosophy of Science* (Chicago: University of Chicago Press, 2003), provides a more detailed discussion.

For classic treatments of philosophy of science, see Karl Popper, *The Logic of Scientific Discovery* (German edition, 1935; English translation, 1959; London: Routledge, 2002), and Thomas Kuhn, *The Structure of Sci-*

entific Revolutions (1st edition, 1962; 4th edition, Chicago: University of Chicago Press, 2012).

For a lucid textbook on the fundamentals of scientific reasoning, see Ronald Giere et al., *Understanding Scientific Reasoning*, 5th edition (Belmont, CA: Wadsworth, 2005). Nate Silver, *The Signal and the Noise: Why So Many Predictions Fail—But Some Don't* (New York: Penguin, 2012), has an excellent, lucid discussion of the difficulty of predicting the future, with many superb examples.

Ben Goldacre, *Bad Science* (London: Faber and Faber, 2010), is a lively survey of unreliable medical claims. Jim Manzi, *Uncontrolled* (New York: Basic Books, 2012), offers a careful analysis the value of social-science research for business and for public policy.

For a detailed but not too technical account of what evidence-based policy requires, see Nancy Cartwright and Jeremy Hardy, *Evidence-Based Policy: A Practical Guide to Doing It Better* (Oxford: Oxford University Press, 2012).

For a detailed and philosophically informed analysis of the climate-change debate, see Dale Jamieson, *Reason in a Dark Age* (Oxford: Oxford University Press, 2014).

Chapter 3

A now classic article that also provides a good overview of the current mind/body problem is Thomas Nagel, "What Is It Like to Be a Bat?" (1974), reprinted in *Mortal Questions* (Cambridge: Cambridge University Press, 2012). John Searle, *The Mystery of Consciousness* (New York Review of Books, 1990), provides philosophical critiques of scientific work on consciousness. (See also subsequent NYRB reviews by Searle and by Colin McGinn.) Daniel Dennett, *Consciousness Explained* (New York: Back Bay Books, 1992), gives Dennett's most thorough defense of his view that the mind is physical.

Alfred Mele, *A Dialogue on Free Will and Science* (Oxford: Oxford University Press, 2013), is a lively introduction to current debates about freedom. Michael Gazzaniga, *Who's in Charge?* (New York: HarperCollins, 2011), is a prominent neuroscientist's defense of freedom.

Daniel Haybron, *The Pursuit of Unhappiness* (Oxford: Oxford University Press, 2008), is an important contemporary philosophical study of happiness informed by work on the psychology of happiness. Martin Seligman, *Flourish* (New York: Free Press, 2011), presents a psychologist's guide to being happy.

On morality, Alasdair MacIntyre, *After Virtue* (Notre Dame, IN: University of Notre Dame Press, 1981; 3rd edition, 2007) brilliantly combines a history of ethics with a critique of modern society. Joshua Greene, *Moral Tribes* (New York: Penguin, 2013), is by an experimental psychologist who also has a Ph.D. in philosophy.

William James is a delightful writer, and his 1907 *Pragmatism* (Indianapolis: Hackett, 1981) is the best introduction to his version of pragmatism (with Chapter 6 specifically on truth). Richard Rorty is also an engaging writer, and his *Philosophy and Social Hope* (New York: Penguin, 2010) is a good introduction to his contemporary version of pragmatism (with Chapter 2 focusing on truth). Dan Sperber and Hugo Mercier further discuss their view in "Reasoning as a Social Competence" in H. Landemore, and J. Elster, eds., *Collective Wisdom* (Cambridge: Cambridge University Press, 2012).

Michel Foucault's work on madness also appears in a more approachable, condensed version (with cuts approved by the author) in *Madness and Civilization* (New York: Vintage, 1965). On current critiques of psychiatry, see the two-part review by Marcia Angell, "The Epidemic of Mental Illness" (June 23, 2011) and "The Illusions of Psychiatry" (July 14, 2011), *New York Review of Books*.

On nothingness, don't miss Jim Holt's entertaining and intelligent *Why Does the World Exist?: An Existentialist Detective Story* (New York: Liveright, 2012).

Chapter 4

Michael Ruse, *Atheism: What Everyone Needs to Know* (Oxford: Oxford University Press, 2015) offers an engaging, even-handed, and very accessible introduction to the topic. For another way of making the new atheist case (with little emphasis on traditional theistic arguments) see Daniel Dennett, *Breaking the Spell: Religion as a Natural Phenomenon* (New York: Viking, 2006).

For a philosophical defense of religion with emphasis on the ontological argument and the problem of evil, see Alvin Plantinga, *God, Freedom, and Evil* (Grand Rapids, MI: Eerdmans, 2007). For full technical details, consult Plantinga's *The Nature of Necessity* (Oxford: Oxford University Press, 1974), Chapters 9 and 10.

For a full-scale treatment of the cosmological argument, see William Rowe, *The Cosmological Argument* (New York: Fordham University Press, 1998), and for a comprehensive and sophisticated critique of theistic arguments, see Graham Oppy, *Arguing about Gods* (Cambridge: Cambridge University Press, 2006).

Chapter 5

Chapter 4 of Denys Turner's *Thomas Aquinas: A Portrait* (New Haven, CT: Yale University Press, 2013) gives a good sense of the challenges of developing a coherent metaphysical conception of God (and of Aquinas's ingenuity).

As a counterpoint to the "testimonials" of believing philosophers, it's informative to read a similar set of essays by atheists: Louise Antony, ed., *Philosophers without Gods* (Oxford: Oxford University Press, 2007). For an instructive debate between two philosophers, one a theist and one an atheist, see William Lane Craig and Walter Sinnott-Armstrong, *God? A Debate between a Christian and an Atheist* (Oxford: Oxford University Press, 2003).

A classic defense of agnosticism (by the person who coined the term) can be found in Thomas Henry Huxley, *Agnosticism and Christianity and Other Essays* (Amherst, NY: Prometheus Books, 1992). Charles Taylor, *A Secular Age* (Cambridge, MA: Harvard University Press, 2007), is no agnostic, but he sees doubt as an accompaniment to reflective belief in today's world, and develops a brilliant critique of secularism.

Chapter 6

Sissela Bok, *Exploring Happiness* (New Haven, CT: Yale University Press, 2010), offers an excellent historical survey of philosophical thought about happiness. The ancient Stoic view is quite accessible in the *Handbook of Epictetus*, trans. Nicholas White (Indianapolis, IN: Hackett, 1983). The classic defense of utilitarianism is John Stuart Mill, *Utilitarianism* (Indianapolis, IN: Hackett, 2002).

For a recent, well thought-out critique of capitalism, see Robert and Edward Skidelsky, *How Much Is Enough? Money and the Good Life* (New

York: Other Press, 2012). Terry Eagleton provides a clear and provocative defense of Marx in *Why Marx Was Right* (New Haven, CT: Yale University Press, 2011). Allan Meltzer, *Why Capitalism?* (Oxford: Oxford University Press, 2012), offers a vigorous contemporary defense of capitalism.

John Rawls, *Political Liberalism*, 2nd expanded edition (New York: Columbia University Press, 1993), develops and revises his position in *A Theory of Justice*. Robert Nozick offers a conservative alternative to Rawls's liberalism in *Anarchy, State, and Utopia* (New York: Basic Books, 1974).

Chapter 7

Amélie Oksenberg Rorty, ed., *Philosophers on Education: New Historical Perspectives* (London: Routledge, 1998), collects an exceptional set of essays on how great philosophers of the past thought about education. Recently, philosophy of education has not been an especially fruitful field. But Harvey Siegel, ed., *The Oxford Handbook of Education* (Oxford: Oxford University Press, 2009), offers a splendid collection of essays by contemporary philosophers on education.

Martha Nussbaum, *Cultivating Humanity* (Cambridge, MA: Harvard University Press, 1997), puts forward a contemporary defense of liberal education based on the classical tradition.

Derek Bok, *Higher Education in America* (Princeton, NJ: Princeton University Press, 2013), is a superb resource, comprehensive and detailed.

Chapter 8

For a brief and intelligent book on Warhol, I recommend Arthur Danto, *Andy Warhol* (New Haven, CT: Yale University Press, 2009). On Danto's philosophy of art, see his *The Transformation of the Commonplace: A Philosophy of Art* (Cambridge, MA: Harvard University Press, 1981).

Jerrold Levinson, ed., *The Oxford Handbook of Aesthetics* (Oxford: Oxford University Press, 2003), contains forty-eight expert essays on major topics and specific art forms. Mathew Kieran, ed., *Contemporary Debates in Aesthetics and the Philosophy of Art* (Hoboken, NJ: Wiley-Blackwell, 2006), offers exchanges on current controversial topics. Peter Kivy, *Introduction to a Philosophy of Music* (Oxford: Oxford University Press, 2002), provides a splendid entry to the field.

Alex Ross, *The Rest is Noise* (New York: Picador, 2007), is a brilliant guide to twentieth-century music, and his *Listen to This* (New York: Farrar, Straus and Giroux, 2010) ranges from classic masters to current popular music. Roger Scruton, *Understanding Music: Philosophy and Interpretation* (London: Bloomsbury, 2009), offers perceptive analysis and strong polemics. On the Beatles–Stones debate (and for a stimulating overview of popular music), see Crispin Sartwell, "Beatles vs. Stones: An Aesthetic of Rock Music", in his collection of essays, *How to Escape* (Albany, NY: Excelsior Editions, 2014).

Chapter 9

Bonnie Steinbock, *Life Before Birth: The Moral and Legal Status of Embryos and Fetuses*, 2nd edition (Oxford: Oxford University Press, 2011), offers a detailed philosophical account of disputes about abortion and related issues.

In *Abortion: Three Perspectives* (Oxford: Oxford University Press, 2012), Michael Tooley, Celia Wolf-Devine, Philip E. Devine, and Alison M. Jagger defend and debate their views.

David Boonin, *A Defense of Abortion* (Cambridge: Cambridge University Press, 2002), responds with philosophical analysis and criticism to a wide range of anti-abortion arguments.

In Robert P. George and Christopher Tollefsen, *Embryo: A Defense of Human Life* (New York: Doubleday, 2008), a law professor and a philosopher offer a sophisticated scientific and philosophical argument against the morality of abortion.

Chapter 10

Richard Kraut, *How to Read Plato* (London: Granta, 2008), offers an introduction through close readings of some key passages. For a comprehensive and detailed treatment, see Hugh H. Benson, ed., *A Companion to Plato* (Hoboken, NJ: Wiley-Blackwell, 2009).

A bit more demanding that its title suggests, Edward Feser, *Aquinas, A Beginner's Introduction* (London: Oneworld, 2009), is a good start for interested readers. Brian Davies, *The Thought of Thomas Aquinas* (Oxford: Oxford University Press, 1993), deals in considerable detail with both Aquinas's philosophy and theology.

Tom Sorrell, *Descartes: A Very Short Introduction* (Oxford: Oxford University Press, 2000), provides a brief but authoritative overview. Gary Hatfield, *Guidebook to Descartes and the Meditations* (London: Routledge, 2002), takes the reader step by step through the six Meditations, supplying context and thorough explanations.

Wilfrid Sellars's writings are notoriously difficult, but here are two helpful ways in: Willem A. deVries, *Wilfrid Sellars* (London: Acumen, 2005), and James R. O'Shea, *Wilfrid Sellars* (Oxford: Polity Press, 2007).

Metaphilosophy, the topic of this chapter, has been mostly neglected over the last century, but interest has revived recently. For a useful survey of problems and positions, see Søren Overgaard, Paul Gilbert, and Stephen Burwood, *Introduction to Metaphilosophy* (Cambridge: Cambridge University Press, 2013). More advanced discussions include Timothy Williamson, *The Philosophy of Philosophy* (Oxford: Blackwell, 2007); and Gary Gutting, *What Philosophers Know* (Cambridge: Cambridge University Press, 2009).

NOTES

1

1. "Nothing to Do with the Deficit", Eschatonblog.com, December 13, 2012.

2. John B. Taylor, "Obama's Permanent Spending Binge", *Wall Street Journal* (online), April 22, 2011.

3. Paul Krugman, "2021 and All That", *The Conscience of a Liberal* (online), April 27, 2011.

4. John B. Taylor, "Paul Krugman vs. Economic Facts," *Economics One* (online), April 26, 2011.

5. "Niall Ferguson on Why Barack Obama Needs to Go", *Newsweek* (online), August 20, 2012.

6. David Frum, "Why I'll Vote for Romney", *The Daily Beast* (online), November 1, 2012.

7. "McCain blasts 'bizarro' Tea Party debt limit demands", CBS News (online), July 28, 2011.

8. Paul Krugman, "Mystery Man", *Conscience of a Liberal* (online), July 29, 2011.

9. Elizabeth Drew, "What Were They Thinking?", *New York Review of Books*, August 18, 2011.

10. Paul Krugman, "Cogan, Taylor, and the Confidence Fairy", *Conscience of a Liberal* (online), March 19, 2013.

11. John B. Taylor, "Spending Rise Has Much to Do with Policy", *Economics One* (online), April 28, 2011.

12. Paul Krugman, "How Did Economists Get It So Wrong?", *New York Times Magazine* (print and online), September 2, 2009.

13. David Christensen, "Disagreement as Evidence: The Epistemology of Controversy", *Philosophy Compass* 4, no. 5 (2009): 756–67.

14. These points were all raised by perceptive readers of a column on political disagreement I wrote for The Stone: Gary Gutting, "On Political Disagreement", *New York Times* (online), August 2, 2012.

15. Bernard Williams and J. J. C. Smart, *Utilitarianism: For and Against* (Cambridge: Cambridge University Press, 1973), pp. 93–100.

2

1. Thomas Kuhn, *The Structure of Scientific Revolutions*, 3rd edition (Chicago: University of Chicago Press, 1996 [first edition, 1962]).

2. "Vitamin D May Prevent Arthritis", *WebMD News Archive* (online), January 9, 2004.

3. "Can Vitamin D Prevent Arthritis?", *Johns Hopkins Health Alert* (online), January 11, 2010.

4. Gene Pittman, "Vitamin D May Not Relieve Arthritis Pain", *Reuters Health*, January 8, 2013.

5. Christopher Weaver, "New Rules for Giving Good Cholesterol a Boost", *Wall Street Journal* (online), January 7, 2013.

6. For a summary of a wide variety of results, see John A. Bargh et al., "Automaticity in Social-Cognitive Processes", *Trends in Cognitive Science* 16 (2012): 593–605.

7. Tom Bartlett, "Power of Suggestion", *Chronicle of Higher Education* (online), January 30, 2013.

8. John Bargh, "What Have We Been Priming All These Years? On the Development, Mechanisms, and Ecology of Nonconscious Social Behavior", *European Journal of Social Psychology* 36 (2006): 147–68.

9. J. A. Bargh et al., "Automaticity in Social-Cognitive Processes", *Trends in Cognitive Science* 16, no. 12 (2012): 593–605.

10. Richard H. Thaler and Cass R. Sunstein, *Nudge: Improving Decisions About Health, Wealth, and Happiness* (New York: Penguin, 2009).

11. Benjamin M. Friedman, "Guiding Forces", *New York Times Sunday Book Review*, August 22, 2008 (print and online).

12. "Where Is Behavioral Economics Headed in the World of Marketing?", *Nudge Blog* (online), October 9, 2011.

13. Nancy Cartwright, "A Philosopher's View of the Long Road from RCTs to Effectiveness", *Lancet* 377 (April 2011): 1400–1401.

14. Nancy Cartwright, "Will This Policy Work for You: Predicting Effectiveness Better—How Philosophy Helps", *Philosophy of Science* 79 (2012): 973–89.

15. See Nancy Cartwright and Jeremy Hardie, *Evidence-Based Policy: A Practical Guide to Doing It Better* (Oxford: Oxford University Press, 2012), pp. 124–26.

16. Jeffrey B. Liebman, "Building on Recent Advances in Evidence-Based Policymaking", April 2013 (online brookings.edu).

17. Raj Chetty, John N. Friedman, and Jonah E. Rockoff, "The Long-Term Impact of Teachers" (online obs.rc.fas.harvard.edu).

18. Nicholas D. Kristof, "The Value of Teachers", *New York Times*, January 11, 2012 (online).

19. Nate Silver, *The Signal and the Noise: Why So Many Predictions Fail—But Some Don't* (New York: Penguin, 2012), Chapter 12, gives a clear summary of the scientific evidence, although its interpretations of that evidence are controversial.

20. "Is There a Scientific Consensus on Global Warming?" (online skep ticalscience.com).

21. Alfred North Whitehead, "Immortality", in Paul A. Schilpp (ed.), *The Philosophy of Alfred North Whitehead* (New York: Tudor, 1951), p. 700.

3

1. Matt Warman, "Stephen Hawking Tells Google 'Philosophy Is Dead'", *The Telegraph* (online), May 17, 2011.

2. This line of thought, often called the "knowledge argument", was first formulated in these terms by Frank Jackson, "Epiphenomenal Qualia", *Philosophical Quarterly* 32 (1982): 127–36. Jackson himself eventually rejected his knowledge argument, but others remain impressed.

3. The most influential version of this line of argument is in David Chalmers, *The Conscious Mind* (Oxford: Oxford University Press, 1996).

4. Daniel Dennett, "The Zombic Hunch: Extinction of an Intuition?", in A. O'Hear (ed.), *Philosophy at the New Millennium* (Cambridge: Cambridge University Press, 2001), p. 37.

5. Daniel Dennett, *Intuition Pumps, and Other Tools for Thinking* (New York: W. W. Norton, 2013), p. 291.

6. Ibid., p. 292.

7. Ibid., p. 350.

8. Ibid., p 353.

9. Valerie Gray Hardcastle, "The Why of Consciousness: A Non-Issue for Materialists", in Jonathan Shear (ed.), *Explaining Consciousness—The 'Hard Problem'* (Cambridge, MA: MIT Press, 1997), p. 61.

10. Quoted in Kerri Smith, "Neuroscience vs. Philosophy: Taking Aim at Free Will", *Nature* 477 (2011): 23–25.

11. Patrick Haggard and Benjamin Libet, "Conscious Intention and Brain Activity", *Journal of Consciousness Studies* 8 (2001): 47–63, quote at 48.

12. For a survey of the possibilities, see Michael McKenna, "Compatiblism", in the online *Stanford Encyclopedia of Philosophy*.

13. Haggard and Libet, "Conscious Intention and Brain Activity", p. 61.

14. Sonja Lyubomirsky, *The How of Happiness: A New Approach to Getting the Life You Want* (New York: Penguin, 2008).

15. One example is the work of Harvard psychologist, Daniel Gilbert, on "miswanting", discussed in John Gertner, "The Futile Pursuit of Happiness", *New York Times Magazine*, September 7, 2003 (online).

16. Jonathan Haidt, *The Righteous Mind: Why Good People Are Divided by Politics and Religion* (New York: Pantheon, 2012).

17. Ibid., p. 85.

18. Ibid., p. 86.

19. Ibid., p. 105.

20. Ibid., p. 137.

21. Hugo Mercier and Dan Sperber, "Why Do Humans Reason? Arguments for an Argumentative Theory", *Behavioral and Brain Sciences* 34 (2011): 57–111.

22. Michel Foucault, *History of Madness*, ed. Jean Khalfa, trans. Jonathan Murphy and Jean Khalfa (London: Routledge, 2006).

23. Ibid., p. 515.

24. Paula Span, "Grief Over New Depression Diagnosis", *New York Times* (online), January 14, 2013.

25. Lawrence Krauss, *A Universe from Nothing: Why There Is Something Rather Than Nothing* (New York: Free Press, 2012).

26. David Albert, "On the Origin of Everything", *New York Times Book Review*, March 25, 2012, p. 20.

27. Ross Andersen, "Has Physics Made Philosophy and Religion Obso-

lete?", interview with Lawrence Krauss, *The Atlantic* (online), April 23, 2012. Krauss later somewhat moderated his views ("The Consolation of Philosophy", *Scientific American* (online), April 27, 2012).

4

1. Richard Dawkins, *The God Delusion* (New York: Mariner Books, 2008), p. 101.
2. Ibid., p. 104.
3. Ibid., p. 105.
4. Ibid., p. 115.
5. For a survey of the main themes see Mark Webb, "Religious Experience", in the *Stanford Encyclopedia of Philosophy* (online).
6. William James, *Varieties of Religious Experience* (Rockville, MD: Arc Manor, 2008; first edition, 1902), p. 51.
7. Dawkins, *God Delusion*, p. 188.
8. Ibid., p. 189.
9. Ibid., pp. 188–89.
10. David Hume, *Dialogues Concerning Natural Religion*, 2nd ed. (Indianapolis, IN: Hackett, 1988), p. 30.
11. Dawkins, *God Delusion*, p. 82.
12. Sam Harris, *Letter to a Christian Nation* (New York: Vintage, 2008).
13. Ibid., pp. 51–52.
14. Ibid., p. 55.
15. Ibid., italics in original omitted.
16. The response I'm suggesting to the problem of evil is an example of "skeptical theism", a position that a number of philosophers have recently developed with great sophistication. See, in particular, Trent Dougherty and Justin P. McBrayer (eds.), *Skeptical Theism: New Essays* (Oxford: Oxford University Press, 2014).

5

1. Alvin Plantinga, *Does God Have a Nature?* (Milwaukee, WI: Marquette University Press, 1980).
2. Una Kroll, "Women Bishops: What God Would Want", *The Guardian* (online), July 11, 2010.
3. Kelly James Clark, ed., *Philosophers Who Believe* (Downer's Grove IL: InterVarsity Press, 1993); Thomas V. Morris, ed., *God and the Philosophers* (Oxford: Oxford University Press, 1994).

4. Morris, ed., *God and the Philosophers*, p. 184.
5. Clark, ed., *Philosophers Who Believe*, p. 36.
6. Ibid., p. 38.
7. Morris, ed., *God and the Philosophers*, p. 37.
8. Ibid., p. 23.
9. Ibid., p. 25.
10. Ibid., p. 28.
11. Clark, ed., *Philosophers Who Believe*, pp. 51–52.
12. Ibid., p. 52.
13. Morris, ed., *God and the Philosophers*, p. 78.
14. Ibid., p. 80.
15. Ibid., p. 78.
16. Ibid., p. 79.
17. Clark, ed., *Philosophers Who Believe*, p. 199.
18. Ibid., p. 181.
19. Ibid., pp. 199–200.
20. Ibid., p. 236.
21. For a detailed discussion of the pros and cons of Plantinga's argument, see James Beilby (ed.), *Naturalism Defeated? Essays on Evolutionary Argument against Naturalism* (Ithaca NY: Cornell University Press, 2002).
22. Morris, ed., *God and the Philosophers*, p. 36.

6

1. Pope Leo XIII, *Rerum Novarum*, Encyclical, 1891 (available online).
2. Robert Nozick, *Anarchy, State, and Utopia* (New York: Basic Books, 1974), pp. 42–45.
3. Aristotle, *Nichomachean Ethics*, book 10, chapter 7 (my translation).
4. Bertrand Russell, "In Praise of Idleness" (1932), in *In Praise of Idleness: and Other Essays* (London: Routledge, 2004), p. 3.
5. For a stimulating discussion of this question, see Robert and Edward Skidelsky, *How Much Is Enough? Money and the Good Life* (New York: Other Press, 2012).
6. See John Rawls, *A Theory of Justice*, 2nd edition (Cambridge, MA: Harvard University Press, 1999), section 15.
7. Jon C. Messenger, Sangheon Lee, and Deirdre McCann, *Working Time Around the World* (London: Routledge, 2007), p. 23, fig. 3.1.
8. Milton Friedman, *Capitalism and Freedom*, Fortieth Anniversary Edition (Chicago, IL: University of Chicago Press, 2002), pp. 133–34.
9. Ibid., p. 133, italics mine.

10. Ibid.
11. Ibid., p. 34.
12. Christopher McMahon, *Public Capitalism: The Political Authority of Business Executives* (Philadelphia: University of Pennsylvania Press, 2013).

7

1. Philip Kitcher, "Education, Democracy, and Capitalism," in Harvey Siegel, ed., *The Oxford Handbook of Education* (Oxford: Oxford University Press, 2009), pp. 300–318.
2. Sam Dillon, "Report Finds Better Scores in New Crop of Teachers", *New York Times* (online), December 12, 2007.
3. Sam Dillon, "Top Test Scores From Shanghai Stun Educators", *New York Times* (online), December 7, 2010.
4. Richard Arum and Josipa Roksa, *Academically Adrift: Limited Learning on College Campuses* (Chicago: University of Chicago Press, 2010).
5. Diane Halpern and Milton Hakel, "Applying the Science of Learning", *Change* (July/August 2003): 37–41.
6. Derek Bok, *Higher Education in America* (Cambridge, MA: Harvard University Press, 2013), p. 187.
7. Nora S. Newcombe, "Biology Is to Medicine as Psychology Is to Education: True or False?" in D. F. Halpern and M. D. Hakel, eds., *Applying the Science of Learning to University Teaching and Beyond* (San Francisco: Jossey-Bass, 2000), pp. 9–18.
8. Bok, *Higher Education in America*, p. 50.

8

1. Peter Schjeldahl, "Going Pop: Warhol and His Influence", *The New Yorker* (online), September 24, 2012.
2. Rainer Crone, "What Andy Warhol Really Did", *New York Review of Books* (online), February 20, 2010.
3. Arthur Danto, *Beyond the Brillo Box* (Oakland CA: University of California Press, 1992), p. 6.
4. Roberta Smith, "The In-Crowd Is All Here: 'Regarding Warhol' at the Metropolitan Museum", *New York Times* (online), September 13, 2012.
5. Danto, *Beyond the Brillo Box*, p. 139.
6. Richard Dorment, "What Is an Andy Warhol?", *New York Review of Books* (online), October 22, 2009.

7. See Jerrold Levinson, "Evaluating Music" in his *Contemplating Art* (Oxford: Oxford University Press), 2006.

8. Gary Indiana, *Andy Warhol and the Can That Sold the World* (New York: Basic Books, 2010), p. 62.

9. Virginia Woolf, "Middlebrow" (1942), in *Collected Essays*, Vol. 2 (New York: Harcourt, Brace & World, 1967).

10. Arthur Danto, *What Art Is* (New Haven, CT: Yale University Press, 2013), p. 41.

11. Ibid., p. 125.

12. Bruce Baugh, "Prolegomena to Any Aesthetics of Rock Music", *Journal of Aesthetics and Art Criticism* 51 (1993): 26.

13. Ibid.: 27.

14. Ibid.: 28.

15. Jeremy Yudkin, *Understanding Music*, 7th edition (San Francisco: Peachpit Press, 2013), p. 207.

16. This description is based on excerpts from Phillip Huscher's program notes for the Chicago Symphony Orchestra performance of Mahler's Fifth Symphony in May 2010.

17. Alex Ross, "Listen to This", *The New Yorker*, February 16 and 23, 2004 (online).

18. For a detailed version of this approach, see Theodore Gracyk, "Valuing and Evaluating Popular Music", *Journal of Aesthetics and Art Criticism* 57 (1999): 205–20.

19. Matthew Arnold, "The Study of Poetry" (1880) (online, poetryfoundation.org).

20. Peter Applebome, "A Humanist and Elitist? Perhaps", interview with George Steiner, *New York Times* (online), April 18, 1998.

21. Richard Taruskin, "The Musical Mystique", *New Republic* (online), October 22, 2007.

22. Noël Carroll, *A Philosophy of Mass Art* (Oxford: Oxford University Press, 1998).

9

1. "Abortion", gallup.com (online).

2. Robert P. George and Patrick Lee, "Embryonic human persons", EMBRO Reports, April 2009 (online, ncbi.nlm.nih.gov).

3. Frances Kamm, Review of Jeff McMahan, *The Ethics of Killing: Problems at the Margins of Life*, in *Philosophical Review* 116 (2007): 273.

4. "Abortion", gallup.com (online).

5. Jeff McMahan, *The Ethics of Killing: Problems at the Margins of Life* (Oxford: Oxford University Press, 2002).

6. Judith Jarvis Thomson, "A Defense of Abortion", *Philosophy and Public Affairs* 1 (1971): 47–66.

7. Don Marquis, "Why Abortion Is Immoral", *Journal of Philosophy* 86 (1989): 183–202.

8. Gina Kolata, "Study Finds 31% Rate of Miscarriage", *New York Times*, July 27, 1988.

9. Jeffrey Stout, *Democracy and Tradition* (Princeton, NJ: Princeton University Press, 2004), p. 69.

10. John Rawls, *Political Liberalism* (New York: Columbia University Press, 1996).

11. Stout, *Democracy and Tradition*, pp. 10–11.

10

1. Stanley Fish, "Does Philosophy Matter?", *New York Times* (online), August 1, 2011.

2. Dorothea Frede, "The Final Proof of the Immortality of the Soul in Plato's 'Phaedo' 102a–107a", *Phronesis* 23 (1978): 27–41.

3. Bas van Fraassen, "Empiricism in the philosophy of science", in *Images of Science*, ed. P. Churchland and C. A. Hooker (Chicago: University of Chicago Press, 1985), p. 258.

4. It's worth noting that some contemporary Aristotelians who carry none of Aquinas's theological baggage still see his work as improving on Aristotle's. Philippa Foot, for example, said, "Often [Aquinas] works things out in far more detail than Aristotle did, and it is possible to learn a great deal from Aquinas that one could not have got from Aristotle. It is my opinion that the *Summa Theologica* is one of the best sources we have for moral philosophy, and moreover that St. Thomas's ethical writings are as useful to the atheist as to the Catholic or other Christian believer" (*Virtues and Vices and Other Essays in Moral Philosophy* [Oakland, CA: University of California Press, 1978], p. 2).

5. René Descartes, *Meditations on First Philosophy*, trans. and ed. John Cottingham (Cambridge: Cambridge University Press, 1996), p. 17.

6. Here I am making use of the historical analysis of John Carriero, *Between Two Worlds: A Reading of Descartes's* Meditations (Princeton, NJ: Princeton University Press, 2009).

7. Wilfrid Sellars, "Philosophy and the Scientific Image of Man", in

Science, Perception, and Reality (London: Routledge and Kegan Paul, 1963), Chapter 1.

8. Ibid., p. 9.
9. Ibid., p. 18.
10. Ibid., p. 20.
11. Arthur Eddington, *The Nature of the Physical World* (London: Macmillan, 1929), pp. ix–x.
12. Sellars, "Philosophy and the Scientific Image of Man," pp. 4, 18.
13. Ibid., p. 39.
14. Ibid., p. 40.
15. Ibid., p. 1.

ACKNOWLEDGMENTS

Each chapter derives from columns I wrote for the *New York Times* philosophy blog, The Stone. I'm grateful to Simon Critchley for inviting me to write for The Stone and to Peter Catapano, an extraordinary editor, whose keen eye and good sense have aided me at every turn.

Parts of Chapters 4 and 5 employ material from my article, "Religious Agnosticism", *Midwest Studies in Philosophy* 37 (2013), 51–67.

Thanks to the philosophical colleagues whose comments on various parts of the manuscript saved me from many mistakes and infelicities: Karl Ameriks, Don Howard, Jerry Levinson, Jeff McMahan, and Paul Weithman. I'm especially grateful to my wife, Anastasia Friel Gutting, who was my constant resource in writing this book. Whenever I hit a rough spot, a conversation with her invariably provided the word, clarification, or argument needed to move forward.

Many improvements were due to lively discussions of an early draft in my seminar with Notre Dame Honors students: Gabrielle Davis, Joseph DeLuca, Madeline Felts, Christian Gorski, Erin Hattler, Katherine Hayman, Andrew Jena, Mary Koptik,

Clare Kossler, Matthew Onders, Thomas Plagge, Petra Rantanen, Elliott Runburg, Alyssa Schlotman, and Lucas Sullivan.

Thanks also to Brendan Curry, my editor at W. W. Norton, for invaluable guidance on the overall shape of the book and acute line editing; to his gracious and efficient assistant, Sophie Duvernoy; to Tara Powers for her careful copyediting; and to Louise Mattarelliano, Nancy Palmquist, and Anna Mageras. Thanks also to Anne Hawkins for much good advice and encouragement.

Finally, I'm grateful to my family: to my splendid children and their spouses—Tasha and Andrew, Edward and Angela, Tom and Andrea; to my delightful grandchildren, Xander and Charlotte; and above all to Anastasia for her love and support of us all.

INDEX

Page numbers beginning with 277 refer to endnotes.